Jews and Feminism

Jews and Feminism

The Ambivalent Search for Home

∽

LAURA LEVITT

Routledge
New York and London

Published in 1997 by

Routledge
29 West 35th Street
New York, NY 10001

Published in Great Britain in 1997 by

Routledge
11 New Fetter Lane
London EC4P 4EE

Copyright © 1997 by Routledge

Printed in the United States of America
Design: Jack Donner

Library of Congress Cataloging-in-Publication Data

Levitt, Laura, 1960–
Jews and Feminism : the ambivalent search for home / Laura Levitt.
p.   cm.   Includes bibliographical references and index.
ISBN 0–415–91444–2 (hb). — ISBN 0–415–91445–0 (pb)
1. Feminism—Religious aspects—Judaism. 2. Women in Judaism.
3. Jewish women—Religious life. I. Title.
BM729.W6L49   1997
296'.082—dc21   97–2757
CIP

≈

In de fremd

        among strangers

iz ir heym

        is her home.

        Do

here
ot do

        right here

muz zi lebn.

        she must live.

—Irena Klepfisz, "*Di rayze aheym /*
  The journey home"

≈

～

For Dana Bialow

～

Contents

~

Acknowledgments

There are many friends/family and colleagues without whom this book would never have been written. First and foremost I want to thank Miriam Peskowitz for her friendship, her courage, and the brilliance of her work. Without her, my first reader, I could never have imagined an audience for this book. I also want to acknowledge David Watt, Susan Shapiro, Deborah Lamb, Ruth Tonner Ost, Aaron Taub, Phyllis and Irving Levitt, and Dana Bialow for their ongoing critical engagement with this project as well as their love and support for me. For crucial comments and suggestions I want to thank Sara Horowitz, Daniel Boyarin, Larry Silberstein, Rob Baird, James Young, Marion Ronan, Evelyn Beck, Rebecca Chopp, Michelle Friedman, Angelika Bammer, Ellen Umansky, David Blumenthal, and Lynne Davidman.

Special thanks also go to Miriam Peskowitz, David Watt, and Susan Shapiro for reading early drafts of my introduction; to Ruth Tonner Ost for her careful reading of parts two and three of the manuscript; Maud Lavin for her careful reading of the entire manuscript; and Tania Oldenhage for her help in compiling my bibliography.

I am especially grateful to Miriam Peskowitz and Daniel Boyarin for their respectful encouragement of my work with rabbinic texts in chapter 2. I thank Miriam for letting me read the manuscript for her book *Spinning Fantasies*, which radically changed the way that I read rabbinic texts. I thank Daniel for sharing with me his reading of Ketubot 39a–b, his manuscript for his forthcoming book *Unheroic Conduct*, and his ground-breaking work on issues of sexuality in talmudic culture in *Carnal Israel*.

I would never have begun writing about identity and home or ventured into feminist theory without Janet Jakobsen and Carrie Jane Singleton. We arrived in Atlanta together; they were there for me through the best and worst of times, and they have been my constant companions through all of the various transformations of this book.

As I completed this manuscript, David Watt and I began a process of reconfiguring our home together. I thank him for his patience, good humor, and labor during all those hours while I was writing.

I would like to acknowledge the ongoing support of my students and colleagues at Temple University, the institution where I work as a scholar and a teacher. Most especially, I want to thank Claudia Schippert, Tania Oldenhage, José Berroa-Saro, Kristin Guzzetta, Jamie Bluth, Jennifer Gubkin, Sharon Ravett, Vassiliki Limberis, Rebecca Alpert, Norbert Samuelson, and Linda Jenkins for their critical engagement. I would also like to thank the Research and Study Leave Committee of the Faculty Senate of Temple University for awarding me a 1995 Summer Research Grant. And finally, I would like to thank all of my students in my feminist theory class at Temple during the fall of 1996 for helping me both let go and better understand what this book is all about.

preface

∼

The Journey Home[1]

This is a book about passionate embraces. It is about the interplay between the need to hold on and the need to let go of the places, relationships, and traditions we call home. It is about the delicacy of all such attachments and the ways we have come to make them seem lasting. In order to place this desire for home in a particular personal and cultural context, I want to begin by considering that peculiar journey known as immigration. In working through this book, I have come to see that immigration, in both a historical as well as a conceptual sense, marks most profoundly my own sense of being especially at home in America. I bear the legacy of my grandparents' journey as well as their fierce attachment to their new home—an immigrant legacy that haunts this project. And, as in immigration, my journey as well as my desire to settle down mark the ambivalence connected to my own longing for home.

In their act of leaving one country to settle permanently in another, immigrants desire both permanence and change. Even within this opposition though, I wonder about permanence as a fixed term. Is anything forever? With this question in mind, I turn to my *American Heritage Dictionary* to look up "permanent." I find the following definitions:

1. Lasting or remaining without essential change: "the universal human yearning for something permanent, enduring, without shadow of change." (Willa Cather)   2. Not expected to change in status, condition, or place. . . .

permanent *n.* A long-lasting hair wave produced by applying a chemical lotion to the hair while wet, winding the hair on rollers, and drying it with heat. Also called *permanent wave.*[2]

The word "permanent" derives from a Latin term meaning to endure, to remain, perhaps also "to survive"?[3] How is it then that, even within these definitions, that which is permanent becomes ephemeral? A note about the history of this word that builds on the ludicrously hopeful final noun form, the permanent as hairdo, addresses precisely this problem, the tension between stability and change with which I began. This note reads as follows:

> In this world of impermanence it seems that we have tried to hold on to a few things at least by using the word *permanent.* Coming ultimately from the present participle *permanens* of Latin *permanere,* "to endure," Middle English *permanent* (first recorded around 1425) also had to do with the enduring and the stable. When we consider some of the applications of this adjective, as in *permanent press, permanent tooth,* we are struck by the relative evanescence of the so-called permanent. But perhaps never more so than in the case of the permanent wave. When asked what this phenomenon was, one journalist wrote in 1932, "(so far as my experience goes): a wave that is anything but permanent."[4]

I focus on "permanent" because it marks the ambivalence at the heart of immigration, the realization that nothing is ever really "permanent"—including home.

This contradiction is at the heart of this book for this is a book about my attempts as an immigrant granddaughter to claim from my various homes the legacies I both lost and found in my parents' home. It is about my attempts to reclaim certain Jewish traditions lost to them as well as my efforts to lay claim to still other liberal and feminist positions in the present. In these efforts I try to both resist the nostalgia of lost pasts as well as the allure of all that is new. I do this by tracing a single journey within and between a series of American and Jewish traditions.

This is not a linear narrative. As with immigration itself, here too the desire to find a place to settle belies its own precondition in the journey. Although I take positions and dig in my heels, I also move on and find other places to stand, at least for a time. This book is about my search for home, a journey that begins with my immigrant Jewish family's ambivalent embrace of America. I seek stability in specific Jewish religious and cultural traditions as well as in the liberal academy. Despite my forays into an ancient Jewish past and back to Europe at various points, this journey both begins and ends in America, that place in the world I continue to call my home.

introduction

∼

Home

Since this book is about the connections between home and identity or identity as a kind of home, I want to begin with the concrete space, the house where I began writing, the first floor of 317 East Ninth Street (it took me a while to recall the exact address; I kept writing down the wrong numbers). I lived at this address from August of 1987 through December of 1991. It was my only home in Atlanta. It was large and sunny. The yard was extremely well taken care of by my landlord, an elderly woman living alone on the second floor. The building was about sixty years old, unrenovated but clean and neat. When I moved in the first floor apartment, all it needed was a new coat of bright white paint, which my parents and I applied during three scorching days that August.

When I moved in the apartment echoed. I liked the emptiness of the space. I had little furniture, and for the first two years I had no soft furniture. I enjoyed the stark beauty of my home. Although it was often difficult to entertain, I was able to do my work. Among the first purchases I made were a computer and a desk, which I settled in the second bedroom. Then, in the summer of 1989, I bought a futon couch and chair. They felt big and bulky, but I got used to them. My home became so much more livable. It was easier to invite friends over, to share my space. In September of 1989, I fell in love with a man who lived just a block a way. He visited often. My home was filled with the promises of a new relationship.

In November of 1989 I was raped in my home by a stranger. After that I considered moving but could not imagine another home. I was angry at having to give up a place that was so much mine, a place where I had a history. I refused to move and chose instead to reconfigure my home. I painted the walls of my bedroom, the site of my rape. There were now two bruised purple walls and green trim. They matched a Botticelli poster on the wall, although, in truth, even the poster did not fully bring the room together again. I also moved the furniture. Since no walls felt safe, the bed floated in the middle of this room until I left Atlanta for good. The futon couch came in very handy, as I could no longer stay at home alone. Friends became a regular presence in this home. I also got a dog who remains my constant companion.

The house was never as neat or stark as it had once been. In the fall of 1990, as I began writing there, I also tried briefly to stay at home alone. I was not comfortable. In October a friend moved in, and I moved my office into a breakfast nook that was small, bright, and sunny. Nestled in between a file cabinet and a window, I felt safe and secure at my desk writing. The house filled up. There were lots of plants and lots of people. Another friend also spent much of this time living with us. With the dog that made four. Of course, there is much more to tell.

This home was the site of a great many conflicting desires. It was a place of both comfort and terror. The knowledge that home could be both de/ and re/constructed was visceral. That knowledge lived in the walls of this place I called my home in Atlanta. From the beginning I was engaged in a process of reconfiguring home on many fronts.

I began writing this book in 1990 in Atlanta, a year after I was raped and just months before I was to end an important relationship. Between then and now I have moved several times; the physical places I have called home have changed. The relationships that offered safety and protection have also shifted. "Home" has become something quite different, and yet some things have also remained constant. This book began as and remains an interrogation of what it means to claim and configure a Jewish feminist identity in the midst of conflicting visions and material conditions. It makes explicit how and in what ways it is crucial to theorize out of the contingent places we call home. Location matters.

It also demonstrates how theory can help explain in nuanced and powerful ways the complexities of our lives. It shows how theory can enable us to explore the seams in the construction of our identities within the constraints of various social, cultural, and political con-figurations of power and desire.

As Gayatri Spivak must revisit French feminism as a way into her cultural criticism,[1] there are specific American feminist texts that have enabled me to write about these issues—to claim my various homes.[2] As I will demonstrate, they form a critical part of my story.

My narrative is also situated within the various promises of a home in America made to Jews, women, and Jewish women.[3] Broadly speaking, I critique these promises as part of liberalism and colonial-ism. I look at how some of these promises have been kept while others have not. What concerns me are the various ways that these grand liberatory dreams have not been met within the parameters of the American social contract or within the liberal academy. In explor-ing some of these disappointments, my narrative is not unique. It is part of a larger "horizon of meanings and knowledges available in the culture at [this] given historical momen[t], a horizon of meaning that includes modes of political commitment and struggle. . . . [as well as] particular discursive configurations."[4] It shares much with Spivak's critique of colonialism.

In these ways this book invites readers into a landscape that is both familiar and unfamiliar—a landscape shaped by a series of tra-ditions, texts, social institutions, expectations, and desires. These are the horizons of meaning and possibility within which, as I under-stand it, American Jewish feminists are living our lives at the end of the twentieth century.

Liberal/Colonial Dreams of Home

A consideration of home raises serious questions for me about my place as a Jew in the West. I begin with a consideration of Jews "in the West," because it was within the promises of the liberal revolu-tions of the late eighteenth century that Jews throughout western Europe and the United States were granted citizenship and offered access to liberal education, through which they could become a part of liberal culture. Emancipation was granted to Jews as individuals. More specifically, liberalism emancipated Jewish men, but inclusion came at a price. It meant they had to relinquish various forms of communal authority: virtually all aspects of Jewish communal life came under the aegis of the liberal state.[5] Out of this history, American Jews have embraced the promises of American liberalism. We have become loyal American citizens.

In the Jewish home I was raised in, Jewish values were liberal values. There was seemingly no difference. Liberalism was filled with promise. It was through liberal lenses that my parents taught me about justice, about fairness, and about liberation. Liberalism had promised my immigrant grandparents a safe home, hospitable soil, a place to grow and to prosper by entering into the American social contract. In my family, being a citizen of the United States was considered sacred.

When my maternal grandmother's citizenship was called into question in the 1970s as she applied for a passport, it was a family crisis. In her sixties at the time, my grandmother had never before considered travel that would require a passport. In fact she was most committed to staying home. Having not been born in this country, she was especially proud to be an American. After spending the vast majority of her life in this country (she was three when she arrived from Russia), she was devastated to receive an alien card in the mail in response to her request for a passport. This reinvocation of her almost, but not quite forgotten, otherness was a problem. For months my family zealously sought proof of her citizenship in the annals of the New York City Hall of Records and HIAS, the Hebrew Immigrant Aid Society. It was understood that being an alien was unacceptable, it was also incorrect. Nevertheless, this incident was a dramatic reminder of just how precious U.S. citizenship was for not only my grandmother but also for so many American Jews.[6] Once my grandmother's situation was finally cleared up and her citizenship reaffirmed, she was never willing to leave this country. Although legally free to travel, she never used her passport, did not venture forth beyond the borders of the United States. There is a photograph of my grandmother taken not long after this crisis, taken on her first trip to Washington, D.C. She is dressed in red, white, and blue. Her arms are outstretched. The dome of the Capitol building is behind her. My mother recalls that her mother cried for joy having finally made it to the Capitol.

There is a statue, built in the 1930s, of George Washington with Robert Morris and Hyam Salomon in Chicago's Herald Square.[7] The men are depicted arm in arm. This is, as I understand it, the only statue of Washington where he is not figured alone. The statue is named for Hyam Salomon, a Polish Jew who died broke after helping finance the American Revolution. While the statue was being constructed, Barnet Hodes, the Chicago lawyer who commissioned the work, pleaded with the sculptor to depict the men locked arm in arm. He was afraid of vandalism, and he thought that linking the figures would assure that the statue would not be defaced. It being the 1930s, he was worried about antisemitism[8] and assumed that Washington's image would protect Salomon.[9] Although there are important differences, this image of protection offered to a loyal American Jew reminds me of my grandmother. It echoes her precarious status in that photograph. Although never quite secure, as an active agent she embraces Washington, metonymically figured in the dome of the Capitol.

I am haunted by these images. They are a reminder of the complicated legacy of liberalism for contemporary Jewish women in the United States. Like my grandmother, many Jewish women fought hard for a place within the American dream and, despite their loyalty, these women, their daughters, and granddaughters have had to face time and again strategic limitations and prohibitions built into liberalism's promise of home.

This legacy of promise and effacement has also characterized Jewish feminist dreams of liberation. As the twentieth century comes to a close, I am arguing that part of this struggle for liberation must include an interrogation of these loyalties.[10] The sheltering arms of Washington are not enough. Although powerful, these images keep us from imagining other possibilities, from seeing the limitations and contradictions built into the discourse of liberalism. I am asking that we begin to let go of these images, that we stop imagining ourselves as always already within this liberal horizon.

Offering American Jews a new vision of home, liberalism opened up both a conceptual and a political terrain within which Jews could participate in American culture. Even as the history of the American Revolution makes clear, this liberal emancipatory project was never just a way of constructing political, social, or cultural relationships in the West. In the North American colonies there was already discursive slippage between "the West," as in western Europe, and a vision that included at least North America. Aside from "West" being a complicated signifier, the distinction between liberalism and colonialism was also unclear. The American Revolution was built on the legacy of European colonialism, and the implications of these connections and complications are only beginning to be appreciated.[11] In part, by speaking about liberalism in terms of a horizon of possibilities I want to indicate the breadth of these connections. Liberalism includes a series of material and discursive cultural configurations of power.[12] As such, liberalism and colonialism are intertwined.

I offer a critique of what I call "the liberal/colonial project," because the pairing of these two discourses has given me a vantage point from which to see the larger implications of my own attachments to liberalism. Like Spivak, I struggle with my commitment to this legacy.

Liberalism and colonialism share an ambivalent promise of emancipation and assimilation. In both, power is organized asymmetrically, and some people are necessarily excluded. Building on cultural critic Homi Bhabha's critique of colonialism, I have come to see the liberal/colonial project in terms of promise and effacement, a kind of mimicry. Like colonialism, liberalism offered formerly subjected peoples a kind of partial emancipation. As Homi Bhabha explains, "By 'partial' I mean both 'incomplete' and 'virtual.' It is as if the very emergence of the colonial [liberal] is dependent for its representation upon some strategic limitation or prohibition *within* the authoritative discourse. The success of colonial appropriation depends on a proliferation of inappropriate objects that ensure its strategic failure, so that mimicry is at once resemblance and menace."[13] In other words, there are limitations built into both liberalism and colonialism. As much as their subjects try to become western or mainstream, they are bound to fail. Asymmetries of power not only remain in place but are essential to the perpetuation of these systems. So, lulled by the promises of a place in the social contract, they keep trying to fit in. No matter how hard the colonial tries, he or she will remain "a subject that is almost the same, but not quite" (126). This is the bitter irony of mimicry: In order to be effective, it must continually produce this kind of slippage or excess (126).

It is my contention that Jews like many others in the liberal West—including women, the poor, various peoples of color, and queers find themselves struggling up against a "strategic limitation" or "prohibition."[14] This is especially true for those who claim identities within and between these various designations of otherness. With this in mind, I have found it helpful to understand the dynamics of Jewish assimilation in the West in terms of mimicry. Jews have desired to fit in, to be like everyone else. The problem is that there is an excess expressed in this desire that is aptly captured in the joke that says that Jews are just like everyone else, only more so; this is the kind of difference that Homi Bhabha was talking about. In other words, as hard as Jews try to be like everyone else, the excess of our effort marks us as different.[15] In my parents' home, this desire often translated into the need to be better than everyone else in our small town. We had to be smarter, better read, more politically active and socially involved in the community in order to be accepted. This dynamic is part of what has made it so difficult for me to talk about my Jewish home in America.

By juxtaposing the two sides of the liberal/colonial coin—sameness and difference—I want to expose some of the gaps in liberalism's narrative of Jewish emancipation.[16] Although we remain grateful to the liberal revolutions of the late eighteenth century for bringing Jews into the dominant cultures of the West, this is not the entire story. Our acceptance remains partial. Ironically it has been the fierceness of our loyalty to the liberal state that has marked many of us as different.

Education as Promise

As part of citizenship, liberalism also laid out a series of cultural promises, with education as a way into western culture. In the United States, "the [western] canon [was] like the Statue of Liberty, transforming the huddled masses into an intellectual community."[17] It offered Jews status, prestige, and authority. As literary critic Marianna Torgovnick eloquently explains, "Universities were sites of acculturation and advancement that serve in the United States. . .[as] the 'melting pot' project of American culture."[18] Building on a rich legacy of Jewish learning, a generation of primarily immigrant Jews made academic achievement their way of getting into American culture.[19]

By reading western canonical texts and writing about them, American Jewish intellectuals in the humanities reinvented Jewish study as a secular practice. Textual study held out the promise of entry into an American intellectual community. Thus, for a luminary like Lionel Trilling who taught literature at Columbia University for almost forty years, the western canon became sacred.[20]

Despite his erudition, much less his devotion to this tradition, even Trilling's status within the American academy was tenuous. As Torgovnick explains, "Thinking of Trilling, I recall immediately certain facts: his immigrant origins, his Jewishness, his embattled status as a young professor at Columbia, which had not previously tenured Jews and told Trilling, when it tried to terminate his contract, that he would be more comfortable somewhere else" (267). Like the colonial subject Bhabha describes, "Trilling tended to be 'always amazed and appreciative of his good fortune' in the profession—even though he had to negotiate his relationship with 'the tradition' and fight, tenaciously, for what he got" (267).

These same ambiguous promises inspired members of my immediate family to pursue the liberal arts. On a much more modest scale, my parents showed their devotion to this tradition by teaching "The Great Books" to high school students in our home for over twenty years. My brother and I were included among these students.

Although I have grown critical of this tradition, my own work remains deeply bound to this legacy of textual engagement. When I came to Atlanta in 1987 to enter a Ph.D. program in religion, like my parents I was committed to reading canonical texts and writing about them; the difference was the texts I chose to study. Because I wanted to understand more about the various dynamics that structure contemporary American Jewish life, I decided to return to Jewish religious texts both ancient and modern for some answers. For me this meant taking seriously the complicated relationships between rabbinic, liberal, and liberal Jewish feminist texts over and against my parents' Great Books. By engaging with these Jewish texts, I hoped to find ways of articulating the complexity of my own position and looked to theology for some answers.

While an undergraduate in religion and a master's candidate at the Reform Seminary, I had done extensive work in theology; I simply planned to continue these studies in Atlanta as a feminist.[21] When I got to graduate school, isolated as a Jewish student in religion, I became increasingly dissatisfied with theology and its answers.[22] Instead, by using feminist and critical theory I found that I could read Jewish texts differently. In working with feminist literary theory in particular, I began to question many of my basic assumptions: my desire for answers as well as my commitment to liberalism's notion of a unified self. I began to appreciate how and why my own positions were partial. Through a feminist critical practice of self-consciousness, I began to appreciate the complexity and contradictions within contemporary Jewish life.

Through their careful reading of "Identity: Skin Blood Heart," an essay by a "white, middle-class, Christian southern, lesbian," poet, and activist Minnie Bruce Pratt, feminist literary critics Chandra Mohanty and Biddy Martin gave me a model for thinking differently about how I read texts. These essays in particular taught me to pay attention to the material and discursive differences among and between women. They helped me begin to rethink many of my assumptions about the necessity of a unified position.[23] They also helped me to appreciate how "feminism" continues to be a site of political struggle that requires my critical engagement.[24] As Martin and Mohanty explain:

> The implicit assumption here, which we wish to challenge, is that the terms of a totalizing feminist discourse are adequate to the task of articulating the situation of white women in the West. We would contest that assumption and argue that the reproduction of such polarities [West/East, white/nonwhite] only serves to concede "feminism" to the "West" all over again. The potential consequence is the repeated failure to contest the feigned homogeneity of the West and what seems to be a discursive and political stability of the hierarchical West/East divide. (193)

By challenging the notion of a monolithic western feminist position, Martin and Mohanty opened up for me complexities within my own position.[25] They explained how the dismissal of these complexities only serves to reenforce the stability of western cultural and political hegemony. They demonstrated how Pratt's partial account of her own identity, "partial in at least two senses of the word: politically partial, and without claim to wholeness or finality," (193) disrupted this economy. [26]

In working with these texts, I learned how, and in what ways feminist theorizing is a politics. By reading Jewish texts differently I learned that I could challenge the assumptions of the liberal/colonial project as they continued to inform contemporary Jewish thought. I also learned how a more partial kind of feminist writing can "demonstrat[e] the importance of both narrative and historical specificity in the attempt to reconceptualize the relationship between 'home,' 'identity,' and political change" (192). I came to see that I did not need a metadiscursive stance to write about contemporary Jewish feminists. Instead I learned how gender figures into not only the liberal/colonial project's promise and effacement of home for Jews but also how and why returning to rabbinic Judaism could not solve this problem.

"a way in"

In the context of claiming a Jewish feminist position, this book illustrates how, as Martin and Mohanty have argued, in relation to Pratt's narrative:

> Change... is not a simple escape from constraint to liberation. There is no shedding the literal fear and figurative law of the father, and no reaching a final realm of freedom. Since neither her [Pratt's nor my] view of history nor her view of herself through it is linear, the past, home, and the father leave traces that are constantly reabsorbed into a shifting vision. (201)

In the chapters that follow I offer close readings of particular texts out of my various Jewish pasts, feminist theory, and contemporary Jewish feminist writing. Each chapter demonstrates how and in what ways "the past, home, and the father" are reabsorbed into a shifting vision of Jewish feminist identity/ies in the present. I take discrete positions within particular contexts while appreciating the contingency of any of these claims, acknowledging the interrelationship between singular and plural positions.[27]

In chapter 1, "Embraces," I offer a reading of Pratt's text. By intertwining Pratt's narrative with my own, this chapter demonstrates how and in what ways reading for home is a feminist practice. I show how Pratt's text has given me a way of claiming an identity in terms of home. I address the difficulties as well as the possibilities of this kind of writing for reclaiming the legacy of an Eastern European immigrant Jewish home in America.

The chapters that follow are arranged in three parts. The first part, "Jewish Women at Home: Rabbinic Judaism, Liberalism, and Liberal Jewish Theology," focuses on the institution of marriage as codified in marriage contracts, rape laws, and contemporary Jewish theology, since these are the sites where Jewish women have often been most visible within these traditions. The second section "Feminist Study: Reconfiguring Jewish Identity," addresses the place of Jews within feminist texts and academic practices. These chapters raise questions about Jewish dreams of being at home within feminist study. By returning to Pratt, Mohanty, and Martin, these chapters both acknowledge the strategic usefulness of some of this feminist discourse for Jews as well as some of its limitations. In section three, "Ambivalent Embraces," I reclaim the various places, traditions, and relationships I have called my homes in America through a reading of specific contemporary Jewish feminist texts.

Part 1 begins in chapter 2 with a close reading of the *ketubbah*, the rabbinic marriage contract. This chapter historicizes the ketubbah through a close reading of a standard rabbinic text. By reading against the grain of this legal text, I highlight the traces of its construction. I also raise questions about the text's normative configuration of Jewish women as wives. I then juxtapose the ketubbah, with a talmudic text about rape in order to show the interrelationship between rabbinic rape and marriage laws in defining Jewish women.

Chapters 3 and 4 offer a specific critique of liberalism by focusing on the relationships between emancipation, Jewish women, and the institution of liberal marriage. Through a reading of Napoleon's questions to the Jewish notables, chapter 3 raises questions about liberal promises of home to Jews as citizens of France. By looking closely at the dynamics of promise and effacement within, especially, the first three of Napoleon's questions, which were the questions about marriage, I raise concern about the limitations of marital fidelity as a trope for defining Jewish citizenship and cultural acceptance.

Chapter 4 further challenges the notion of civil emancipation by denaturalizing liberalism's sexual contract. Building on the work of feminist political theorist Carole Pateman,[28] I draw connections between this contract and liberal rape laws in order to show how the dynamics of promise and effacement within liberalism explicitly define the position of Jewish women in the West as wives.

Building on the critique of liberalism in chapters 3 and 4, chapter 5 "Covenant or Contract? Marriage as Theology" discusses the internalization of liberal values within contemporary Jewish theology. Through a close reading of the work of my teacher Eugene Borowitz, an important liberal Jewish theologian, I show how the trope of liberal marriage has come to define the relationship between God and the Jewish people. I then problematize this theological move by showing how this same trope also continues to define material relations within Borowitz's liberal Jewish ethics.

In chapter 6, I draw on Judith Plaskow's feminist critique of liberal Jewish theology and its implications for Jewish women. Through a close reading of her ground-breaking Jewish feminist theology of sexuality I make clear the promise, as well as the limitations, inherent in her liberal feminist approach to right relationships. By returning to feminist literary theory at the end of this chapter, I argue for a more thorough feminist critique of Jewish liberalism. In this way, I return to feminist theory in order to envision other, not necessarily theological, possibilities for claiming Jewish feminist positions.

Chapter 6 marks the point of transition from Part 1 to Part 2. Chapter 7, "Feminist Dreams of Home," is framed by a reading of Nancy K. Miller's "Dreaming, Dancing and the Changing Locations of Feminist Criticism, 1988." I begin with this essay because it is one of the only texts in feminist literary theory that explicitly addresses questions of Jewish inclusion. I then offer a reading of feminist literary critic Teresa de Lauretis's introduction to *Feminist Studies/Critical Studies*, a classic introduction to the field. By reading this text in relation to Miller's essay, I examine my own dreams of being at home in academic feminist study. Through a close reading of de Lauretis's account of the 1985 feminist conference out of which her volume emerged, as well as Miller's account of this same conference, I raise serious questions about the place of Jews in feminist studies.

In chapter 8 I focus on "Personal Histories," the second half of Miller's essay. Through a close reading of this section of her essay, I demonstrate how I believe it is possible to read, write, and speak as a Jew in feminist classrooms and at feminist conferences.

Part 3 begins in chapter 9 with a return to Atlanta. I come back to Atlanta through a reading of Jewish feminist poet and activist

Melanie Kaye/Kantrowitz's poem "Notes of an Immigrant Daughter: Atlanta." I use this poem to reconsider my relationship to the place where this book began in the form of a textual embrace.

In chapter 10, "Claiming America," I offer a reading of Part 3 of Irena Klepfisz's prose poem *"Bashert."*[29] I use this text as a way of reimagining my own relationship to this country. The ambivalences within my embrace of America become even more explicit in chapter 11, "What's in a Name?" Here I reconsider Jewish and feminist acts of naming in terms of being at home in America. Finally, in my conclusion, "Writing Home," I offer an account of where I have come to in my own journey home. Here I reflect on what it has meant for me to embrace all of these homes in this writing and to let them go.

one

~

Embraces

On the map of my many homes, in this book I try to locate my physical homes in Atlanta and Philadelphia, my liberal Jewish home in America, and my academic homes within and between the disciplines of Jewish studies, feminist studies, and religion. These are the sites of my particular preoccupations with safety, agency, and desire. These homes have allowed me to venture forth into an interrogation of the promises of my various Jewish, liberal, and feminist traditions. Although throughout much of this book I am critical of these legacies, I do not abandon them, for I do not believe that that is possible. Like 317 Ninth Street, where I no longer physically live, other homes past and present—my parents' home, rabbinic, liberal Jewish, and liberal Jewish feminist Judaisms—remain part of the landscape I call home, as do my homes in Philadelphia, the ideology of liberalism, and feminist study.

Echoing feminist literary critics Chandra Mohanty and Biddy Martin, I re-ask the question: What's identity got to do with home? In order to answer this question for myself, I want to bring the pieces of my story together now in a slightly different way from how I did it in my introduction. Although I hope that I have made clear that my rape was not the only motivation for this book, it has been constitutive. It, perhaps more than anything else, has called into question so many of my beliefs about what constitutes home. These include my construction of my heterosexuality, my notions of family, of domesticity, of agency, and of personal safety and protection. To say I am a Jewish feminist in light of all that has happened to me, in light of all that I have done, and to make some sense of these disparate experiences is what this book is about. I have posed to myself the challenge to be honest about the complexity and contradictions of my experiences. The fact that the resources of my various traditions were not able to do this for me in any simple way has led me to this more partial, less absolute account of my identity as a kind of home.

I started thinking about home and identity as feminist questions in the spring of 1988 in my first course in feminist theory.[1] It was here that I was introduced to Chandra Mohanty and Biddy Martin's essay "Feminist Politics: What's Home Got to Do with It?" and Minnie Bruce Pratt's "Identity: Skin Blood Heart."[2] Pratt's evocative essay is a specific account of a feminist politics. It demonstrates in concrete terms how the personal and political are intertwined with struggles against antisemitism and racism. Mohanty and Martin's reading of Pratt's essay makes clear the challenges Pratt's essay poses for feminist theorizing. Their essay shows how Pratt's personal narrative opens up the complexities within feminist politics. Although my understanding of these essays and other works in feminist theory continues to evolve, these particular essays have colored this project, informing my own thinking about the intersection of politics, identity, and home. I have remained especially attached to Pratt's rich personal narrative. Although Martin and Mohanty raise cautions about how applicable Pratt's narrative approach is for other feminist theorizing, warning that "we do not intend to suggest that Pratt's essay, or any single autobiographical narrative, offers 'an answer',"[3] I remain tied to her text. For me it is not so much "an answer" but a partial strategy for putting together a life. For me, Pratt's narrative has operated as an invitation. It has given me permission to speak honestly about the complexities of my own life. This was especially important to me after the disruption of my rape.

Through reading and writing about Pratt's text, I have been able to find and stake out my own positions—an interaction that has been critical. Held up by the strength and power of Pratt's essay, I have found my own footing. Her essay has provided weight, authority, and precedent for me to write about my own identity and homes. This interaction, as a feminist practice, is what I have referred to elsewhere as a kind of textual embrace.[4] In what follows, I will demonstrate how this kind of interaction works by writing about myself in relation to Pratt's essay.

The Blow

Not long after I was raped, a series of letter bombs were sent to liberal judges across the South, some of whom were killed. Accounts of these incidents were all over the Atlanta news. Those people who claimed credit for these attacks were white supremacists, who professed to have acted on behalf of white women who had been raped by black men.[5] Since I had been raped by a young black man, these claims spoke to me in direct ways. These men said they had acted on my behalf. They committed acts of violence and used my experience as their justification. In a previously published essay about my rape, I had chosen not to write about race. As part of the final edit, I was convinced by an editor that simply writing that I had been raped by a black man with a note that briefly addressed some of my ambivalences about relaying this information was not a sufficient way of addressing the complexity of these issues: I would simply be reinscribing the kind of racist assumptions my note was attempting to avoid.[6]

Since complexity is so much a part of what I am addressing in this book, I return to this issue. My race is an issue especially in light of these bombings. My initial reaction to them was shame and anger: How could these white supremacists act on my behalf? Who gave them permission to invoke my experience? Rereading Pratt's essay, I have had to think again about this construction of these events in terms of "that soundless blow, which changes forever one's map of the world" (33). My being raped had done this for me.[7]

What Pratt says about the event that shattered her vision of safety caused me to pause once again in trying to come to terms with my rape. Pratt writes:

> For me the blow was literal, the sound was rifle-fire. In broad daylight, in Greensboro, North Carolina, about 50 miles from where I lived, Klansmen and Nazis drove into an anti-Klan demonstration, shouting "Nigger! Kike! Commie bastard!" They opened fire, killing five people: four white men, two of them Jews, one Black woman; labor union organizers, affiliated with the Communist Workers Party. The next day I saw in the newspaper an interview with Nancy Matthews, wife of one of the Klansmen. She said, "I knew he was a Klan member, but I don't know what he did when he left home. I was surprised and shocked. . . ." But the Klansmen

defended their getting out of their cars at the rally, rifles in hand, by saying they saw the car holding some Klanswomen being attacked and were "rushing to their rescue." (33)

I quote Pratt at length here in order to make clear that, not unlike the letter bombers, the klan invoked the notion of protection to justify its acts of violence. In Greensboro, blacks, Jews, and communists were all at risk together. In my case these alliances were less clear. I was a white Jewish woman raped by a black man. How or in what ways did those letter bombs relate to my experience? Pratt reminded me that my Jewishness could be an issue in the South. Am I a white woman or not? How and in what ways did this matter to either my attacker or to the white men who sent those bombs?[8]

In my struggles to figure out who could protect me and at what costs, like Pratt who returns to her various Southern homes to come to terms with what happened in Greensboro, I too looked to the traditions and physical places I had called my home for some answers.

Between November of 1989 and November of 1990, I learned not to be surprised that the same men who offered to act violently in the name of the violation of "their" women were, more often than not, also deeply implicated in the abuse of these same women. I learned that American women are at most risk when they are at home. Not only are they more likely to be beaten, raped, or killed at home, but also those who commit these acts are rarely strangers. Perpetrators are most often husbands, boyfriends, fathers, and uncles, the men we live with.[9]

Since my rape, I have also learned about the interconnection between pledges of protection, on the one hand, and acts of violence on the other. When I went to the American legal system for help, I discovered just how little justice it had to offer me. It made me think again about liberalism's social contract, the voluntary subjection to state and civil authority in exchange for protection upon which this country had been founded. Through a combination of frustrating interactions with the police and a great deal of reading on rape laws and feminist political and social theory, I learned that rape has been constructed within the parameters of proper heterosexuality. In this system, rape and marriage are paired within a sexual contract. Marriage is the positive term that is defined over and against the negation of rape. Marriage is scripted as protective and consensual while its other, rape, is defined as illegal, threatening, and nonconsensual. This economy of proper hetero/sexuality is naturalized through the institution of marriage. As in the social contract, in exchange for protection, a man acquires sexual access to his wife's body, a right protected within the boundaries of his home.[10]

In a man's home in America, the dynamic of threat and protection is replicated in relation to children, who are also defined in terms of needing protection. This need forms the basis of a man's legal relationship to his wife and children within the liberal state. Under this logic, he both controls and protects his family. What happens to women and children inside their homes is rarely questioned. Protection is simply assumed. In other words, under this system, the liberal state has no compelling interest in what goes on within a man's home. This so-called private sphere remains off-limits to the state, making it difficult for those of us whose bodies have been violated at home to seek justice. Even in cases like mine, where women are raped by strangers—cases that presumably re-enforce this logic of protection—the legal system rarely offers resolution. In my case this meant that the man who raped me was never pursued. Despite the fact that I had immediately reported the crime, made a statement to the police, and even had evidence from a rape exam done the night of my rape, there was no follow-up. The police did not investigate the case. There was no suspect, no arrest, and no trial. Like thousands of other reported rape cases in Fulton County, Georgia, and throughout the United States, my case was simply dropped.

Until this happened to me, I had not fully understood how much I had trusted in American liberalism's promise of protection. I came to realize just how much I had believed in this country's vision of liberal justice. Perhaps because my case never even resulted in an arrest, I learned just how illusory these promises of protection and justice can be.

When I first read Pratt's essay in 1988, I seemed to skip over these passages; I had not yet had a "blow that would change forever my map of the world." At that time, I focused on Mohanty and Martin's reading of Pratt. I was especially interested in their enthusiasm for a notion of ever-shifting identities, for I had ambivalent feelings about such claims. The passage from Mohanty and Martin's text that then disturbed me most presented Pratt's fluid account of identity in opposition to her father's more rigid position. These seemed to be the only options: either identity was stable and constant or it was in perpetual motion. They wrote:

> What she has gained . . . is a way of looking, a capacity for seeing the world in overlapping circles, "like movements on the millpond after a fish has jumped, instead of the courthouse square with me at the middle, even if I am on the ground.". . .[H]er difference and "need," emerges as the contrast between images of constriction, of entrapment, or ever-narrowing circles with a bounded self at the center . . . and . . . the images of the millpond with its ever shifting centers. (201)

As a Jew, I felt uncomfortable with these sharp distinctions between what is fixed and what is able to change. In 1988 I was keenly aware of how history had marked Jews in ways that were not negotiable. In other words, I experienced some aspects of my own Jewishness as fixed. In many ways, I understood my being Jewish as a given, as not a matter of choice. My Jewishness meant that my narrative was different from Pratt's a white, southern, middle-class, Christian-raised, lesbian, feminist poet and activist with a Ph.D. in English. And, yet, I very much identified with her. I shared much of her privilege—her class position, education, cultural capital, and white skin—but I also had another privilege—my heterosexual desire. Thus, from the beginning, my identification with Pratt was complicated by differences. I knew this in 1988, but was not sure what to do with it.

When I returned to Pratt's text later, I made new connections. I was struck by her discussion of the interplay between violence and protection. I found new links between our narratives and wrote about the following passage from Mohanty and Martin's text:

> During the height of the civil rights demonstrations in Alabama . . . her father called her in to read her an article in which Martin Luther King Jr. was accused of sexually abusing young teenaged girls. "I can only guess that he wanted me to feel that my danger, my physical danger, sexual danger, would be the result of the release of others from containment. I felt frightened and profoundly endangered, by King, by my father: I could not answer him. It was the first, only time, he spoke of sex, in any way, to me." (204)

I used this text to make connections between my interrogations of rape and marriage laws in rabbinic, liberal, and liberal Jewish theological sources and Pratt's conflictual relationship with her racist father. In that version of this text, these links were inferred, not spelled out. At that time I was unable to fully articulate these connections.[11]

In returning to Pratt's essay in the context of writing this book, I am more able to articulate these connections as well as new distinctions. Pratt's response to the incident in Greensboro was to return home, to see what the traditions that she had been raised in had to teach her about not only this tragedy but also her own violation—the loss of her children in a bitter custody battle, which happened after she came out as a lesbian and left her husband.[12] In response to this loss, Pratt's strategy was, I now realize, not unlike my own. I too have had to return home to work through not only my own disappointments with liberalism but also my disappointments with my various Jewish traditions.[13] And, like Pratt, I have not let go of any of these places. I continue to love them even as I read them differently.[14]

The passage about Martin Luther King Jr. that Mohanty and Martin referred to comes as part of Pratt's discussion of her sense of what change would entail. After Greensboro she began to realize not only that she was a victim of injustice but also that she too was implicated in histories of injustice done to others. As she writes, "I felt myself in a struggle with myself, *against* myself. This breaking through did not feel like liberation but like destruction" (35–36). Pratt connects this double message to a childhood memory of staying up late at night reading Edgar Allen Poe: "I was scared but fascinated by the catastrophic ending; when the walls of a house split, zigzag along a once barely noticeable crack, and the house of Usher crumbled with 'a long tumultuous shouting sound like the voice of a thousand waters'" (36).

Pratt uses Edgar Allen Poe's story, a story also very much about a woman who is buried alive and whose confinement has every thing to do with the demise of a southern home, as a way of talking about her own complicated feelings about her childhood home in Alabama.[15] Recalling the historical moment in which Poe wrote—"the 1840s a time of intensifying Southern justification of slavery" (36)[16]—Pratt makes connections to her experience of growing up in Alabama in the 1950s. She continues, "Poe's description of the dread, nervousness, fear of the brother, pacing through the house from 'whence for many years, he had not ventured forth' could have been a description of my father, trapped inside his beliefs in white supremacy, the purity of (white) women, the conspiracy of Jews and Blacks to take over the world" (36).

Like the woman in Poe's story who was entombed, Pratt saw her own place in her father's home as similarly constricted: protection came at the cost of confinement. To live in her father's house meant "physical, spiritual, sexual containment" (36). The only way out was, therefore, necessarily destructive. It is at this point in her narrative that she writes about Martin Luther King Jr. and her father. The whole discussion of King is framed by a critical reading of the "protection" that men in her culture used to keep "their women" pure (36). She writes: "It was this protection that I felt one evening during the height of the civil rights demonstrations in Alabama, *as the walls that had contained too many were cracking*" (36; my emphasis). Like Poe, Pratt is aware of the end of a certain way of life. A new order is being ushered in that will offer both liberation and destruction.

What she loses as she breaks out of her father's house is her own once-romantic reading of the protection he had offered. She eloquently ties together the tale of a romantic knight that Poe's characters read to each other on that stormy night when the house of Usher fell, and the southern knights who continue to fight for "the sanctity of the home," and who struggle to "protec[t] the homes and women of the South" (37) even as these edifices are crumbling. By enumerating the various kinds of violence that kept the walls of her father's home intact, Pratt's narrative returns to Greensboro. By exploring this history, she lets go of "the fear of others' release from containment" that her father had tried to frighten her with in talking about King. Yet, these passages are characterized by a deep sense of loss. Liberation requires an end to her father's way of life; his is a home that has fallen. In its wake, Pratt begins to see whole new possibilities for making a life that is different. She remakes a series of homes that she can live in, at least for a time. I understand this process. It continues to echo many of my own efforts and, yet, there are many important differences between our stories and our projects.

The *Unheimlich*

Leaving my father's home, I began my formal study of Judaism, learning about my Jewishness in the context of religion. In so doing, I let go of my father's rational and highly secular vision of the world, at least in part. Although there was still so much I clung to that was his—particularly his faith in liberalism and the promises of America—the framework was different. The liberal values he had taught me as being American and Jewish I made into a religious faith, theologizing his position as my own. God was not so much a part of my father's view of the world; theology was my innovation. I needed the authority, the power of such claims to escape certain vulnerabilities, and religious faith gave me some security. I needed to ground my values in something more firm than what my father had given me.

There is a sadness that washes over me as I write about these things. I am not sure for whom I am most sad, him or me. I do not know the particulars of my father's vulnerabilities, his fears, where they come from. I only have pieces—a mother's death, poverty, shame, foreignness, war, horror, disappointments. I do not often write about my father, but as I struggle to figure out how to make the transition from these issues of identity and home to a larger critique, like Pratt, I find myself struggling with him.

Pratt writes at the end of her essay that she bears the weight of her father's legacy; it comes to her in a dream just before he dies:

On the night before my birthday, I slept and thought I heard someone walking through my apartment; I wanted it to be my lover, but it was my father, walking unsteadily, old, carrying something heavy, a box, a heavy box, which he put down by my desk: he came through the darkness, smoking a cigarette, glints of red sparks, and sat down on my bed, wanting to rest: he was so tired; I flung my hands out angrily, told him to go, back to my mother; but crying, because my heart ached; he was my father and so tired; he left, and when I looked the floor was a field of sandy dirt, with a diagonal track dragged through it, and rows of tiny green seed just sprouting. (52–53)

I quote this passage in full because it makes me think about my father: "crying, because my heart ached; he was my father and so tired." I too feel this way about my father. He too is tired and aging, and my heart aches for all I will never know about him.

I love my father with his vulnerabilities and limitations, but my father is not like Pratt's father in very important ways. My father is not a man who has wielded a great deal of power in his life. There is no great big house to come crashing down. Nor is his legacy to me so clearly shaped by distinctions of gender and race. Unlike Pratt, I cannot speak of the responsibilities my father has bequeathed to me in terms of "my responsibility for what the men of my culture have done, in my name, my responsibility to try to change what my father had done, without ever knowing what his secrets were" (53). There are secrets that my father holds close to his heart that I will never know, but they bear the traces of a very different history. There are things that my father has done even in my name that I might want very much to undo, but not so much because they have hurt other people(s) but because they have harmed us.

These things that my father has done to us, to me, are not peculiar to him. Along with many other Eastern European Jewish men and women of his generation, my father gave up much of our collective past in order to become American. In becoming acculturated, he surrendered the language and traditions of his parents—a loss that has made my efforts to claim a Jewish position that much more difficult. To even begin to get at what the men of my culture have done to Jewish women, I have had to work against this loss as well as within it. My father gave me some critical distance from certain aspects of that Jewish past while also teaching me other ways of being an American Jew.

What my father gave me was an American identity that was contingent upon a disavowal of all that his parents had been before coming to this country. Because of this, I have no direct access to the culture of my grandparents.[17] And so, as I have returned to study Jewish texts outside of my family, I have had to continually come to terms with this complicated legacy, what Freud has called the *unheimlich*, that which was once familiar *(heimlich)* that has been repressed and is now no longer homelike. As Freud explains, the *unheimlich* is that which ought to have remained hidden and secret about the familiar but which has come to light.[18] In my case this has been a self-conscious process. I have worked hard in order to reclaim some of the historical meanings of certain Jewish traditions that exist within my family but whose historical meanings have been lost. In these ways, my discussions of Jewish traditions in the chapters that follow are uncanny. They are about the absent presence of certain traditions within American Jewish families like my own, traditions that are both familiar and strange.

Returning to Pratt and a difference between our projects, the traditions I claim are somewhat removed from my own father. In many ways, I have come to know more about these Jewish legacies than he does.[19] In this book the legacy I focus on is that of marriage as it continues to define Jewish women. I struggle with the traces of various traditions of Jewish marriage precisely because marriage remains a constitutive, critical piece of even my own family's notions of home. It is the central life-cycle event that continues to reconstitute home. As ritual, weddings offer moments of contact and continuity over, against, and within many different kinds of losses. As occasions for celebration, they hold out the promise of continuity.

In my family, weddings are important enough to spend large sums of money on lavish affairs. Even when distant relatives get married, the occasion is so crucial as to make expensive travel and lodging arrangements in order to attend. Diets, elaborate wardrobes, and expensive gifts are all planned months in advance. Weddings count. The more expensive the better.

Trying to figure out how this relates back to my work on marriage laws has been complicated. Because I call into question the asymmetries within marriage as they continue to define Jewish women, I have had to let go of the centrality of marriage in defining my own relationship to my family and to Jewish community. Nevertheless, as critical as I am of various forms of marriage, I believe that the centrality of marriage even within negotiations for Jewish emancipation remains significant. It has helped me explain some of the lingering excess around weddings, even in my own assimilated American Jewish family.

By focusing on my family's indirect connections to these legacies, I want to foreground the role of nostalgia, ignorance, and shame in my own efforts to both reclaim and critique these same legacies. In what follows, I consider what is lost and/or gained in a critical reclaiming of various notions of marriage as an identity and home for Jewish women. I argue that this version of community and family is not the only option.

part one

Jewish Women at Home

Rabbinic Judaism, Liberalism,
and Liberal Jewish Theology

two

~

Reading Ketubbot

The ketubba is perhaps the most important document for the study
of Jewish marriage and family law and the changing status of
women throughout the ages.

—Mordechai Akiva Friedman,
The Jewish Marriage in Palestine

Why marriage and the *ketubbah,* the rabbinic marriage contract?[1] Why
this traditional legal document and the ancient rabbinic discussions
about marriage in the section of the Talmud named for these documents, "Ketubbot"? In what follows I offer a feminist reading of a
standard ketubbah text. I read this text at the end of the twentieth
century from my place within an ambivalent liberal Jewish tradition
in America. I come to this text primarily through the mediation of
various kinds of translations and secondary sources, those sources
available to American Jewish readers who, like me, find themselves
somewhat removed from the rabbinic traditions out of which the
ketubbah text emerged. In so doing, I both reclaim and critique this
legacy as it continues to define "the changing status of women"
within various contemporary Jewish traditions.

When I first began to read and write about the ketubbah, I was
struck by the contrast between my desire to look critically at this
document as a legacy lost to me, an unfamiliar piece of my Jewish tradition, and my growing refamilarity with that same document in a
very different context. When I began to study Jewish texts in Israel in
the early 1980s, I was introduced to the ketubbah as a revitalized tradition. I learned about illuminated medieval manuscripts as well as
recent efforts to re-create the ketubbah as a new Jewish art form in

the context of contemporary Jewish practices.[2] It was an option I might someday consider appropriating. I might someday get married and have a kettubah made for me. One of the women in my yeshiva program was an artist who made ketubbot. She was concerned about the visual effect of the documents she created. Her ketubbot were beautiful and individualized. She created documents that illustrated the interests and commitments of each couple she worked with and for. She was not that interested in the content of these works as legal contracts.

When I began to look for information about the origins and meaning of the ketubbah some years later, the books I found offered little information. The authors of these texts were, like the woman I had studied with in Israel, more interested in the visual effects than the content of these contracts.[3] Others were interested in proper sexuality and the various rituals around weddings. Many of these texts translate contemporary guides to good marital relations into authoritative advice for liberal and more traditional Jews who are getting married.[4] What I did not find were many books about the content of the ketubbah as an historical contract or about its ongoing implications for Jewish women.

Although many of the ketubbot created by contemporary artists are now "egalitarian"—texts in which the English and/or the Aramaic content of the contract has been altered to reflect a presumably more balanced relationship[5]—the question of the ketubbah as contract, an exchange of property, and its historical role in the construction of Jewish women's identities have not been fully addressed. Along with these questions one might ask why historically, ketubbot were made to look so beautiful? What is the relationship between the aesthetic and the legal, this particular contract and its decoration?[6]

This chapter addresses some of these questions, and it does so at a moment when the popularity and visibility of this traditional document even among liberal Jews continues to grow. Within the context of contemporary Jewish weddings, the ketubbah, a hand-made piece of art, has become an expected element within the marriage ceremony.[7] It is becoming one of various investments contemporary Jewish couples make when getting married. Unlike a fancy wedding dress and just the right invitation, this work of art not only figures within the wedding ceremony but also becomes an ongoing presence in the couple's home, where it is often prominently displayed.[8] In these and other ways, the ketubbah continues to define Jewish women.

What is a Ketubbah?

"Ketubbah" comes from the Hebrew root of the verb "to write." The term literally means a writ or deed most often associated with marriage contracts. As the noted historian S. D. Goiten explains, the ketubbah is a

> "written statement" (on the obligations of the husband toward his spouse). Although the actual document spells out also the duties of the future wife, mostly in general terms, the essence of the ketubba is the husbands's financial responsibility, wherefore it is the wife who receives and keeps the ketubba.[9]

So, the kettubah is the legal document that makes a marriage official within rabbinic law. It sets the terms of the agreement and explicitly states a husband's financial commitment to his wife. According to the terms of the contract, a husband asks his wife to "be my wife according to the law of Moses and Israel. I will work, honor, feed, and support you in the custom of Jewish men, who work, honor, feed, and support their wives faithfully."[10]

In one form or another, ketubbot have been used to set the terms of Jewish marriages as far back as the second century C.E. Despite disparities between texts, we have evidence of their use from a variety of ancient sources, including fragments from the Judean Desert,[11] and citations within early rabbinic sources, including the Mishnah, the earliest authoritative rabbinic text, and various early midrashic collections.[12] Despite this evidence, however, there is no complete ketubbah text preserved in any of these early sources, nor is there a complete formulary preserved in either the Babylonian or Palestinian Talmuds.[13] This striking absence of documentation raises questions about the origins of and variations between these ancient contracts.[14]

The texts used today by most orthodox Jews, by Jews in the State of Israel, and, with varying degrees of modification, even by liberal Jews in the United States are basically versions of a Babylonian formula. According to Jewish historian Mordechai Friedman, this document became standardized by about the twelfth century C.E.[15] Before this time, however, there seems to have been a great deal of variation between the contracts of different Jewish communities. The ketubbah texts Friedman and Goiten examine from the Cairo Geniza, for example, are quite different from Babylonian texts from approximately the same period.[16]

In some of these Geniza documents, marriage is a two-party contract in which both bride and groom take on obligations to each other. In many of the fragments, the bride presents her own set of obligations to her husband. And, even more significantly, within many of these texts it is stipulated that both husband and wife can initiate a divorce,[17] a sharp contrast to the Babylonian tradition.

By keeping some of these historical variations in mind, it becomes easier to challenge some of the normative claims made about the role of wife within a standard contemporary text. In my reading of such a standard ketubbah, I question precisely these kinds of normative claims. I use some of this historical evidence in conjunction with a close rhetorical reading of the text to raise questions about how this particular document has defined what it means to be a Jewish woman.[18]

Examining a Ketubbah

The ketubbah text I examine here is a standard European text in the Babylonian tradition that follows a formula that became standard by the Middle Ages.[19] It reads as follows:

> On the . . . . . . day of the week, the . . . . . . day of the [Hebrew] month of . . . . . . , the year . . . . . . after the creation of the world, according to the manner in which we count [dates] here in the community of . . . . . . , the bridegroom . . . . . . son of . . . . . . said to this virgin, ... daughter of . . . . . . , "Be my wife according to the law of Moses and Israel. I will work, honor, feed and support you in the custom of Jewish men, who work, honor, feed, and support their wives faithfully. I will give you the settlement (mohar) of virgins, two hundred silver zuzim, which is due you according to Torah law, as well as your food, clothing, necessities of life, and conjugal needs, according to the universal custom."
>
> Miss . . . . . . agreed, and became his wife. This dowry that she brought from her father's house, whether in silver, gold, jewelry, clothing, home furnishings, or bedding, Mr. . . . . . . , our bridegroom, accepts as being worth one hundred silver pieces (zekukim).

Our bridegroom, Mr. ...... agreed, and of his own accord, added an additional one hundred silver pieces (zekukim) paralleling the above. The entire amount is then two hundred silver pieces (zekukim).

Mr. ..... our bridegroom made this declaration: "The obligation of this marriage contract (kethubah), this dowry, and this additional amount, I accept upon myself and upon my heirs after me. I can be paid from the entire best part of the property and possessions that I own under all the heavens, whether I own [this property] already, or will own it in the future. [It includes] both mortgageable property and non-mortgageable property. All of it shall be mortgageable and bound as security to pay this marriage contract, this dowry, and this additional amount. [It can be taken] from me, even from the shirt on my back, during my lifetime, and after my lifetime, from this day and forever."

The obligation of this marriage contract, this dowry, and this additional amount was accepted by Mr. ......, our bridegroom, according to all the strictest usage of all marriage contracts and additional amounts that are customary for daughters of Israel, according to the ordinances of our sages, of blessed memory. [It shall] not be a mere speculation or a sample document.

We have made a kinyan from Mr. ...... son of ...... our bridegroom, to Miss ...... daughter of ......, this virgin, regarding everything written and stated above, with an article that is fit for such a kinyan.

And everything is valid and confirmed.

...... son of ...... Witness
...... son of ...... Witness (105–106)

In what follows, I offer a close reading of this document, section by section.

The Preamble

The opening section of the ketubbah begins by situating the contract in time and space. Time is first set according to the Jewish calendar and then in terms of the dominant culture and its calendar. The community or place where the ketubbah was signed is then named (even if this is different from the place where the marriage ceremony will take place).

Next the couple is named in Hebrew: first the groom and then the bride, as the son or daughter of X. The bride is further identified according to her sexual status. Is she a virgin? If not, in what capacity had she been sexually involved with men? This is a critical issue for the completion of the contract. The community must be certain about the bride's virginity in order to set the value of her dowry and other additional amounts due her as part of the contract. The relationship between these monetary values and a woman's virginity are presented as biblically sanctioned amounts and are specified within the terms of the contract. The biblical text used to set these amounts is Exodus 22:16, which explains that the "dowry of virgins" was to be distinct from that of nonvirgins (109), translating into a sum twice that of a nonvirgin. This sum determines the amount a woman is entitled to in the event of her husband's death or a divorce.

In these ways virginity is made normative.[20] The wording of the contract both asks for explicit verification of a bride's virginity while also presuming that brides are virgins. All other cases are presented as exceptions.[21] If she is not a virgin, amends for this exception must be made at each of those points throughout the document where specific sums of money are specified. Each time, attention is given to both the norm and the fact that in this case there is an exception.

The Groom's Obligations

The text reads as follows:

> "Be my wife according to the law of Moses and Israel. I will work, honor, feed and support you in the custom of Jewish men, who work, honor, feed, and support their wives faithfully. I will give you a settlement (*mohar*) of virgins, two hundred silver zuzim, which is due you according to Torah law, as well as your food, clothing, necessities of life and conjugal needs, according to the universal custom." (105)

This passage follows immediately after the identification of the bride and groom. Here the text shifts to the first person and is written in the voice of the groom. Although there are many things to say about this passage, I want to focus on just one aspect of this statement, its repetitiveness.[22] Why does the text say in a number of different ways essentially the same thing? It is this excess that interests me. I am struck not only by the reiteration of the groom's obligations but also by the various ambiguous references to Jewish law contained within this statement.

In the opening clause, becoming a wife is connected to "the laws of Moses and Israel." This legal reference is initially ambiguous. Is this a reference to biblical and/or rabbinic law? In conflating these types of Jewish law, the text seems to add authority to a rabbinic construct. In so doing, additional authority is given to this construction of what it means to be a Jewish wife.

Beyond this, there is yet a second, quite specific reference to Jewish law that parallels this ambiguous opening statement. A biblical practice, the *mohar* or bride price, is presented as "Torah law."[23] Here I want to call attention to an additional conflation set up by this reference and the previous reference to the law of Moses and Israel. What interests me is the gap between them. By drawing a parallel between these two kinds of Jewish law, differences are effaced and authority is solidified despite the fact that these are not the same thing.[24] In this instance, the authority of the latter is lent to the former. The text conflates a general, albeit ambiguous statement of Jewish law and a very specific reference to a biblical practice.

The need to secure authority on all these fronts suggests contestation. In other words, the legal definition of the relationship between a husband and a wife is by no means self- evident. What these references highlight instead, is the fragility of these claims to authority. Moreover, in the second part of this passage, communal practice is added to the authority of both the law of Moses and Israel and Torah law. These additional appeals to authority only exacerbate this confusion. In this now third instance of parallelism, custom and Jewish law are equated. But is the law of Moses and Israel the same as the custom of Jewish men in relation to their wives? The differences between these assertions of authority are also quite telling. Even more striking is the precise repetition of the following obligations: "to work, honor, feed and support." The first reference appears to be tied to the initial invocation of the laws of Moses and Israel and Torah law; the second mention seems to be more clearly tied to the practices of Jewish men. By means of this exact repetition, the material gap between law and custom is filled. Within the logic of the text, law and practice become one and the same thing. Thus, what God demands of Jewish men is precisely what Jewish men are already doing.

If these statements were to be reversed, their ideological agenda would become more apparent. In other words, what they tell us is that Jewish men's power over Jewish women through the institution of marriage is divinely sanctioned. Through parallelism and repetition this dependant relationship takes on a self-evident quality. And yet, by going out of its way to state and restate this definition of marriage, the text also reveals its vulnerability. Instead of reflecting some already agreed-upon common practice, I am suggesting that it makes more sense to read this text rhetorically as an attempt to naturalize a particular type of relationship that may never have been universally practiced.

This statement is then followed by yet another rendition of the groom's obligations, paralleling the previous one in two ways. First, it begins with an invocation of Jewish law, and then it specifies yet another reading of the rule of custom. In this second statement, however, the formula includes additional obligations, "your food, clothing, necessities of life and conjugal needs" (105). This time, along with food and clothing, the groom spells out in even more detail what his obligations will be. Most importantly, he pledges to provide for his wife's "necessities of life" as well as her sexual needs.[25] Why does the text repeat itself in this instance? More importantly, what do the variations from the formula above signify?

To begin with, once again repetition is used to make a connection between law and custom. This time the custom—here, the specificity of the biblical law of the bride price—presumably a universal practice is juxtaposed with a very specific Torah law. The assumption of a bride's virginity upon marriage as well as her subjugation within the terms of the contract are, therefore, brought together. In this final parallel, sexuality is highlighted. The references to "virginity" and "conjugal needs" make clear that the husband having sole access to his wife's body is part of the contract.

Thus, in various ways, this passage presents an asymmetrical heterosexual relationship as the one and only sanctioned version of marriage carrying both religious and communal authority. In other words, these arrangements are both divinely commanded and natural, the way of the world, and yet the repetitions remind us of the insecurity of these basic claims. Despite this instability, the text provides a very clear picture of what it means to be a wife: within the text's vision of marriage, the relationship set up and reinforced by these two powerful statements is one of domination. There are clearly two unequal parties involved, a man and his wife, with the wife depicted here as completely dependent upon her husband for all of her most basic needs. At its best, this vision of marriage imagines a paternalistic relationship of dependence. What is especially disturbing, and perhaps liberating, about this particular series of passages is the excess of these claims. Through so many repetitions, the text reveals what literary critic Mieke Bal has called the "burden of domination," its fundamental instability and vulnerability.[26] As Bal suggests, it is for this reason that domination can be challenged. "Insecurity is not a prerogative exclusively of the dominated. . . . Traces of the painful process of gaining control can therefore be perceived in those very myths" (110). Thus, by highlighting the traces of this process of securing control in the language of the ketubbah, we can begin to unravel its mythic claims to authority.

The Bride's Obligation

The next, short section of the ketubbah is where the bride presumably speaks. "Miss . . . . . . agreed, and became his wife" (105).

Two things are striking about this "consent." The first of these is the fact that the bride is given a title, *marat*, Miss, which parallels the title to be given the groom, *mar*, Mr. The second is what the bride agrees to. Literally she agrees to "become his wife." More than this, she does this in the past tense. The document does not tell us that she is actively participating in this contract at the time of its signing but, rather, that she has already agreed to its terms at some unspecified time in the past. Her consent is, therefore, not being attested to by the witnesses present. Those signing this document only attest to the groom's consent. The date specified in the preamble refers to what he does. In other words, only the groom acts in the present tense. Thus, what this clause reminds us, as did the previous section, is that these scripted roles are not equal. In becoming a "wife," the bride is not even a party to the contract.[27]

The Bride's Property

The *nedunya*, or the dowry that the bride brought with her from her father's house, is then specified. (Here again the text presumes that the bride is a virgin.) As the text states, this includes "silver, gold, jewelry, clothing, home furnishings, or bedding." These items are listed and a monetary value is given to them. In this way, what the bride brought with her into the marriage is acknowledged as being, in some sense, her property.[28] Although her husband gains access to these assets upon marriage—he can use them to invest, for example—they remain her property and are never fully his. In the event of the dissolution of the marriage, the assumption is that the full original value of this property will revert to the woman. The ketubbah seems to assure this by carefully specifying what these assets are at the time of the marriage.

The final clause of this section is the groom's acceptance of this obligation. Here a monetary sum of 100 silver pieces is given as a minimal value for these assets, although here again there is much disagreement about this claim.[29] This sum, the *nedunya*, like the *mohar/kesef*, presumes that the bride was a virgin and sets the amount at 100 silver pieces. If the bride is not a virgin, she was only entitled to half of this amount.

Additional Obligations

Following the arrangements for the bride's *nedunya*, the groom pledges to provide an extra sum know as the *tosephta*, the addition. The text reads, "Mr. . . . . . . agreed, and of his own accord, added an additional one hundred silver pieces (*bekukim*) paralleling the above [the *nedunya*]. The entire amount [the *tosephta* plus the *nedunya*] is then two hundred silver pieces." This sum is an additional obligation that the groom takes on formulaically "of his own volition." It is in addition to what is required of him by law— the *mohar*, the initial settlement as biblically stipulated for virgins, and the *nedunya*. Here again, all calculations are based on the virginity of the bride.

Finalizing of Contractual Obligations

The Groom

The next section of the ketubbah finalizing these obligations sets out to assure the payment of these sums to the woman if the marriage ends. The text reads as follows:

> Mr. . . . . . .our bridegroom made this declaration: "The obligation of this marriage contract (*kethubah*), this dowry, and this additional amount, I accept upon myself and upon my heirs after me. It can be paid from the entire best part of the property and posses-

sions that I own under all the heavens, whether I own [this property] already, or will own it in the future. [It includes] both mortgageable property and non-mortgageable property. All of it shall be mortgageable and bound as security to pay this marriage contract, this dowry, and this additional amount. [It can be taken] from me, even from the shirt on my back, during my lifetime, and after my lifetime, from this day and forever. (105–106)

This statement is yet another reiteration of all that precedes it. Here the groom restates each of the debts he has agreed to take on by virtue of the contract: the *mohar*, the *nedunya*, and the *tosephta*, monies and property that he has agreed to give to his bride in case of his death or a divorce. In this statement, however, the means by which each of these debts would be repaid are explicitly addressed. The obligated parties are named, first the groom and, in case of his death, his (male) heirs. The text then specifies how these debts would be handled. "It can be paid from the entire best part of the property and possessions that I own under all the heavens, whether I own [this property] already, or will own it in the future." This statement makes clear that no property can be exempt from these obligations. If the groom divorces or dies, all of his property can be assessed to pay this debt since, as the text explains, "both mortgageable and non-mortgageable property" are included. Furthermore, the text states that "All of it [his various properties and possessions] shall be mortgageable and bound as security to pay this marriage contract, this dowry, and this additional amount."

This property assessment, as specified in the ketubbah, was presumably all-inclusive. Not only was a husband's real estate subject to this lien, literally all of his possessions were included. We know this from the final phrase, "even from the shirt on my back." This statement indicates that even portable property could be assessed.

The final part of this declaration reiterates the ongoing nature of this financial obligation. The obligation begins once the ketubbah is signed and continues throughout the groom's life, if the marriage ends by divorce, or "after his lifetime," if the marriage ends as a result of his death. In either event, these obligations are to be met by whatever means necessary.

Much like other key statements in the ketubbah, the next section parallels the statement preceding it. It is yet another version of these same obligations. It reads as follows:

The obligation of this marriage contract, this dowry, and this additional amount was accepted by Mr. . . . . . . , our bridegroom, according to all the strictest usage of all marriage contracts and additional amounts that are customary for daughters of Israel, according to the ordinances of our sages, of blessed memory. [It shall] not be a mere speculation or a sample document. (106)

The first part of this passage is a reiteration of the declaration that precedes it. Here, in the past tense, we read that the groom has accepted the three financial obligations specified by the terms of the contract. The difference, however, is that he has done so by custom in a fastidious manner. In other words he does these things following the strictest of all rabbinic laws and customs and the Rabbis' provisions for the daughters of Israel.[30]

The second part of this statement follows a talmudic formula, which apparently gives the groom no way out of these obligations despite the fact that they are here specified as only rabbinic law and custom. In order to make this precarious law binding, the text once again goes out of its way to make clear that the groom cannot at some later time argue that the contract was too strict, that he was tricked into signing, or that he is somehow not bound by these laws and obligations. Thus, with this final clause, he relinquishes his ability to appeal to any of a number of excuses to deny his obligations to the contract.[31]

The Witnesses

The final section of the ketubbah makes the contract binding. Here the witnesses become active participants in the contract.

We have made a *kinyan* from Mr. . . . . . . son of . . . . our bridegroom, to Miss . . . . . . daughter of . . . . . . , this virgin, regarding everything written and stated above, with an article that is fit for such a *kinyan*. (106)

In this way the witnesses confirm that the groom not only took on all the obligations already stated in the contract, but that he had made a legal transaction, a *kinyan*, with them as well. I will discuss the specifics of this transaction below. For now, it is important to note that there are two references to *kinyan* within the ketubbah. The text specifies, first, that the *kinyan* was made and, second, that it was done in an appropriate manner, "with an article fit for such a *kinyan*." Both of these ritual acts had to be confirmed before the ketubbah could be signed. Once this happened, a talmudic formula signifying that all that is in order was invoked, "and everything is valid and confirmed." This was followed by the signatures of the two witnesses.

Kinyan

Kinyan, deriving from the root of the verb meaning to establish, create, acquire, own, to take possession of, it means to make sure, to obligate a person by a special symbolic act, or to enter into an obligation by a special symbolic form.[32] According to Aryeh Kaplan, a traditional Jewish commentator:

> The word *Kinyan* literally means purchase or acquisition, and it denotes a legal transaction based on the rules of barter. The method of sealing a transaction is mentioned in the scripture where it says, "This, was the ancient practice of Israel . . . to confirm all things: a man would take off his shoe and give it to the other party. This among the Israelites, would create obligation" (Ruth 4:7). While the Biblical custom may have involved a shoe, a handkerchief or other article could have been used. Thus, if a person wanted to gain any right or obligation from another, he would give the person a handkerchief, napkin, scarf, or similar item.[33]

Although the earliest references to kinyan are biblical where it was most often associated with the acquisition of land through money,[34] it is also used in the context of men "taking" wives. It is this connection that helps explain what happens in the context of the ketubbah.[35]

The Kinyan Between the Groom and Witnesses

The transaction between the groom and the witnesses had to take place before the wedding ceremony. Once the ketubbah was read in front of these two witnesses (usually different from the two witnesses involved in the wedding ceremony),[36] the groom performed an exchange with them. According to Kaplan, the witnesses give the groom a handkerchief or napkin of theirs that he had to take hold of. Once he does so, it becomes his property, signifying that an exchange has taken place and, through this exchange, that he has taken on all of the obligations and privileges spelled out in the ketubbah.[37] The witnesses were then able to say, as specified in the document, that "we have made a kinyan."[38] This is the final clause of the contract.

As I have explained, this ritual act signifies that the groom has gained both rights and obligations from another. The question is, from whom? According to Kaplan, the witnesses take the place of the bride, although the rights and obligations attested to are symbolically between the bride and groom. The witnesses take the place of the bride since she was not present for the signing.[39] This raises an additional set of questions about why the bride is not present for the signing.[40]

In contrast to Kaplan's explanation of the first question, I believe that the groom contracts not so much with the bride but more with the community. This means that the witnesses act on behalf of the community. Through them the groom obligates himself to the community as opposed to the bride. This interpretation makes additional sense when we consider the role of the witnesses. They are never described as agents for the bride or her family but, rather, as upright and learned members of the community. With the witnesses understood thus, the absence of the bride need not be accounted for. She is not important to this legal procedure.

The Ketubbah in the Marriage Ceremony

The final part of the ketubbah's enactment is its reading during the marriage ceremony. After the groom recites the traditional formula, "Behold, you are consecrated to me with this ring according to the law of Moses and Israel,"[41] and gives the bride a ring, the ketubbah is read out loud. The reading of the ketubbah also marks the middle of the ceremony, separating what were once two distinct rituals, betrothal, *kiddushin*, and the full fledged marriage, *nisu'in*.[42] The recitation of the contract signifies that the legal transaction has already taken place. After the ketubbah is read it is given to the bride.

Women, Consent, and Silence

It is commonly argued that historically the ketubbah protected women from being easily divorced and provided them with financial and social security in the event of a divorce.[43] Yet I am not convinced that this was the case. Why, for example, does this text imagine that Jewish women need protection in the first place? And from whom does it think they need to be protected? By naturalizing Jewish women's vulnerability as wives, the ketubbah both creates and justifies precisely this situation.[44] The same paternalistic impulse to protect women from being abandoned or uncared for by men also effaces other possibilities.

The question of whether Jewish women agreed to this situation is not clear from the evidence of the ketubbah, a contract to which they were not a party. It is also not clear from the terms of the marriage ceremony where, as elsewhere, "The woman's consent . . . does not require definite articulation. Silence on the woman's part may be construed as consent (*shkikah ke-hodayah*). In other words, if a woman is given a sum of money or an article as a token of betrothal [as in the marriage ceremony] and does not protest the act, she is betrothed."[45]

This consent by silence is especially disturbing, because it relates not only to marriage but also to issues of rape and sexual violation within rabbinic sources.[46] In tractate Ketubbot of the Talmud[47] as well as other rabbinic sources, laws about rape and sexual violation are linked directly to questions of marriage. In these texts, lack of consent is construed as active verbal protestation. Only if there is evidence that a woman cried out is the sexual assault a rape.[48] As will become clear, this ambiguity around a woman's sexual desires and the complicated relationship between these desires and her consent are at the heart of chapter 3 of tractate Ketubbot of the Talmud and its discussion of liability for the pain of rape.

Rape, Pain, Desire, and Consent

When I first set out to look for a ketubbah text, I began reading tractate Ketubbot of the Talmud devoted to questions of marriage.[49] I was looking for a copy of this illusive rabbinic contract. Strikingly, I never found a copy of this document within tractate Ketubbot. Despite the fact that this entire section of the Talmud is about rabbinic marriage and is named for this contract, the text does not include a version of it. There is no specific ketubbah offered within either the Babylonian or the Palestinian Talmuds, although these texts offer discussions about various aspects of the marriage contract.[50]

Instead, as I read through these rabbinic texts that were presumably about marriage, I was startled to come upon a discussion of the pain of rape. Needless to say, I was surprised. This was not the place

I expected to find this kind of information, but it is how I first came to connect the ketubbah, the rabbinic marriage contract, with chapter 3 of tractate Ketubbot of the Babylonian Talmud, a text about the pain of rape.[51]

In working through this rabbinic text about rape, I had to rethink the vision of home the Rabbis had held out to me. Like the ketubbah, this text offered me little comfort. Despite the fact that it was about the pain of rape, I found little here that echoed my own experience. In chapter 3 of tractate Ketubbot of the Babylonian Talmud, what the Rabbis address are the financial implications of rape. They discuss the cases of rape and seduction and the fines payable in each. Despite the various rabbinic positions presented in this text, no one expresses the outrage of the women involved. The woman's pain and anger remain unexplored.

Through a close reading of this text, I will now show how, in these instances, violence and sexuality are indelibly linked. I will also show how issues of desire and consent are related to the pain of rape. The text reads as follows:

> Mishnah. The seducer pays three forms [of compensation] and the violator [rapist] four. The seducer pays compensation for indignity and blemish and the [statutory] fine, while the violator [rapist] pays and additional [form of compensation] in that he pays for the pain.[52]

Given the way this Mishnah, the initial legal statement, is worded, I expected to hear about the pain involved in rape for the woman, but this was not the case. Instead, the Gemara, the commentary that follows, reads:

> Gemara. [For the] Pain of what?- The father of Samuel replied: For the pain [he has inflicted] when he thrust her upon the ground.
>
> R. Zera demurred: Now then, if he has thrust her upon silk stuffs would he for a similar reason be exempt? And should you say that the law is so indeed, was it not [it may be retorted] taught [in a baraita]: "R. Simeon b. Judah stated in the name of R. Simeon, A violator does not pay compensation for the pain [he has inflicted] because [39B] the woman would ultimately have suffered the same pain from her husband, but they said to him: One who is forced to

intercourse cannot be compared with one who acts willingly?" [The reference] in fact, said R. Nahman in the name of Rabbah b. Abbuha [is to the] pain of opening the feet [legs], for so it said in Scripture, *And hast opened thy feet to every one that passed by.* R. Nahman replied in the name of Rabbah b. Abbuha: The case of one who has been seduced may be compared to that of a person who said to a friend, "Tear up my silk garments and you will be free from liability." "My?" Are they not her father's? This, however, said R. Nahman in the name of Rabbah b. Abbuha, [is the explanation]: The smart woman among them declare that one who is seduced experiences no pain. But do we not see that one who is seduced experiences pain?- Abye replied: Nurse told me: Like hot water on a bald head. Raba said: R. Hisda's daughter told me, Like the prick of the blood-letting lancet. R. Papa said: The daughter of Abba of Sura told me, Like hard crust in the jaw.[53]

What is the pain that is being addressed here? "Thrust upon the ground." This commentary begins by connecting the pain of rape to the assault and not necessarily to the sexual violation. But this position is quickly called into question. What if a rape takes place and the woman is apparently not harmed in the process of being accosted? This is the question raised by the example brought by R. Zera. What happens when she is "thrust upon silk stuffs" and, presumably, not harmed in the process? Is this or is this not rape? In other words, if the woman is not also beaten, has she been raped? In their attempts to figure out what it is that is so painful about rape, the Rabbis, like many of today's legal reformers, seem to make a distinction between battery and sexual assault.[54] They acknowledge that rape can be additionally violent if a woman is also beaten. But, as this passage continues, the Rabbis, unlike some contemporary legal thinkers, do not simply define rape as violence, i.e., only as an assault. Instead they focus not so much on the assault but the sexual violation. R. Zera's question or comment asks the question directly: Is the pain about being thrown to the ground, or is it the sexual violation whether any other harm is also committed? As the commentary continues, it makes clear that the pain of rape is about the sexual violation. Even if assaulted on silk stuffs, it is a rape. Before shifting arguments, the text states clearly that rape is primarily a sexual violation. It does this by making an analogy between rape and intercourse within marriage.

R. Simeon b. Judah, speaking in the name of R. Simeon, explains this by citing a *baraita*, an early authoritative legal text from the first two or three centuries of the common era but not found in the Mishnah.[55] It says that "a Violator does not pay compensation for the pain [he has inflicted] because the woman would ultimately have suffered the same pain from her husband." In other words, the *baraita* claims that rape and first intercourse with one's husband are one and the same thing. But this statement raises additional questions. It makes an overt connection between rape and marital intercourse.[56]

In response to this question, the text makes a further distinction. In the name of the majority opinion, the focus of the argument begins to shift. The reply to R. Simeon b. Judah's position is that there is a difference between desired and undesired intercourse. The references shift from a young girl who is accosted to a discussion of women more generally,[57] and from the question of whether there is pain in first intercourse to a determination of the degree of pain in both desired or undesired intercourse. The text presumes that there is always a degree of pain involved at least in first intercourse.[58] Again, this is a remarkable admission. In effect, it means that R. Simeon b. Judah's position is not completely refuted. As I read it, both a raped woman and a wife experience pain in intercourse. Just how much pain a woman experiences is determined by how willing a participant she is in the sexual encounter. Thus, instead of staying with the case of rape, the text moves on to explore the parameters of desired intercourse.

In the argument that follows, the text continues to distinguish between desired and undesired intercourse, with implications for both rape and marriage. R. Nahman claims that the pain a woman experiences is simply in "opening the feet [legs]." He argues that the pain discussed in the Mishnah with regard to rape is simply the pain of intercourse. He cites a biblical text, Ezekiel 16:23, to bolster his position. By citing as proof this biblical text about marital infidelity and betrayal, he ends up raising an additional set of disturbing questions. The Ezekiel passage uses the imagery of marriage to describe Israel's idolatrous relationship with God. In the biblical text, Israel is described as God's whoring wife. God is presented as an angry, jealous, and powerful husband. "The power of this image derives from the exclusivity of that relationship, which forbids the wife to have sexual relations with any other man; thus by analogy, Israel is forbidden to worship other gods."[59] In Ezekiel 16:23, Israel "opens the legs" to every passerby, thereby multiplying her harlotries. The issue here is not so much pain as sexual transgression and sinfulness. In the Ezekiel text, the power dynamics are reversed. The woman is not the victim but rather the perpetrator. She inflicts pain on her husband; God is the injured party[60]—the pain is "His."[61] By acting like a harlot, the woman brings not pain, but shame upon herself. Her pain is not at issue. In the biblical text, she chooses to play the harlot. In this way the text returns to the question of volition: What does it means for a woman to choose to have intercourse outside of the structure of marriage? This is precisely the problem the talmudic text goes on to address.

In cases of seduction, the text argues that women allow themselves to be "hurt." According to the imagery in the Gemara, the later rabbinic commentary on the Mishnah dating from approximately the fourth to the eighth centuries of the common era, a woman literally gives her seducer license to damage her stuff or, more importantly, her body. But this time there is another problem. Who legally controls a woman's body or indeed her property? Does she have the authority to either damage or give away any of these properties? In the name of R. Nahman in the name of Rabbah b. Abbuha, the text continues with a parable: "A person who said to his friend, 'Tear up my silk garments and you will be free from liability.' 'My?' Are they not her father's?" According to this account, a woman's virginity is not hers to give away because it belongs to her father.[62] Given this, her seducer is not liable to her, but to her father. Here the woman's agency is called into question, since permission can only be granted by her father.[63] What becomes clear is that desire and consent are not the same thing. Desire determines the degree of pain involved in intercourse, but it does not mean a woman's consent. Desire becomes legally efficacious in the case of rape. Damages must be paid for the pain involved in an act of undesired heterosexual intercourse.

Returning to the terms of the Mishnah, the earlier source, my question is, why does the seducer not pay damages for the pain of intercourse? Here again, the text makes a distinction between desired and nondesired intercourse. Because there was some kind of volition in the case of seduction, the pain is considered minimal. Given this, R. Nahman argues that the "smart woman"[64] might go so far as to claim that there was no pain at all in the case of seduction.[65] This appeal to the expertise of women is used to strengthen the distinction between rape and seduction as expressed in the Mishnah but otherwise obscured by the Gemara. According to some commentators, "By her consent to suffer the pain the woman [in the case of seduction] has exempted the man from paying compensation."[66] She does this not so much by having the legal right to give herself to her seducer; rather, by expressing her desire she can alter the degree of pain involved. As a willing participant, she experiences very little pain and, therefore, she does not receive compensation.

The Gemara ends with a discussion of the relative pain of especially first intercourse. This pain is described as minimal. Here the text offers three concrete examples, each in the name of a particular woman: for Nurse, it is "like hot water on a bald head," for R. Hisda's daughter "like a prick of the blood-letting lancet," and, for Abba of Sura's daughter, "like hard crust in a jaw."[67]

By presenting this argument in the names and voices of women, the text seems to make up for the fact that, up until this point in its argument, no women were consulted about these issues. But even when they do appear, their voices are mediated by particular Rabbis who speak for them. Confirming what they themselves can never know, the Rabbis use these women's names to add weight and authority to their speculations about women's desires and women's pain. I find their fantasies about these matters (the entire discussion of the Gemara) quite disturbing.[68] To presume that even desired intercourse is painful not only effaces the possibility of sexual pleasures for women but also reinforces a narrow construction of a normative heterosexuality. Pain becomes an imagined norm. As I return to the question of compensation for the pain of rape, the question with which the Mishnah began, I am disappointed. That pain is never addressed. The Gemara's discussion of rape offers me little comfort.

Conclusions

The evidence of the ketubbah, seen alongside this single rabbinic text about rape, offers a disturbing picture of Jewish women. These texts reveal certain rabbinic preoccupations with control and authority as well as a series of fantasies about sex, violence, and pleasure. Within the terms of the marriage contract, wives are defined as utterly dependent. The asymmetrical power relationship described within the terms of the contract is given tremendous authority. Despite the pre-

cariousness of these claims, this relationship is presented as both natural and divinely sanctioned.

Chapter 3 of tractate Ketubbot links this normative definition of
what it means to be a good Jewish woman, a wife, to the crime of
rape. It does this by highlighting the relative pain of intercourse both
within and outside of marriage. The talmudic text constructs its own
fantasies about sex and violence, not from the standpoint of creating
normative relationships, but from the site of prohibition. It defines
rape and seduction in relation to sex in marriage through a fantasy
about women and pain. The text blurs important distinctions
between desire and coercion by assuming that women always experience at least first intercourse as somehow painful.

I have taken apart these two legal texts in order to expose some of
the dangers they pose for Jewish women. By reading rhetorically, I
have called attention to some of the ambivalences within these claims
to authority and suggested a more cautious reading. I have not suggested simply rejecting this legacy, as I do not believe that that is possible. These are normative traditions that have defined Jewish women
for centuries, and their assumptions have been repeated so many
times that they have become natural. They continue to define even
contemporary Jewish understandings of gender in terms of these
kinds of sexual relationships. I have taken the time to re-read these
texts because I believe that they continue to define what it means to
be a Jewish woman. Thus, although I can not simply reject this legacy,
I can express my disappointment.

Despite the fact that contemporary Jews continue to appeal to liberalism as an answer to this problem (by, for example, rewriting the
ketubbah in more egalitarian terms), I do not see this as an answer to
the kinds of problems raised in this chapter. As disappointed as I am
with the Rabbis, I came to them as an alternative to liberalism and its
limited vision of identity and home.

three

~

Becoming Liberal

The French Revolution marked the transformation of the nation from a focus of often divided loyalty to an all-embracing principle.

—George Mosse, *Nationalism and Sexuality*

It is as if the very emergence of the colonial is dependent for its representation upon some strategic limitation or prohibition *within* the authoritative discourse.

—Homi Bhabha, *Of Mimicry and Man.*

This chapter begins with the French Revolution in 1879, which marked the beginning of Jewish emancipation.[1] With the revolution, France was the first nation to grant Jews citizenship and a place within the liberal state, to offer them a new national home. As historian George Mosse explains, the revolution came to solidify national loyalties into an "all embracing principle." The question was, were Jews able to adhere to this principle? To what extent were they Frenchmen like all other Frenchmen? In this chapter, I am interested in what, from the beginning, distinguished Jews from their fellow citizens and how this difference already challenged the revolution's promise of inclusion. By returning to France, I try to look at the inception of some of my own deepest commitments to the promises of liberal emancipation.

Like Homi Bhabha's emerging colonial subject, the emergence of the liberal Jewish subject in France was also dependent for its representation upon certain strategic limitations. In France, this limitation was scripted in terms of fidelity. By blurring the boundaries between nation and family, marriage and citizenship, the question for Jews was one of loyalty. Could Jews be trusted? Did they have dual loyalties? Would or could they ever really become citizens of France like everyone else?

From the beginning of Jewish emancipation, Jewish citizenship and cultural acceptance went hand in hand. Liberalism promised both a new cultural and a new civic home, linking these public and private desires. Citizenship, the pledging of one's loyalty to a particular nation-state, became both figuratively and literally a familial obligation. In France, fidelity not only marked the relationship between citizens and the state but also defined the proper (state-sanctioned) marital relationship between a husband and his wife. Marriage became the foundation for the liberal state. By making the nation-state a kind of home, it made public and private loyalties into two sides of the same coin. Thus, the granting of political rights and obligations to Jews came with a series of "private" demands.[2] After the revolution, Jews were required to speak French, attend French schools, and adhere to French middle-class notions of propriety, including notions of taste, decorum, and comportment. They were to do this even within the private realms of family and religious life.

Given the all-encompassing nature of these requirements, there were, necessarily, limitations. Although, as historian Paula Hyman argues, "the majority of French Jews cherished bourgeois values of family, property, and patriotism with the ferocity of parvenus eager for acceptance,"[3] there were no guarantees of acceptance. Ironically, Jewish zeal in these matters marked Jews as different and ensured the failure of their efforts to ever fully assimilate into French society.

In what follows, I flesh out this limitation by looking specifically at the terms of Jewish political emancipation. I do this first through a brief reading of "Concerning the Amelioration of the Civil Status of the Jews," a 1781 tract in defense of Jewish betterment by Christian Wilhelm Dohm, an enlightened historian, economist, and Prussian government official,[4] and, second, by focusing on the 1806 exchange between Napoleon and a gathering of Jewish notables on the question of Jewish emancipation.[5] Through a careful reading of this discussion, I point to some of the ambivalences within liberal discourse and its claims to liberation, especially as regards Jews, and call attention to the role of submission within these negotiations.

More specifically, I look at the critical role of marriage in Napoleon's first three questions. These questions highlight the role of gender in these negotiations for Jewish emancipation. They also explain how, by bringing together ritual and law, custom and morality, family, and patriae, marriage came to define the relationship between Jews and liberal states.

The Liberal Solution to the Jewish Problem

The French Revolution brought liberalism's social contract from theory into practice, opening up the possibilities of political power to those of the property-owning class, which eventually included Jews.

In the period leading up to the French Revolution, there were many questions raised about the status of the Jews in France. [6] Even those who came to the defense of Jews often conceded that there was a "Jewish problem." They argued that exclusionary policies toward Jews led to their degradation, and that this "Jewish problem" could be solved by making Jews into productive and loyal subjects or citizens. As Christian Wilhelm Dohm wrote, as quoted in Chazan and Raphael's *Modern Jewish History*:

> We have found in the oppression and in the restricted occupation of the Jews the true source of their corruption. Then we have discovered also at the same time the means of healing this corruption and of making the Jews better men and useful citizens. With the elimination of the unjust and unpolitical treatment of the Jews will also disappear the consequences of it; and when we cease to limit them to one kind of occupation, then the detrimental influence of that occupation will no longer be so noticeable. [7]

Dohm went on to present a series of concrete suggestions about how France might go about changing these policies. Many of these suggestions became the basis for Jewish emancipation and included the granting of political rights, the opening of various occupations formerly closed to Jews (especially agricultural, public service, and guild positions), [8] the providing of liberal educational opportunities and civil rights to Jews, as well as the right to worship according to their own faith. In return for these rights and privileges, rabbinic authority was to be ceded and, in its place, Jews were expected to adhere to the authority of the state. The French Revolution's emancipation of the Jews built on these suggestions. In these ways, France became the first western nation to grant Jews citizenship. [9]

French Jewry is, in fact, a child of the Revolution. As a result of the revolutionary upheaval in the concept of the nation-state, the 40,000 Jews resident in France in 1789 became the first in the West to achieve full emancipation—that is, acceptance as equal citizens with all the civic and political rights and obligations which citizenship entailed.[10]

Despite this promise, Jewish liberation did not happen immediately:

The debate regarding the emancipation of the Jews was prolonged and acrimonious because of doubts as to the willingness and ability of the Jews to assimilate within French society and fulfill the obligations of citizenship.[11]

Given these tensions, by the time Napoleon came to power there was already a precedent for questioning the efficacy of Jewish emancipation. From the beginning, the question of Jewish loyalty—whether it would be possible for Jews to truly become French citizens—was at issue. The liberal solution was to give, in the words of Clermont-Tonnerre before the National Assembly in 1789, "To the Jews as individuals—everything; to the Jews as a group— nothing. They must constitute neither a body politic nor an order; they must be citizens individually."[12] This demand echoed liberalism's dominating and indeed revolutionary focus on the presumably undifferentiated individual as the building block of the liberal state. This was also a position that Jews would never quite be able to take. Instead, Jewish entry into liberalism's social contract was partial, both incomplete and virtual. Given this, Jews were considered dangerous to the state. For, like colonial subjects outside of Europe, liberal Jewish subjects were dependent for their representation upon a strategic limitation within liberal discourse.[13]

Because Jews resembled but were never quite French, they were considered suspect. Fears about Jewish loyalty were present even in the earliest debates leading up to the granting of Jewish emancipation during the revolution.[14] This same trepidation was repeated as a matter of grave and precipitating concern for Napoleon, whose suspicions about Jewish allegiances were nowhere more apparent than in his first three questions to the Jewish notables about Jews and marriage. By bringing together national and marital fidelity, literally and figuratively, these questions made explicit the overarching nature of liberal emancipation as both a public and private enactment and manifested that marriage was the model for the proper relationship between Jews and the liberal nation-state. They also demonstrated the critical role of Jewish women within this emancipatory wager.

Napoleon's Queries: At What Price Jewish Emancipation?

In 1806, Napoleon ordered an Assembly of Jewish Notables and, after that, a Great Sanhedrin to convene in Paris in order to determine the ongoing viability of Jewish citizenship.[15] According to the decree:

> The conduct of many among those of your persuasion have excited complaints, which have found their way to the foot of the throne; these complaints were founded on truth. Nevertheless, His Majesty has been satisfied with stopping the progress of the evil, and he has wished to hear from you on the means of providing a remedy.[16]

For Napoleon, there were still questions about the alleged inappropriate behavior of some Jews, particularly around issues of commerce, for which all Jews were to be called into account. Although these assemblies were ostensibly convened to secure the rights of Jews as individuals within Napoleon's France, ironically the primary task of these assemblies was to call the Jews to speak in one collective accountable voice. Like Dohm and the revolutionary assembly, Napoleon's strategy was also to use citizenship as the means to a solution. Noble Jews were enlisted to help enact this plan.

As the decree continues: "You will, no doubt, prove worthy of so tender, so paternal a conduct, and you will feel all the importance of the trust thus reposed in you."[17] The decree demanded that the Jews assembled pledge the complete loyalty of every individual Jew to the state.

> Our most ardent wish is to be able to report to the Emperor that, among individuals of the Jewish persuasion, he can reckon as many faithful subjects, determined to conform in everything to the laws and to the morality which ought to regulate the conduct of all Frenchmen.[18]

Along with the explicit demand for group loyalty, those assembled were also asked to answer Napoleon's questions as honestly and openly as possible.

The decree then posed twelve specific questions.[19]

1. Is it lawful for Jews to marry more than one wife?
2. Is divorce allowed by the Jewish religion? Is divorce valid, although not pronounced by courts of justice and by virtue of the laws in contradiction with the French Code?
3. Can a Jewess marry a Christian, or a Jew a Christian woman? Or has the law ordered that the Jews should inter-marry among themselves?
4. In the eyes of the Jews are Frenchmen considered as brethren or as strangers?
5. In either case what conduct does their law prescribe toward Frenchmen not of their religion?
6. Do the Jews born in France, and treated by the law as French citizens, acknowledge France as their country? Are they bound to defend it? Are they bound to obey the laws, and to follow the directions of the civil code?
7. What kind of police jurisdiction have the rabbis among the Jews?
8. What judicial power do they exercise among them?
9. Are the forms of the elections of rabbis and their police juris-diction regulated by the law, or are they only sanctioned by custom?
10. Are there professions from which the Jews are excluded by their law?
11. Does the law forbid the Jews from taking usury from their brethren?
12. Does it forbid or does it allow usury towards strangers?[20]

The Jewish Notables Response

Given the preoccupations of the decree, the notables' answers to Napoleon's questions were carefully framed within an overall state-ment of Jewish loyalty to the emperor. Moreover, the declaration was defined in halakhic terms, as Napoleon had requested. The principle of Jewish law invoked was an ancient injunction demanding Jewish obedience to the laws of a prince. Thus, in gratitude to Napoleon, the Assembly of Jewish Notables declared

that they are fully determined to prove worthy of the favors His Majesty intends for them, by scrupulously conforming to his paternal intentions; that their religion makes it their duty to consider the law of the prince as the supreme law in civil and political matters; that, consequently, should their religious code, or its various interpretations, contain civil or political commands at variance with those of the French Code, those commands would, of course, cease to influence and govern them, since they must, above all acknowledge and obey the laws of the prince.[21]

This declaration makes clear the deferential stance taken by the Jewish notables. Although this is not surprising given the task before them, there is a deep irony herein: Despite the overt promise of liberation, the whole interaction between the Jewish notables and Napoleon was framed in terms of paternalistic deference. For his benevolence, Napoleon would be granted complete authority. The Jews' emancipation came at the price of subordination. With Napoleon's rise to power, citizenship was literally guaranteed on the basis of loyalty to a prince, a much earlier rabbinic stance toward non-Jewish authority.

According to this rabbinic principle, if there were conflicts between Jewish and princely authority, princely authority would take precedence.[22] Given this, even with liberal emancipation, the structural relationship between Jewish and non-Jewish authority remained constant. With the revolution, the French Code simply took the place of "the law of the prince" only to be reapplied to an emperor with Napoleon's rise to power. Thus, despite the radical nature of much of what Napoleon and, indeed, the revolution had offered French Jews, the mechanism through which rights and privileges were granted did not change. Jews remained at the mercy of those non-Jewish authorities with power over them, grateful for whatever rights and privileges were granted them, however limited.[23] As the notables wrote:

> That, in consequence of this principle [obedience to the law of the prince], the Jews have, at all times, considered it their duty to obey the laws of the state, and that, since the revolution they, like all Frenchmen, have acknowledged no others.[24]

The ancient strategy was given new life with emancipation. Because Napoleon demanded a halakhic response, a legal precedent, the principle of obedience to the law of a prince with all of its ambiguity, worked perfectly. It gave Napoleon what he wanted. The dilemma was that, if Jews were to remain beholden to Napoleon in precisely the same way in which they had been to other princes—who had allowed them to live in their lands without political emancipation—to what extent did emancipation really free the Jews?

The Marriage Questions

The notables' responses to Napoleon's questions about marriage are emblematic not only of the emperor's desire for a kind of marriage between the Jews and the state but also of the notables' strategy of deference to Napoleon.[25] As I will now demonstrate, the notables' answers to the following three questions clearly signal the ambivalences within France's embrace of Jews.[26]

1. Is it lawful for Jews to marry more than one wife?
2. Is divorce allowed by the Jewish religion? Is divorce valid, although not pronounced by courts of justice and by virtue of the laws in contradiction with the French Code?
3. Can a Jewess marry a Christian, or a Jew a Christian woman? Or has the law ordered that the Jews should intermarry among themselves?

The framing of these questions asked Jews to submit not only to French legal authority in the matter of marriage but also to French middle-class customs and norms in regard to proper heterosexuality. The first question asked literally if Jews were monogamous. The second demanded that the French state have authority over Jewish marriage and divorce proceedings, while the third demanded social integration through marriage.[27] Seen as a whole, these questions challenged the ongoing viability of a separate Jewish community in France. They proposed Jewish assimilation and/or conversion into the dominant culture.

Questions 1 and 2 demanded clear lines of jurisdiction be drawn around the transaction of marriage. First the law of the land demanded undivided loyalty; polygamy was the opposite of such a stance, overtly challenging the notion of fidelity not only to a spouse but to the state. If Jews had multiple family loyalties, how could they be trusted as faithful citizens of a single nation? Here marriage brings together a vision of long-term commitment to both the state and one's family. It conjoins both public and private notions of fidelity and belonging.

On another level, however, this question was also about adherence to particular French laws and customs. There was no polygamy in France. Would the Jews, a foreign people known sometimes to allow their men to have more than one wife, follow the laws of France in these most intimate of matters? Here, the fear was grounded in both a historical understanding of Jewish communities allowing polygamy as well as in evidence of polygamy as an ongoing practice outside of Europe. Was there a legal precedent for supporting Jewish adherence to monogamous French practices?

The notables' answer to this first question was yes. They did this by first invoking as law the custom of European Jews since the eleventh century, by which Jews had been monogamous. Second, they appealed to colonial assumptions about the backwardness of eastern practices as a way of acknowledging that there were still Jews who practiced polygamy at that time; outside of Europe there had been near-contemporary Jewish communities that practiced polygamy. The notables used this acknowledgement of a difference between Jews in order to assuage Napoleon's fears about infidelity. By claiming that polygamy was an eastern practice, they were able to distinguish themselves as Europeans.

But behind this question was, as I have already indicated, a more basic concern about the persistence of Jewish difference in France. Would Jews conform to French social practices? Polygamy marked Jews as other in a crucial realm: the private sphere, upon which civil society was based. Indiscretions in this sphere were particularly dangerous to the stability of the state as a family unit, and the notables had to clearly renounce this practice precisely because marriage and family had already become central tropes in defining the nation.[28] In this way, monogamy reinforced a vision of national loyalty as an all-embracing principle.

Question 2 demanded loyalty to the law of the land. In this case, the initiation and dissolution of marriage had to be carefully controlled by the state. The question asked who would have jurisdiction over these critical transactions. The second part of this question is especially telling. "Is divorce valid although not pronounced by courts of justice and by virtue of laws in contradiction with those of the French Code?" The clear point of this question was to assure the absolute authority of the French Code in all such matters.

In answering this question, the initial statement of the Jewish notables was quite clear. "Repudiation is allowed by the law of Moses[29]; but is not valid if not previously pronounced by the French Code."[30] This general statement was then followed by a reiteration of the principle of Jewish loyalty and submission to princely authority. More specifically, the notables referred to oaths taken by French Jews after the revolution. This reminded Napoleon that the Jews of France had already pledged their loyalty to French authority in all such matters. Given this, the notables reassured Napoleon that both initiation and repudiation of marriage rights were to remain under state jurisdiction:

> The rabbis could not impart the matrimonial benediction till it appeared to them that the civil contract had been performed before the civil officer, in like manner they cannot pronounce repudiation, until it appears to them that it has already been pronounced by a sentence which gives it validity.[31]

The notables went on to proclaim that Jewish tradition was at one with the civil code in all such matters for which the rabbis had no authority of their own. Given that civil contracts became critical with the French revolution and Jewish emancipation, the notables reiterated that formal control of the institution of marriage had already shifted from rabbinic to civil authority.

The liberal marriage contract became Jewish precisely because "it may be justly affirmed that the Jewish religion agrees on this subject with the civil code."[32] Through this statement of accommodation, the notables relinquished control over the institution of marriage, bringing Jewish women under the aegis of the liberal state. By upholding the terms of the liberal marriage contract women would play a crucial role in Jewish emancipation. Like their Jewish husbands, brothers, and fathers, they also entered into a liberal contractual arrangement that demanded fidelity in the form of subordination.

Question 3 proved to be the most difficult question of all for the notables to answer:

> The truth would insult French Christians while an accommodation would ignore fifteen hundred years of clear Jewish legislation against intermarriage. The answer, which divided Jewish law into nonexistent categories, was unique in its historical importance as well as its ingenuity.[33]

The question of intermarriage made explicit the public/private nature of emancipation for both Jewish men and Jewish women. The question asked not only if Jewish men could marry Christian women but also if Jewish women could marry Christian men.[34]

For Napoleon, the question of intermarriage necessarily went both ways. Part of what made this question so troubling for the notables was that it made even more explicit the desire for, as well as the impossibility of, Jewish social integration. In this instance, bringing Jews into French culture was quite literally figured as a family matter, a matter of bringing Jews into French homes and families. Implicit in this question was both the promise of integration as well as the fear of Jewish difference. Assimilation was to be accomplished explicitly through the institution of marriage. By marrying into the dominant culture, one individual at a time, be it male or female, the hope was that Jews would slowly cease to exist as a separate people and become a part of the French family.[35] Jewish women would no longer be Jewish, because their identities would be subsumed under those their non-Jewish husband's. For Jewish men, the lure was ultimately social acceptance through family connections—either through religious conversion or, at the very least, new family affiliations—through which they would abandon their ties to a separate Jewish community.

Not surprisingly, the notables' reply to this question was strained. It began by stating unequivocally that "the law does not say that a Jewess cannot marry a Christian, nor a Jew a Christian woman; nor does it state that the Jews can only intermarry among themselves."[36] Following this statement, the notables went on to discuss biblically forbidden unions. They argued that these restrictions were only to have applied to Jewish men in relation to peoples who no longer exist. "The prohibition in general applies only to nations in idolatry. The Talmud declares formally that modern nations are not to be considered as such, since they worship, like us, the God of heaven and earth."[37] This statement was presumably the proof text for the notables' initial assertion that intermarriages were permitted according to Jewish law. Nevertheless, no specific talmudic text was cited. This discussion was then accompanied by a qualification that explained that there was a dispute between the rabbis and lay leaders assembled and that the rabbis' position was not unlike that of Catholic clergy on these matters.[38] Like their Catholic counterparts, the rabbis held that marriage was a religious ceremony and, as such, required both bride and groom to share a single faith.

In contrast to the notables' answer to question 2, this answer suggested that there were important differences between religious and civil ceremonies despite the Jews' commitment to state authority. In order to temper this claim of difference, however, the position was only made in the name of the rabbis present and not of the entire gathering of notables.

The answer continued by stating that one does not cease to be a Jew by marrying a non-Jew or even by having a civil ceremony. Here again, some of the gaps between the practices and the beliefs or, for that matter, between the public statements and the private practices of those Jews assembled became increasingly apparent. Despite intermarriage, Jews remain Jews. From this answer it was clear that some ambiguity about whether Jewish weddings were in fact ever exclusively civil ceremonies remained open to debate.

In considering intermarriage, the rabbis made explicit the gap between Jewish and civil authorities. In cases of intermarriage Jewish difference continued to make a difference and, ironically, the only way to alleviate the problem was to insist upon even more civil intermarriage. The more intermarriage, the less need there would be for particularistic authorities altogether. Although this strategy of assimilation through marriage held much promise in the nineteenth century in France, it already made explicit ongoing ambivalences toward liberal emancipation for Jews. The persistence of Jewish difference, the need for "intermarriage" and not just "marriage" continued to disrupt any smooth vision of Jewish integration within the liberal state.[39]

Studying this historical state desire for assimilation through intermarriage in France made me think again about marriage as a liberal institution. I began to see parallels between how liberal states attempted to homogenize Jews and what happened to women within liberal marriage. In chapter 4, I use feminist political theorist Carole Pateman's analysis of liberalism's sexual contract in order to extend this critique of liberalism.[40] I offer a more pointed account of the power dynamics within liberal marriage in order to further question the notion that liberalism emancipated Jewish women. By examining liberal marriage in conjunction with liberal rape laws, I will argue that liberalism actually both reinforced and made invisible the subordination of women through its sexual contract.

four

The Sexual Contract

Both nationalism and respectability defined the role of women too, and the different ways in which these roles were defined has a direct bearing upon the definition of normality and abnormality in bourgeois society.

—George Mosse, *Nationalism and Sexuality*

The two spheres of civil society are at once separate and inseparable. The public realm cannot be fully understood in the absence of the private sphere, and, similarly, the meaning of the original contract is misinterpreted without both, mutually dependant, halves of the story. Civil freedom depends on patriarchal right.

—Carole Pateman, *The Sexual Contract*

Although the dream of liberalism that I shared with my father was for universal emancipation, this was not necessarily the case for the nineteenth-century Jews of France or for many others elsewhere in the West, including women. As the liberal state and its laws evolved over the course of the nineteenth century, marriage and rape laws became focal points for defining contractual relationships and loyalties to the state. In order to get at this particular legacy for women, in this chapter I use the example of the sexual contract in British and American common law because it is, in many ways, the legal tradition I know best: it is the specific tradition that disappointed me after I was raped and went in search of justice. By looking closely at this legal tradition's marriage and rape laws, I try to make unfamiliar precisely these promises of equality and justice. I also make clear the double bind that this liberal legal tradition, a tradition built on the social contract and notions of free association, poses for women.

Jewish women came under the aegis of these liberal states through what political theorist Carole Pateman has described as the sexual contract, the social contract that gave free men access to women's bodies through the contract of marriage.[1] At the end of the eighteenth century, this form of state-sanctioned marriage brought Jewish women into the sexual contract by making explicit the interrelationship between the public and private spheres of civil society within the terms of Jewish emancipation. So, instead of viewing Jewish emancipation as liberatory, I question here such assumptions by asking what happened to women within the institution of liberal marriage. Following Pateman, I argue that liberalism's sexual contract created and perpetuated its own form of consensual subordination.

Given that even contemporary Jewish feminists like me continue to move back and forth between liberalism and rabbinic Judaism as an answer to our oppression, in this chapter I once again argue as strongly as possible against a return to liberalism.[2] By describing some of the asymmetries of power that continue to define liberal marriage, I question the efficacy of liberalism as a liberatory discourse for women.

Jewish Women, Liberal States

It is difficult to speak about the place of Jewish women within liberal states. With Jewish emancipation came a demand that not only should Jewish women as well as Jewish men uphold the morality of "the Jews" but also that they demonstrate fidelity to the state through the institution of liberal marriage. Calling attention to the inequities within these relationships again challenges a vision of liberal inclusion. The precariousness of the position of women within this institution has meant letting go of a dream of liberation, my own belief in the possibility of being at home within the liberal West. Letting go of this fantasy has demanded that I reimagine belonging and liberation in other than liberal terms.

In her analysis of feminism and the marriage contract, Carole Pateman presents a series of arguments against feminist appeals to contract theory as a means to liberation.[3] She argues that it is not simply a question of making a better contract, and instead shows how this contract is complicit in the ongoing domination of women within liberal states. Pateman's analysis presented me with a schematic, demonstrating to me what was most disturbing about this contractual arrangement for women. Although I came to this critique cognizant of a long tradition of accomplishments by Jewish women within liberal states since Jewish emancipation, these individual success stories were not enough.[4] I have also come to see that these accomplishments need to be tempered by an acknowledgment of certain persistent limitations. For me this has meant recognizing certain problems within liberal notions of consent.

The Problem of Consent

Within the term "consent" there is an ambiguity. According to the *American Heritage Dictionary*, to consent is "to give assent, accede; agree. To agree in opinion; be of the same mind." As a noun, it means "voluntary acceptance or allowance of what is planned or done by another; permission."[5] Built into these definitions is a contradiction between agreement and coercion. On the one hand, consent connotes assent. On the other hand, if one asks what is being agreed to, one is only being asked to agree to something that someone else has already determined. Thus, how much agency does consent really imply? By highlighting these internal contradictions, the centrality of consent to the liberal marriage ritual becomes somewhat more clear. In this ritual, a woman is literally asked to voluntarily accept what another has arranged for her. Within a liberal marriage ceremony, a woman need only voice her assent to becoming a wife, thus agreeing to the terms by which the liberal state has already defined what a wife is supposed to be. As I will now explain, she agrees to become a subordinate to her husband.

On the question of consent, John Locke, a classic figure within liberal contract theory, wrote in the seventeenth century that "'free and equal individuals' . . . own the property in their persons and their attributes, including their capacity to give consent. The individual is the 'guardian of his own consent.'"[6] Pateman reads this passage literally in order to make clear that even the liberal individual, much less a woman who marries, has an ambiguous relationship to his consent. Although Locke's individual owns his consent, he must remain on guard. The most interesting aspect of this passage is precisely this contradiction, a contradiction built into even Locke's notion of "consent." The need "to be a guardian" points to an insecurity. As such, the ground upon which even Locke posits consent is shaky. Read this way, Locke's statement is quite defensive. Liberal consent theory does not offer any guarantee of volition, and in Locke's text, freedom requires guardianship, a constant vigilance—it is always a risky business. In other words, even in Locke, "freedom isn't always free."[7]

Given this classic statement of liberal contract theory, Pateman suggests:

Contemporary consent theory has no room for two fundamental questions: first, why consent is of central importance to liberal theory and practice; second, how far theory and practice coincide, and whether genuine consent is possible within the institutions of the liberal-democratic state.[8]

As Pateman explains, the very question of consent points to a fundamental problem within liberalism, a problem not unlike the kind of strategic limitations I described in chapter 3. The question of "genuine consent" is an embarrassment because, despite its centrality within liberalism, there is little to assure that such consent is ever really granted.[9] Instead, liberal contract theorists often avoid precisely these fundamental questions by resorting to a kind of "hypothetical voluntarism." They simply posit consent as a given and never address how or when citizens actually perform this act, or they completely avoid the question of who gets to consent by "gloss[ing] over the ambiguity, inherent in consent theory from its beginnings about which individuals or groups are capable of consenting and so count as full members of the political order."[10] In other words, they either assume voluntarism as a given and never theorize about it, or enact a series of exclusions so that the fundamental question of consent is never posed. The problem of women and consent makes explicit this crucial problem, and nowhere is this more apparent than within the marriage contract.

In returning to a consideration of the problem of consent for women, I return to the question of consent in marriage. "The marriage contract is distinguished by reserving for wives 'the gratuitous degradation of swearing to be slaves.'"[11] To freely agree to be a slave is not an act of volition. In this transaction there is a tension between freedom and coercion not unlike that experienced by Locke's individual in the passage cited above. In marriage, consent signifies two things. First, it justifies the contractual nature of the institution by making marriage appear to be an equal exchange. The problem is what such a reading effaces. By using consent in this way, the institution of liberal marriage covers over the historical necessity of the institution for women with few other cultural, economic, or social options. Second, once married, it is precisely a woman's consent that can be used to justify all subsequent infringements on her agency by her husband.[12] This is especially true in the case of marital rape. Not only does a wife lose her sexual agency, or in Locke's terms the property in her person, she also loses her right to equal protection under the law.[13] Under the laws of coverture that remained in effect in the West until the mid- to late nineteenth century, once a woman consented to marriage her legal voice literally was subsumed by her husband. Legally, they were considered, as my dictionary suggests, of "one mind"—the man's. This is the ambivalent legal tradition that Jewish women entered into with the emancipation of "the Jews" in the West at precisely this moment.

The Sui Generis Contract

Little is known about the origins of the liberal marriage contract. According to the *Oxford English Dictionary*, under the entry for "contract," the specific listing for "marriage contract" states that marriage "has been seen as a contractual relationship since at least the fourteenth century."[14] This definition, however, begs the question of what is meant by a "contractual relationship," a question further complicated by the legacy of the social contract, which in the eighteenth century radically altered the meaning of the term "contract" and, with it, the institution of marriage.

Even when the marriage became a civil contract, as Blackstone suggests, there was still some confusion about what was meant by the term "contract." The question remains, to what extent is marriage a contractual relationship like other legal contracts? Moreover, even if it is a legal contract, can consent be presumed? Even in the nineteenth century, marriage did not fit neatly into the legal category of contract. As Schouler, a nineteenth-century legal scholar, claimed,

> We are then to consider marriage, not as a contract in the ordinary acceptation of the term; but as a contract *sui generis*, if indeed it be a contract at all; as an agreement to enter into a solemn relation which imposes its own terms.[15]

For these reasons, marriage remains ambivalently contractual. Unlike the ketubbah, whose defining characteristic was that it was a written document, the [liberal] marriage contract does not exist as a written document that is read and then signed by the contracting parties. Generally, a contract is valid only if the parties have read and understood its terms before they commit themselves.... Instead, the unwritten contract of marriage, to which a man and a woman are bound when they become husband and wife is codified in the law governing marriage and family life.[16]

As an unwritten agreement, the liberal marriage contract carries certain legal implications. Since the terms of the agreement are never clearly spelled out, it is difficult to argue that any specific practice or behavior goes against the agreement. Thus, although there are laws governing marriage and family life in general, there is no specific text to which one can refer when there are disputes.

Moveover, without a written text, there are questions about what makes the contract binding. Without signatures and a document, the terms upon which liberal marriages are constituted—a prescribed ceremony followed by a physical enactment—raise additional questions.

The ceremony is a public event. The couple is required to come before an agent of the state with at least one witness present in order to perform a speech act. Each party is asked to take an oath of commitment to the solemn relationship. By saying "I do," they each agree publicly to subject themselves to the terms of the state's version of proper marriage, but this does not complete the transaction.[17] There is a crucial second part of the process, a sex act that makes the speech act valid. Quoting Kant, Pateman makes clear that this contract can only be validated by an act of heterosexual intercourse:

The Contract of Marriage is completed only by conjugal cohabitation. A contract of two Persons of different sex, with secret understanding either to abstain from conjugal cohabitation, or with the consciousness on either side of incapacity for it, is a *simulated Contract*; it does not constitute a marriage.[18]

In other words, consummated heterosexuality is mandated by the state for a marriage to be valid.[19] Not only has the sexual contract of marriage come to define the proper roles of men and women as rigidly heterosexual, but there also continues to be overt hostility towards other forms of social organization and sexual expression.[20]

Beyond this, the relationship of marriage is asymmetrical. Under the terms of the liberal contract, wives are placed in subordinate positions vis-à-vis their husbands. As was the case in France, liberal states continue to invest a great deal in the stability of these institutional arrangements. In other words, marriage continues to play a crucial role in maintaining social order.

Finally, a third factor that continues to make liberal marriage different from other contracts is the legacy of coverture.[21] Under coverture, the couple became one legal entity and not two. Thus, "for a man to contract with his wife, 'would be only to covenant with himself: and therefore it is also generally true, that all compacts made between husband and wife, when single, are voided by the intermarriage.'"[22] Given this, a wife literally had no legal rights of her own.

Even if a woman had legally agreed to enter into marriage, once married, her consent was no longer efficacious. Marriage imposed its own terms. And even without formal coverture, this legacy continues to inform liberal marriage and family law, making it virtually impossible for a wife to make legal claims against her husband.[23] This power dynamic has also been reinforced by a literal vow of obedience. As part of the marriage vows, until very recently, women pledged not only to love and cherish their husbands but also to obey them. Although this too is no longer an explicit part of the vow, as Pateman makes clear, it also continues to inform cultural expectations about marriage. Here again, what is expected is that a wife will submit to the authority of her husband. Despite feminist efforts at reform, this continues to be a legal norm.

The Link Between Marriage and Rape

In rabbinic and liberal jurisprudence, the institution of marriage regulates, facilitates, and sanctions sexual access to individual women's bodies by individual men. Rape violates these arrangements. To what extent does liberalism's construction of rape as a criminal act, however, also reinforce these institutional arrangements? To address these questions, I now turn to some of the legal problems posed by rape, the other side of the sexual contract.[24] In this section I build on the problematic role of "women's consent" within the sexual contract in order to make explicit the dangers these arrangements pose for women, above all when they are sexually violated. As I move through this material, I will draw some comparisons between liberal legal texts and the rabbinic sources presented in chapter 2. I am not doing this to idealize the rabbinic tradition, but rather to make clear how, despite its claims to the contrary, the liberal legal tradition has been far from liberating.

Consent marks the difference between rape and marital or sanctioned hetero/sex in liberal legal discourse even as it did for the rabbis. The difference is that liberal consent overtly presumes the efficacy of a woman's volition in such matters. The language of "contract" within the liberal tradition demands such a reading; but, as I have already indicated, the difference between volition and coercion is often obscured under the sign of consent.

The case of rape is supposed to exemplify the opposite of consent, a situation where the woman has no sexual agency. She is seized, taken off, and forced to submit to sexual intercourse.[25]

> A man commits rape when he engages in intercourse (in the old statutes, carnal knowledge) with a woman not his wife; by force or by threat of force; against her will and without her consent. That is the traditional, common law definition of rape, and it remains the essence of even the most radical reform statutes.[26]

Even within this legal definition, it becomes difficult to talk about what happens to a woman who is married to the man who has raped her—a case I will return to shortly. For now, however, I want to clarify the general difficulties involved in cases of rape under common law. Given this legal definition, in order to prove that a rape was committed, the woman involved must show that the assault was against her will and/or without her consent. The problem is how these criteria have been interpreted within common law.

In the eighteenth century, "the English Lord Chief Justice Matthew Hale warned that rape is a charge 'easily to be made and hard to be proved, and harder to be defended by the party accused, tho' never so innocent.'"[27] Justice Hale's word came to codify certain already existing practices in this regard. They set the precedent for all subsequent cases of rape, making it extremely difficult for women to press charges, much less bring rape cases to court and win them. Hale argued that, given how difficult it is for a man to establish his innocence, the burden of proof must be on the woman to prove *her* innocence. As feminist legal scholar Susan Estrich explains, "Under Hale's approach, the one who so 'easily' charges rape must first prove her own lack of guilt" (5). This, in turn, set up a whole series of inquiries into the reliability of the victim as witness to the point that, in order to prove her innocence, a woman first had to be interrogated and put on trial.

More than an apparent inversion of justice, this whole procedure was built on a series of disturbing assumptions about women. To begin with, women are presumed to be unreliable witnesses. As Pateman explains:

> It is . . . very difficult for a woman to convince a court that she did not consent when standard works on evidence reinforce the view that women, especially "unchaste" women, are "naturally" deceitful and prone to make false statements, including false accusations of rape.[28]

Hale's precedent raises other questions as well. By making false distinctions between different groups of women, Hale's position assumed a split between the "good victim" and the "bad woman." According to Hale's logic, the "unchaste woman" deserves what she gets; only the "good victim" may even begin to demand justice, but even here very few cases ever come to court. As a result of this, even in the United States at the end of the twentieth century, women as a class remain at risk. Despite stiff penalties, very few rapists are ever arrested or prosecuted, as happened in my case. At best, the courts offer women a pretext of protection, but this protection comes at a cost when and if these cases ever come to trial.[29]

For a woman must prove that she was assaulted not only "against her will" but also "without her consent." The proof of nonconsent has become another burden placed on the victim. She must have marks that show that she physically resisted her assailant. According to this criterion, the evidence of sexual assault is not enough; a woman must also provide evidence that she was maimed or beaten in order to prove that she was raped. Ironically, this problem has been exacerbated by the passage of feminist-sponsored reform measures. In these cases the slogan "rape = violence" has been deployed to redefine rape as an assault, a change reflected in the discursive shift in legal discourse from "rape" to "sexual assault."[30] In order to make clear the violence of rape—that rape is not simply a crime of passion, a sexual indiscretion—emphasis has been placed on the violence of the act. The problem with this legislation is that it does not take into account how this criterion can be made legally quantifiable. In attempting to focus on the violence of rape, the interconnection between violence and sexuality within rape has become obscured. As a result, sexual violation has become less of a cause for prosecution, and the fact that rapists are sexually aroused by attacking their victims has also been obscured.

In cases of sexual assault, struggle is everything. Without it, many rape victims find they have no case. This is especially true in cases of acquaintance rape, where little credence is given to what is often most devastating about these rapes: the coercion and manipulation involved in the assault.[31] Here, acquaintance all too often literally signifies consent. Under current statutes, there are few ways of demonstrating how not all of the violation of rape is physical. In this way the problem of women and consent re-emerges. As in marriage, the lines between submission or coercion and consent are blurred. The liberal contract theory upon which these laws were built cannot make clear distinctions between consent and nonconsent. It is this confusion within the sexual contract that continues to place women at risk, especially in cases of marital rape.[32]

Marital Rape

In considering marital rape, I return to Justice Hale. Not only did he set the terms under which rape cases continue to be prosecuted, he is also responsible for framing the marital rape exemption. In this instance, Hale's distrust of women is most evident.

> The marital rape exemption originated at common law in the seventeenth century[33] with Lord Matthew Hale's declaration that "the husband cannot be guilty of a rape committed by himself upon his lawful wife, for by their mutual matrimonial consent and contract the wife hath given up herself in this kind unto her husband, which she cannot retract." Hale has long stood as the accepted authority on marital rape in the United States.[34]

As this passage suggests, this precedent continues to shape common law, for in most cases, married women still cannot successfully prosecute their husbands on charges of rape.

Because the liberal marriage contract defines marriage as an asymmetrical power relationship, a husband is still granted tremendous power over his wife. What makes the case of marital rape so striking is that it calls into question precisely this arrangement. Because men like Hale have continued to define the law on these matters in favor of men, by and large husbands remain exempt from prosecution: ipso facto, there is no such thing as "marital rape." As Hale argued, consent is given once and for all time within the marriage ceremony. In turn, this claim sets up its own logic and its own truth.

> Therefore, when men say "a husband cannot rape his wife," they speak the truth. When women accuse their husbands of rape, they lie. Because women are perceived as liars, they remain silent. The dominant discourse of truth thus evolves from the reality of ongoing subjugation.[35]

Under this logic, a wife cannot be raped by her husband, nor will she be believed if she attempts to make such claims. Only the husband can determine what counts as a legal truth.

Conclusion

As liberal wives, Jewish women's identities were redefined in terms of the sexual contract. Jewish women entered this contract when Jewish men became citizens of liberal western states. As in chapter 3, it is still difficult for me to let go of liberalism's promise of emancipation. This legacy is still so much a part of my self-understanding, and yet so are the dangers and disappointments I have described. In the chapters that follow I show how, and at what cost, this legacy of marriage has become a part of liberal Jewish theology.

five

~

Covenant or Contract?
Marriage as Theology

The Jewish community has found no more central and significant form for the individual Jew to live in . . . than the personal covenant marriage. In its exclusiveness and fidelity it has been the chief analogy to the oneness of the relationship with God as the source of personal worth and development. In marriage's intermixture of love and obligation the Jew has seen the model of faith in God permeating the heart and thence all one's actions. Through children, Jews have found the greatest personal joy while carrying out the ancient Jewish pledge to endure through history for God's sake.

—Eugene Borowitz, *Exploring Jewish Ethics*

Clearly one aspect of the [colonial] project was carried out in the overt articulation at both institutional and discursive levels, but there was also another, perhaps mystified element that was expressed as the self-attributing superiority of the colonizer and the attribution of inferiority to the colonized. The moves to usurp the consciousness of the colonized by attempts to remake the self, evidenced, for instance, in the active suppression of indigenous systems of metaphysics or in the constant preoccupations with the manners and "the Character of the Negro" [like "the Character of the Jew"] . . . were simultaneously aimed at dislodging resistance, reorganizing daily life, reconstituting identity, indeed remaking the sexual identity of those subjected to colonial rule.

—M. Jacqui Alexander, "Redrafting Morality"

While I was in Israel in 1983, I learned a great deal about rabbinic Judaism and my own complicated place within a community of practicing Jews. I spent that year as part of an intense community of primarily American rabbinical students and other recent graduates of American universities who also wanted to know more about their Jewishness. We were each, in our own way, looking for alternatives to the kinds of Jewish homes we had grown up in. All the participants in this program had chosen to spend a year away from home to learn about and engage in classical (rabbinic) texts and practices. Although the dominant position among both the students and faculty in my program was for us to become more traditional, to follow more rabbinic practices, many of us were gnawed by questions about the distance between what we had learned in our American Jewish families about being Jewish and what we were being taught in this program. It was during this time in Israel that I began to acknowledge my need to reconcile the relationship between rabbinic Judaism and liberalism.

I also learned not only about contemporary ketubbot or marriage contracts but also about covenantal theology as a liberal Jewish theology of marriage. During one of many intense conversations with my friend Morris, a rabbinical student at the time, he told me about the work of Eugene Borowitz,[1] a leading contemporary liberal Jewish theologian. For over twenty-five years he has been the theological spokesman for the Reform movement in America, a leading advocate for liberal Judaism.[2] Morris described Borowitz's covenantal theology as a different and more satisfying way of bridging the distance between rabbinic Judaism and liberalism. He offered me Borowitz's work as an alternative to simply becoming observant. Covenantal theology, a term coined by Borowitz for his relational theology, could allow me to bring together various strands of rabbinic and biblical Judaism with the works of various modern Jewish thinkers. Through a notion of covenant that resembled liberal marriage, Borowitz offered me a middle position that was both rabbinic and liberal.

For me, Borowitz's work was a tremendous relief and comfort. It meant not having to choose between the authority of the Rabbis and my family. He not only offered me a way of reconciling these aspects of my Jewishness but also made clear to me that liberal Judaism was indeed a legitimate historical Jewish tradition and that I need not be ashamed of what I had inherited. Even now, I continue to feel grateful to Borowitz for helping me work through these issues despite the fact that I no longer find his appeal to a marital covenant compelling. He continues to offer one of very few models for how to reconcile liberalism and rabbinic Judaism. By internalizing the values of liberalism as Jewish, he gives contemporary Jews a way to engage with the legacy of rabbinic Judaism without denying their liberalism.

Eugene Borowitz was not just an important liberal Jewish thinker whose books and articles I read voraciously, he was also, quite literally, my teacher. I spent a year working with him on my master's degree at the Reform Seminary in New York. He was a generous, respectful, and engaging mentor and was the person most responsible for encouraging me to continue my own graduate work in theology, for which I am greatly indebted to him.[3]

In many ways, this chapter has grown out of this relationship. It is my way of both holding on to and letting go of Borowitz's legacy to me. In what follows, I offer a rigorous critique of his covenantal theology and ethics, specifically in relation to issues of gender and sexuality. In so doing, I address many of the limitations I have found in his marital model. I offer this critique as a constructive attempt to imagine a different vision of Jewish community. Thus, even as I retain Borowitz's promise of reconciliation, I insist on using other than liberal metaphors for embracing the traditions of liberalism, rabbinic Judaism, and liberal Jewish theology.

What I have found most disturbing in Borowitz's theology is how he makes liberal marriage into the model for the relationship between God and the Jewish people, "the chief analogy to the oneness of the relationship with God."[4] I will show how the kinds of problems I posed in relation to liberal marriage in chapter 4 get exacerbated within Borowitz's covenantal theology. The sexual contract poses particular problems for Jewish feminists like me, who want to imagine Jewish communities that are more respectful of Jewish women. This is not the case in Borowitz's liberal theology of marriage. His covenantal theology as a theology of liberal marriage turns out to be oppressive to Jewish women. It is also quite literally unable to embrace queer Jews as a part of Jewish community.

The quote at the opening of this chapter from M. Jacqui Alexander bears on these problems because, here again, I have found that, by thinking about liberalism and colonialism together, I have been able to gain some perspective on these issues. I have been able to see most clearly the limitations of liberalism as a home for Jews even in a theology as promising as Borowitz's. M. Jacqui Alexander's text has been a reminder to me of how liberalism became Jewish, how the history of Jewish emancipation in the West is reflected in Borowitz's theology. It has helped me remember that part of the problem is that Borowitz's work continues to be marked by the limitations of liberal discourse for Jews. In other words, Borowitz's covenantal theology not only remakes Jewish metaphysics as a version of liberalism, it also continues to demonstrate a preoccupation with the sexual manners and character of the Jews by its focus on marriage. In other words, his efforts, like my own, stand in a long line of liberal Jewish attempts to fit into western culture by remaking Jewishness into a series of liberal beliefs and practices, and this is how, within Borowitz's covenantal theology, the sexual contract becomes Jewish.[5] Here, there are no references to the rabbinic contract of marriage.[6] Instead, by offering a unified liberal position with a single set of relational norms, Borowitz makes rabbinic Judaism and liberalism appear to be one and the same thing, a more encompassing form of liberalism. Jewish marriage and liberal marriage are no longer distinguishable.

For these reasons, Borowitz's theology is not a place I can continue to call home in any simple way. In what follows I offer a close reading of Borowitz's work in order to make clear some of the dangers in his particular version of Judaism. I take the time to demonstrate these problems point by point precisely because I know their allure.

Rabbinic = Liberal

According to Borowitz, the rabbis "saw in generative, heterosexual marriage a major, if not the major, human embodiment of the Covenant between God and Israel."[7] For him, liberalism's version of procreative heterosexual marriage is the norm. He builds on modern Jewish thinker Martin Buber's notion of the intimacy of the "I-Thou" relationship as his theological ideal.[8] Borowitz argues that the covenant between God and the Jewish people becomes "the bidding that arises from intimacy; in other words, he [Buber] replaces *halakhah* with the marital I-Thou" (213). As Borowitz explains:

> We have an old-new model for such open, unsettled, but mutually dignifying relationships, namely, "covenant," now less a contract spelled out from on high than a loving effort to live in reciprocal respect. As the pain of trying to create egalitarian marriages indicates, we cannot know early on what forms and processes most people will find appropriate to such relationships. We can, however, accept covenantal relationship as a central ethical challenge of our time and pragmatically learn how we might sanctify ourselves by living it. For some such reason, I take it, God has given us freedom and opened history to our determination. (223)

In this way, Borowitz's own work offers marriage as a model for describing the relationship between God and Israel. As will become clear at the end of this chapter, it also plays a crucial role in his ethics.

Despite Borowitz's enthusiastic embrace of marriage as the "I-Thou" relationship of choice, this particular passage also suggests some of the ambivalences within his position. According to Borowitz, the marital covenant both is and is not "a contract spelled out from on high." Despite this qualification, the asymmetries of the original contract remain intact.

By appealing to a less rational and more loving category of value, Borowitz tries to affirm right relationship without being too specific about the content of this engagement.

Covenant as Unique Relationship

I now turn to the internal workings of Borowitz's notion of "covenant." What constitutes a covenantal relationship? What distinguishes it from all other relationships? Uniqueness is critical. According to Borowitz:

> The first and most formative experience in the development of Jewish spirituality was entering the Covenant. As traditionally put, the one God of the universe made a pact with Abraham, renewed it with his descendants, confirmed it in the Exodus, and made it specific in giving the Torah to the people of Israel at Mount Sinai.[9]

Borowitz argues that the history of the Jewish people as a distinct people is characterized by their unique relationship with the one God of all creation who sought them out among the nations. It involves a special loyalty and a special promise. Through Abraham and his descendants, "all human beings might one day come to know—that is to obey—God. In return, God promised to make Abraham's family a mighty nation, to give them a land, and to protect them throughout history."[10] In other words, God secures Abraham with not only a home but also a future. He promises him immortality.[11] In Borowitz's contemporary reading of this covenant, submission to God is transformed into heterosexual procreative marriage. By talking about "a marital I-Thou relationship" and not directly about submission in marriage, Borowitz tries to have it both ways (the old and the new). He obscures the absolute power differential between the parties to the covenant and how these connections translate into the relationship between a husband and wife. He simply repeats the pattern.

Contract or Covenant?

In order to show the connections between his theological covenant and the liberal marriage contract, I now focus on a few key passages from Borowitz's latest theological work, *Renewing the Covenant: A Theology for the Postmodern Jew*, that demonstrate his position and its limitations, as I understand them. According to Borowitz, the covenant between God and Israel is not a "contract" but a "relationship." Nevertheless:

> the autonomous self makes sense only in terms of each person's ineluctable bond with God, the source of our dignity and the criterion of its correct use. Our tradition spoke of this as the (Noahide) covenant, a term whose legal origin conveyed a sense of seriously contracted specific obligations. (285–286)

Despite his reluctance to speak about covenant as contract, Borowitz acknowledges its legal/contractual roots and affirms them.

Borowitz then uses the language of relationships as a way of tempering his understanding of God's power over Israel within this contract:

> Opposing a heteronomic understanding of it (covenant), I reinterpret the term through the metaphor of personal relationships, which communicates duty without depriving either participant of selfhood and autonomy—an experience as characteristic of direct relationship with God as with persons through whom we know God indirectly. (286)

Although Borowitz's explicit reason for turning to the language of relationship is to rethink the power dynamics between the partners in the covenantal relationships (God and humankind, and God and Israel), there is a contradiction. On the one hand, Borowitz supposedly gives up the language of contract in order to oppose a heteronomic understanding of covenant that gave God power over God's partners, while, on the other hand, as the earlier part of this particular passage makes clear, Borowitz is committed to reaffirming God's absolute power; this is what troubles me.

Even in Borowitz's resistance to the language of contract, there is an uncanny resemblance between his covenant and the sexual contract. Here too it is not clear "if indeed it be a contract at all; as an agreement to enter into a solemn relation which imposes its own terms."[12] In other words, Borowitz's covenant also sets its own terms. For him, there is a tension between the desire for loving egalitarian relationships and an abiding commitment to a God who continues to have power over Israel.

Borowitz wants it both ways. As he explains,

> God and the individual self are the two axes around which my faith pivots, but I do not consider them to be of *equal* significance. For all my insistence on a somewhat curious "independence" of the self, I know that it derives its value from and is *subordinate* to God. Primacy can never be in serious doubt here since the One creates and the other is created. Yet the creatures have such stature with God that, on occasion, they may argue God's justice, as it were, face to face.... Summoned by God to personal responsibility, my piety expresses itself as a personal activism that finds its motive and standard in my being privileged to *serve* God as a covenantal partner. (31) (my emphasis)

In this passage, Borowitz brings together autonomy and heteronomy. Since human dignity is contingent upon human createdness, God must always remain primary. God's power, as such, is not lost in the transition from the language of "contract" to "relationship." The shift in metaphor simply affirms a greater degree of autonomy for human beings without challenging the basic structure of the covenant as a relationship between unequal partners. God's ultimate power is never questioned; autonomy simply gets scripted as an act of God's benevolence, which allows Borowitz to speak of his own piety as "privileged servitude." It is only "on occasion" that it *might* be possible to address God "face to face."

This double move of promise and effacement is also evident in Borowitz's attempts to align himself with traditional Jewish thinking:

> Our tradition supplies us with a most evocative metaphor for this awesome tie between the Transcendent and the human: *brit*, covenant. The Torah daringly asserts that, despite the disparity between them, the one God of all the universe enters into intimate

partnerships with humankind. It understood God's covenants with the Children of Noah—humankind—and the Children of Israel as contracts between partners mutually bound by the stipulations of their agreement. (107)

Here again he only makes a metaphorical distinction. He remains committed to a God who has power over him in order to prove that there is no difference between what he terms as "liberal and ortho-dox faith."

> Both [liberal and Orthodox faith] affirm the transcendent preeminence of God and ascribe some independent dignity to humankind. We radically diverge, however, over the issue of the proper balance or relative significance we ascribe to God's sovereignty and to human will. (241)

The structural arrangement is the same; the difference is only a matter of degree. In fact, Borowitz goes on to say that

> different social circumstances aside, the underlying relationship between God and the people of Israel has remained substantially the same.... Hence much of what they did as their Covenant duty will likely still lay a living claim on us. (291)

I have highlighted these passages in order to make clear both the selectivity of Borowitz's reading of rabbinic tradition as well as the tension between his claims to continuity and to change. I have also highlighted these passages because they make clear what is troubling about Borowitz's theology for Jewish women: his theological reiteration of the asymmetries within the sexual contract pose dangers for Jewish women precisely because they are uttered in the name of love.[13] As in the sexual contract, liberalism offers a means to make both of these claims simultaneously.

The Persistence of the Liberal Marriage Contract

Borowitz argues that through his old-new approach to the covenant, he can get rid of the most egregious aspect of the rabbinic tradition without fully doing so. Instead, under the sign of "relationship," he continues to reaffirm God's power over Israel.

This dynamic becomes clearer in looking at how Borowitz uses the term "marriage." On the surface, the kind of marriage he seems to advocate is egalitarian, but he also argues that love commands. In terms of marriage, this translates into the power husbands hold over their wives. By talking about this inequity in terms of love, Borowitz avoids any discussion of power. He conceals the fact that marriage, as analogous to the covenant with God, demands submission. In this way, Borowitz not only replicates the liberal dynamic I have already described but even makes it holy.

As Carole Pateman argues, liberal marriage also links consent with subordination. "Contract is presented as freedom and as antipatriarchal, while being a major mechanism through which sex right is renewed and maintained."[14] Similarly, Borowitz's covenant also gestures toward equality while reinforcing structural inequities. Thus, as Pateman argues, "with the establishment of marriage and the pretence of a contract, men's domination is hidden by the claim that marriage allows equal, consensual sexual enjoyment to both spouses."[15] Here again, men's domination of women is cloaked and disguised. It is precisely because of this that I have insisted on giving close readings of Borowitz's text to make explicit how these dynamics operate in his text.

In Borowitz's case, the cloak is love, relationship as opposed to contract, which only makes the issue of power that much more illusive. Unlike Pateman, who argues against feminist appeals to contract because "the feminist dream is continuously subverted by entanglements with contract,"[16] Borowitz presumes that relationships can offer freedom, although he never fully relinquishes his reliance on contractual inequities to define this relationship. Since Borowitz's assessment of contract is so close to Pateman's, this repetition is particularly striking as well as disappointing. As Pateman explains, "Contract always generates political right in the form of relations of domination and subordination."[17] By contrast, Borowitz writes: "When the biblical motif of covenant is restated as relationship rather than contract—giving expanded scope to the human partner—this hallowed notion can effectively symbolize our postmodern spirituality."[18] Despite this, as in liberal marriage, there is an inequity of power given to the subordinate partner by the one who continues to command. The fact that there is still a partner who commands is crucial to the perpetuation of the relationship.

In order to strengthen the connection between covenant and marriage, in *Renewing the Covenant* Borowitz reveals a romantic portrait of this ideal relationship, which again I not only find unconvincing but extremely disturbing. In Borowitz's account marriage becomes miraculous:

> We also easily speak of relationships extending through time despite the harsh reality that the immediacy of encounter begets only a temporary certainty. It sometimes manifests such quality that we hope it will recur, allowing acquaintance to ripen into friendship, perhaps even love, or almost *miraculously*, the love that elicits the pledge of self for the life we call marriage. (275–76) (my emphasis).

Here Borowitz values endurance and certainty. Even in the worst situations of neglect and abuse, only marriage is fully suited to achieve such a holy relationship.

> We often do not understand why those most dear to us occasionally hurt us, sometimes very deeply. Little injures us more than parents, children, friends, lovers, or spouses not being there when we need them; should they withdraw willfully, we will suffer most intensely. Yet, miraculously, love often survives such traumas. Every relationship lives out of the faith that the meaning we once knew together might at any moment return and thereby be renewed—and that is as true of religion as it is of the love of persons. Though we cannot make sense of their acting this way, we may be willing to "bear" with them, to accept the burden of the pain they have caused us—not the least by showing themselves capable of betrayal—and to forgive them. Sometimes we can do that because of what we have meant to one another; sometimes we do it freely, staking our lives on what this torment has taught us about the depth of our love. (130)

This passage says much about Borowitz's understanding of love as submission. What makes this passage even more disturbing is that it is presented as part of a larger discussion of Buber's response to the Holocaust, which Buber describes as a breach in the relationship between God and the Jewish people. Borowitz relates his vision of love as submission to Buber's understanding of the Holocaust.[19]

After the Holocaust, Buber could no longer make people the exclusive source of interpersonal evil. He now daringly suggested that there are some terrifying times when God, as it were, withdraws from us despite our seeking God. Absence is the worst evil. For Buber the problem of theodicy then becomes not understanding "how" or "why" our good God ever countenances our suffering or "hides his face" from us, but contemplating how we might still maintain or regain a loving relationship with God despite our anguish. (130)

Borowitz suggests an analogy between God's absence in the Holocaust and when a loved one withdraws. He then goes on to use this analogy to argue that those who have been hurt, even deeply abused, must be forgiving of their abusers. In the face of the Holocaust, he writes, "we try to respond to God in love though evil overwhelms us, caring despite not understanding" (130). Borowitz concludes this section of his book by reaffirming his commitment to this vision of submission to God as a loving relationship. He writes: "Nurtured by that love, we pray to be able to go on trusting God even when we are wounded and do not understand our momentarily unrecognizable Lover" (131).

According to this analysis, Borowitz accepts the premise that either blames the Jews for God's absence, or makes God's absence a matter of God's capriciousness in the Holocaust. In so doing he accepts that suffering and abuse are not only necessarily a part of loving relationships but also a part of the covenant with God.

In response to this problem, Borowitz offers the miracle of love, which ultimately operates outside of the realm of human agency. Love must be given by God. This disturbing vision of submission to God within a covenantal home offers little comfort to those who suffer, and makes it that much harder for them to leave an abusive home. What bothers me about this model of Jewish covenantal community and home is that, aside from effacing aspects of the rabbinic tradition, it ends up perpetuating a liberal fallacy in its efforts to make Judaism contemporary. It assumes that marital relationships are loving and safe even in the face of powerful evidence to the contrary. For me this does not offer much security.

From Theology to Ethics: "Proper Sexuality"

Marriage links Borowitz's ethics with his theology. In his ethics, covenant translates literally into the demand to marry. In this way it operates as the normative unifying core of his liberal Jewish position, "the chief analogy to the oneness of the relationship with God."[20]

Even before he began to address the issue of queer[21] Jewish relationships in his ethics, Borowitz had defended monogamous, procreative heterosexual marriage over and against both feminism and the sexual revolution of the 1960s. In "Reading the Jewish Tradition on Marital Sexuality," an essay originally published in 1982,[22] he asked:

> If women should now similarly channel much of their sexual drive into the pursuit of success and power, what will become of the sexual primacy of the marital bed? How, we must now wonder, can liberal Judaism today combat the destructive power of a society bent on exploiting the new sexual freedom for women? (268)

So as early as 1982, Borowitz was worried about the traditional marriage bed. In this essay, he recognized that marriage was not the exclusive context in which sexuality was being expressed but, nevertheless, he reaffirmed its centrality and importance to the liberal Jewish community. In order to be more inclusive, he set up a hierarchy in which he included the following options: the freedom of a "mutual-consent ethics," the restrictions of a "love standard," and the even greater restriction demanded by a "marriage standard."[23]

This gradation allowed Borowitz again to have it both ways. He could recognize a series of different sexual ethics while still maintaining his commitment to the one and only marital ideal. "What we require, therefore, is something far more pluralistic, a *ranking* rather than a comprehensive rule, a hierarchy rather than a single, synthesized principle" [my emphasis].[24] Thus, Borowitz made explicit the hierarchy within liberal pluralism. Only from a single unified position could he tolerate other possibilities.[25] The liberal position he takes necessarily reduces, translates, and harmonizes differences—an approach that becomes even more apparent in his response to gay and lesbian Jews.

Queer Covenants

Given that heterosexual procreative marriage is the critical metaphor in Borowitz's theological and ethical writing, it is not surprising that the issue of queer Jews in the rabbinate would be so troubling for him. In his essay, "On Homosexuality and the Rabbinate, a Covenantal

Response"[26] his metaphor for the covenant becomes prescriptive. To sanction queer Jewish expressions of love would require an explicit interrogation of this central tenet of his liberal theology and ethics.

As in his earlier essays on sexuality, differences are tolerated and not sanctioned. In addressing the question of whether gay and lesbian Jews should be rabbis, he first deals with right relationships and then with the role of the rabbi in relation to other Jews. Marriage is not just the ideal sexual relationship it is also a model for the asymmetrical relationship; between a rabbi and his or her congregation.

When it comes to sexual relationships, Borowitz is utterly consistent. Heterosexual procreative marriage remains his ideal. In this essay he writes, "Positively, I hear us asserting that the special imperatives that devolve upon Jews because of the covenant necessitates our special devotion to the heterosexual, that is, the procreative family" (279). As for rabbis, they too are accorded special privilege:

> (1) to be a rabbi is not a Jewish right but a title bestowed as a special Jewish honor; (2) rabbis, in fulfillment of their special community status, ought to set an example of Jewish ideals. . . . [R]abbis ought, more than all other Jews, to be exemplars of living by the Covenant. . . . [It] is as model more than anything else that the rabbi teaches Judaism. (281–82)

Because rabbis must embody the covenant, they must engage in the kind of sexual relationship most clearly associated with covenantal responsibility: heterosexual procreative marriage.[27] By looking at the question of ordination in this way, Borowitz leaves himself little choice but to reject the possibility of queer rabbis, essentially defining them out of contention.[28]

> If we are dedicated to the Covenant with its special standards, then we should require of our rabbis, insofar as we are able, that they exemplify them. I am, therefore, against the ordination of homosexuals as rabbis. (282)

Despite his efforts throughout the essay to account for other positions, queer relationships are excluded from his definition of covenant. Instead, he goes so far as to encourage bisexual Jews who want to become rabbis to choose to be straight:

Does our Judaism have a preference as to the decision a fully bisexual person makes with regard to his or her sexuality? To me, the answer is quite clear. Given the choice, the Covenant requires Jews to elect the heterosexual option because in that mode they can, at least in principle, directly fulfill their duty to create the Jewish biological future. (281)

Additionally, Borowitz demands that lesbian and gay potential rabbinical students remain closeted, offering them a version of "don't ask don't tell."[29] His position is that Hebrew Union College—Jewish Institute of Religion, the Reform Jewish Seminary, should not accept all students "without regard to sexual preference"[30] and argues that if gay and lesbian students are to be accepted, they should not openly reveal their sexual orientation:

A far less desirable but nonetheless workable additional alternative is for homosexuals to come to the College as a number have done over the years, staying "in the closet" until ordination. (283)[31]

This is as generous as he gets. Borowitz suggests that it may be possible for closeted gay and lesbian rabbis to eventually become a critical mass who could promote change from within the Reform movement.

In a parenthetical comment, Borowitz tells queer rabbinical candidates that it will not be so bad spending five years of their lives in the closet. "This depersonalizing situation will be somewhat mitigated these days by the significant number of students who will give such colleagues their full personal support during their studies" (283). This final statement is especially telling, for instead of providing institutional support for these students, Borowitz uses the personal good will of other students as a way of mitigating the most egregious aspects of his own institutional position.[32]

Finally he claims that his objections to queer families is about protecting the biological future of the Jewish people:[33]

Homosexual families can model the Covenant insofar as it involves interpersonal faithfulness in a lifetime. But when it comes to procreation, they divorce loving faithfulness and the generation of

Jewish children. The love comes down along one line, so to speak, the generativity along another. To be sure, Jews who cannot have children are encouraged to adopt them; a pattern of such split relationships is known among us and has been transcended, but it is not our preferred state. (279)

Even within heterosexual families, he is worried about maintaining the terms of the sexual contract. "These ethical imperatives [the equality of women and children's rights] have resulted in a restructuring of the family that is still under way, a restructuring that has subjected the Jewish family to great strain" (280). Given this turmoil, Borowitz argues that liberal Jews like him "are loath to do anything that might weaken it [the family] further" (280). The question is, who is really threatened by such changes?

What is striking to me about these assertions is that they illustrate the instability of the sexual contract even, and perhaps especially, as a theological position. I have raised these issues to make clear how narrow and confining I have found even Borowitz's covenantal theology. Given the singularity of his position, Borowitz provides me with little space to participate in what he calls "covenantal community." By drawing connections between Borowitz's unified liberal theology and ethics, I have tried to make clear the material implications, the limitations, and the dangers posed by this kind of theologizing of the sexual contract as a vision of Jewish community and home.

Conclusion

Unlike my father who was never quite able to put together liberalism and Jewishness in any sustained way, Borowitz offered me a model for doing just this. He offered me a theological position that included both rabbinic Judaism and liberalism. With Borowitz, I thought that I did not have to choose between the Rabbis and liberalism. His work gave theological weight and authority to my own liberalism. The problem was that his position did not offer me enough room to grow and change.

By presenting a theological version of the sexual contract as Jewish, Borowitz's work incorporates rabbinic Judaism under the cloak of liberalism, where there is presumably no more difference. I have offered a close reading of Borowitz's work in order to make clear the dangers involved in such efforts. Although Borowitz's work offered me a more secure vision of liberalism as a Jewish home with God, it did not offer me liberation, justice, or even protection. In chapter 6, I look to Judith Plaskow's feminist theology for an alternative vision of home.

six

Marriage as Feminist Theology?

> Homosexuality . . . does not necessarily represent a rejection of Jewish values but
> the choice of certain Jewish values over others—where these conflict with each
> other, the choice of the possibility of holiness over control and law.
>
> —Judith Plaskow, *Standing Again at Sinai*

In sharp contrast to Eugene Borowitz's liberal Jewish theology, Judith
Plaskow's *Standing Again at Sinai: Judaism From a Feminist Perspective*, the first full-length Jewish feminist theology, directly
addresses the kinds of exclusions I describe in my reading of
Borowitz's work.[1] For Plaskow, the problem is primarily within the
rabbinic tradition and its vision of the covenant.[2] In Plaskow's work,
rabbinic Judaism is presented as legal and controlling, which presents
a problem for Jewish women. This focus on the legally binding limitations of rabbinic Judaism is at the heart of Plaskow's feminist critique. In response to these problems, Plaskow argues that liberalism
offers Jewish feminists a more promising intimate model of sexuality
and holiness. Because rabbinic Judaism—and specifically its readings
of the biblical tradition—lack many voices, including those of Jewish
women, she argues that the Rabbis offer an incomplete vision of
covenantal community. By contrast, liberalism allows Plaskow to
address this absence. By appealing to liberalism, she is able to offer a
fuller vision of the relationship between God and Israel, a vision that
includes Jewish women.

Although I admire Plaskow's critique of the Rabbis, I am troubled
by her liberalism. As I have already argued, I do not believe that lib-

eralism in and of itself can offer Jewish feminists an answer to the problem of what it means to claim a Jewish feminist position.

Critiquing the Rabbis

Plaskow begins her critique in *Standing Again at Sinai* by revisiting the covenantal relationship with Abraham and the patriarchs. As Plaskow explains, in sharp contrast to the stories of the patriarchs, little is known about the relationship between the matriarchs and God.

> It is not the women who receive the covenant or who pass on its lineage. . . . Their relationship to God, in some way presupposed by the text, remains an undigested element in the narrative. What was the full theophany to Rebekah and how is it related to the covenant with Isaac? The writer does not tell us; it is not sufficiently important. And so the covenant remains the covenant with Isaac, while Rebekah's experience floats at the margins of the story. (4)

Plaskow uses this insight to explore the links between the covenant with Abraham and the covenant at Sinai:

> When . . . God enters into a covenant with Abraham and says to him, "This is my covenant, which you shall keep, between me and you and your descendants after you: Every male among you shall be circumcised" (Gen. 17:10), women can hear this only as establishing our marginality. Even if circumcision is not itself the covenant but only the sign of the covenant, what role can women have in the covenant community when the primary symbol of the covenant pertains only to men? (82)

In Plaskow's account, even at Sinai women are excluded by the language of covenant. "The covenant at Sinai is spoken in male pronouns . . . and its content assumes male hearers" (82). By returning to Sinai, Plaskow's theology tries to reimagine this relationship in more inclusive terms.

For Plaskow, the communal covenant at Sinai is "the root experience of Judaism" (26). The biblical verse Plaskow finds most disturbing is Exodus 19:15, "Be ready for the third day; do not go near a woman," because it makes clear that Jewish women were not addressed at Sinai. As Plaskow explains, "At the very moment that the Jewish people stand ready at Sinai to receive the covenant—not now with individual patriarchs but with the people as a whole— ... Moses addresses the community only as men" (26). Despite this legacy of exclusion, Plaskow's position is that Jewish women were in fact present at Sinai and have something to say about this experience. Plaskow's theology is an attempt to recognize and fill in this gap in the tradition.

Like Borowitz, Plaskow uses the connection between the covenant between God and Israel and the covenant of marriage to frame her critique of Jewish marriage. For her, the problem of domination is especially acute when tropes of family and marriage are used to describe the relationship between God and Israel:

> The prophetic metaphors for the relationship between God and Israel are metaphors borrowed from the patriarchal family— images of dominance softened by affection. God as husband and father of Israel demands obedience and monogamous love. He repays faithfulness with mercy and loving-kindness, but punishes waywardness, just as the wayward daughter can be stoned at her father's door (Deut. 22:21). (7)

She then shows how these tropes are coupled with more blatant images of political power—God as king or warrior as well as husband. She brings these images together to show the link between political and patriarchal expressions of domination and argues that, within the rabbinic tradition, these images are used to sanction such relationships. For Plaskow, images of God as patriarchal husband and king are directly related to the subordination of Jewish women.

> Family and political models of dominance and submission are recapitulated and rendered plausible by the dominance and submission of God and Israel. The silence and submission of women becomes part of a greater pattern that makes it appear fitting and right. (8)

Plaskow appeals to liberalism as a response to this legacy. Her answer is a more inclusive liberal community, which she calls feminist. As she explains:

Feminism demands an understanding of Israel that includes the whole of Israel and thus allows women to speak and name our experiences for ourselves . . . [that] we replace the normative male voice with a chorus of divergent voices, describing Jewish reality in different accents and tones. (9)

Although, as Miriam Peskowitz has argued, there are serious questions about what it means to "let women speak," Plaskow claims this liberal strategy as a feminist practice.[3]

Plaskow's Covenant

In this section, I address two distinct issues in Plaskow's understanding of the relationship between God and Israel: the issue of domination and how Plaskow proposes to overcome it, and the question of inclusion. For me these questions are intertwined as two sides of the limitations of liberal inclusion. Domination persists within liberalism precisely because it cannot tolerate differences. Instead, liberalism demands that differences be harmonized within a greater vision of the whole. Thus, Plaskow figures differences among and between Jews in the section of her book on the people Israel in terms of pieces. The community is figured as many pieces of a single whole. She figures different images of God in her section on God within a more inclusive monotheism, and various strands of rabbinic and biblical traditions in her section on Torah as incomplete pieces of a single Torah. In other words, for Plaskow, there is one people Israel, one God, and one Torah. Differences are incorporated into a theological vision of wholeness.

In her account of the relationship between God and Israel, she distinguishes between "domination" and "covenant" in order to offer a liberal solution to the problem of domination. In the chapter titled "God: Reimaging the Unimaginable," Plaskow writes:

While the portrait of God as dominating Other seems to fit well with the traditional understanding of the chosenness of Israel, it also threatens to undermine the relationship between God and Israel—a partner who enters into an alliance that involves commitment on both sides. The language of domination, however, is in tension with the language of covenant, because it denies the reality of human power and responsibility that the covenant presupposes. (133)

Plaskow assumes that "covenant" as a liberal "contract" is free from coercion, but, as I have already argued, liberal contracts are also asymmetrical power relationships. Pateman even suggests that liberal contract theory itself "turned a subversive proposition into a defense of civil subjection."[4] Despite this feminist critique, however, Plaskow offers liberalism as her feminist answer to a rabbinic legacy of domination. She never challenges the inequities within liberal contracts.

What distinguishes Plaskow's effort from Borowitz's is that, unlike him, she is not satisfied with an old-new model. She wants to get rid of domination and tries to do so by pinning domination on the Rabbis, which allows her to appeal to liberalism as an alternative. Nevertheless, her contractual strategy is limited.

Even in Plaskow's feminist text, liberalism's ambivalence toward women remains a problem. By maintaining God as an all-powerful figure in relationship with Israel, Plaskow offers a liberal feminist modification of domination.

> I have argued that metaphors of God as Other . . . mirror and sustain destructive social relations that ought never to be sanctified by religious usage. But rejecting such metaphors does not entail abandoning God's "moreness"; it simply challenges us to imagine that moreness in nonhierarchical terms. (167)

She does not get rid of domination; she just remakes it as liberal:

> Just as a community is more than the sum of its members, for example, without necessarily controlling or dominating them, so God as the ultimate horizon of community and source of unity is more than all things—also without needing to control or dominate them. (167)

The model Plaskow advocates is a kind of liberal monism that incorporates different images within the one God of Israel.[5] As she explains, "God incorporates the qualities and characteristics of . . . the whole pantheon, with nothing remaining outside (151).[6] She continues this line of argument by stating that "only when our metaphors for God are sufficiently inclusive that they reflect the multiplicity both of a pluralistic Israel and of a cosmic community will God truly be one—which is to say all in all" (151). In this way, Plaskow can ultimately *only* envision differences as a part of a greater whole. In order to maintain this liberal stance, as in Borowitz's theology, certain differences cannot be affirmed and the terms of liberal inclusion remain limited.[7] Thus, although Plaskow offers an important critique of certain legacies of domination, the relationship between God and Israel that she advocates perpetuates another form of domination, which I find particularly unsatisfying.

Toward a New Theology of Sexuality

The most powerful section of Plaskow's theology is her discussion of sexuality. Here, more than anywhere else in her work, she sets out her vision of right relationships, a more inclusive version of liberal marriage as mirrored in the relationship between God and Israel. Unlike Borowitz, Plaskow's discussion of sexuality not only takes into account a diversity of sexualities but also explicitly argues against marriage as an exclusively heterosexual contract. By calling for respect, responsibility, and honesty, she opens up the possibility of affirming different kinds of sexual relationships.

Before going any further, however, I think it is important to be explicit about Plaskow's direct advocacy of the "erotic" as a theological value. Relying on work of black feminist poet and activist Audre Lorde, Plaskow argues that sexuality is a source of liberation.[8] Citing Lorde, she writes: "And when we fail to understand sexual feelings as an expression of the power of the erotic, we reduce them to mere sensations that we then fear and seek to suppress."[9] In this respect, Plaskow's work is explicitly about sexuality, addressing its moral and spiritual power. Plaskow reads Martin Buber's *I and Thou* and the biblical *Song of Songs* as charged with the power of the erotic, a power that she describes as an ambivalent presence within rabbinic Judaism.[10]

Like the rest of her theology, her writing about sexuality also begins with an explicit critique of the Rabbis' ambivalence toward sexuality. She identifies three key problems. First, she argues that the Rabbis address sexuality under the guise of an "energy/control" model, according to which "sexuality is an independent and sometimes alien energy that must be held in check through personal discipline and religious constraints. While the sexual impulse is given by God as a normal and healthy part of human life, sanctified within its proper framework, sexuality also requires careful, sometimes rigorous control in order that it not violate the boundaries assigned it."[11]

Plaskow sees the second problem as the Rabbis' too-narrow definition of sexuality, in which heterosexual marriage is the only proper venue for Jewish sexual expression. Yet, Plaskow, like Borowitz, does not write about the ketubbah.

The third problem she describes is that Jewish women are the explicit concern of most rabbinic accounts of sexuality. As she explains: "To speak of control is necessarily to speak of women—of the need to cover them, avoid them, contain them in proper (patriarchal) families where their threat is minimized if it cannot be overcome."[12]

In each case, Plaskow argues that the Rabbis acknowledge and give power to sexual expression, but use this power to control Jewish women and not liberate them. Plaskow rejects this legacy and offers a liberal alternative.

Like Borowitz, Plaskow uses Martin Buber's I-Thou relationship to describe a kind of mutuality. For her, this relationship need not be marital. As she explains, "Relationships between human beings need not hover at the 'threshold of mutuality' but can express themselves in language, so that acknowledgment of the other as a person can be both given and received."[13]

This vision of mutuality is also echoed in Plaskow's liberal reading of the *Song of Songs*. "Unabashed by their desire, the man and woman of these poems delight in their own embodiment and the beauty surrounding them, each seeking the other out to inaugurate their meetings, each rejoicing in the love without dominion that is also the love of God."[14] As her use of Audre Lorde's notion of the erotic suggests, for Plaskow, the erotic is both holy and powerful. The question is, what kinds of relationships does Plaskow envision as possible outside "the sacred garden" and "in the midst of daily demands" in the present?

Plaskow argues that her mutual vision of the erotic stands in sharp contrast to "the structures of marriage as Judaism defines them."[15] Although these arrangements still define Jewish women as subordinate to Jewish men, she writes that they fail to recognize "the possibility of loving same-sex relationships."[16] In response to this, Plaskow explains: "A first concrete task, then, of the feminist reconstruction of Jewish attitudes towards sexuality is a radical transformation of the institutional, legal framework within which sexual relations are supposed to take place."[17] She does this by not only advocating lesbian and gay relationships but also by calling for a reaffirmation of consent as a criterion for her liberal feminist position:

> In the modern West, it is generally assumed that such a decision [mutual consent] constitutes a central meaning of marriage, but this assumption is contradicted by a religious (and secular) legal system that outlaws homosexual marriage and institutionalizes inequality in its basic definition of marriage and divorce.[18]

Thus, Plaskow opens up the legal definition of marriage to include gay and lesbian relationships but, at the same time, does not alter the structure of liberalism's legal framework. For Plaskow, marriage continues to be about consent, which she also uses as an answer to patriarchy:

> "Marriage" will not be about the transfer of women or the sanctification of potential disorder through the firm establishment of women in the patriarchal family, but the decision of two adults— to make their lives together, lives which include the sharing of sexuality.[19]

Here Plaskow's argument begins to break down, because she can not fully distinguish between the modern western legal tradition and her feminist alternative. Plaskow cannot account for the fact that the patriarchal family is not just a rabbinic problem. Even her efforts to affirm lesbian and gay relationships are based on a liberal premise of inclusion. These relationships are affirmed in their likeness to liberal marriage and not their queerness.

Plaskow's Erotic Ideal

According to Plaskow, sexuality and spirituality are linked:

> I believe that radical mutuality is most fully possible in the context of an ongoing, committed relationship in which sexual expression is one dimension of a shared life. Long-term partnership may be the

richest setting for negotiating and living out the meaning of mutuality, responsibility, and honesty amid the distractions, problems, and pleasures of every day.[20]

Plaskow qualifies her assessment of "radical mutuality" while also choosing "long-term partnerships" as a means to that end.

Within the framework of everyday life as she experiences it in the United States at the end of the twentieth century, ongoing committed relationships like marriage make sense although such relationships may be neither desirable nor possible for others. Thus, "to respond to the realities of different life decisions and at the same time affirm the importance of sexual well-being as an aspect of our total well-being,"[21] Plaskow offers criteria for making sexual choices.

We need to apply certain fundamental values to a range of sexual styles and choices. While honesty, responsibility, and respect are goods that pertain to any relationship, the concrete meaning of these values will vary considerably depending on the duration and significance of the connection involved.[22]

As opposed to Borowitz, Plaskow offers contingent criteria that are potentially inclusive of various sexual possibilities. I affirm these moves. When she begins to apply these criteria to specific relationships, however, Plaskow's position shifts away from its initial contingency, that aspect of her efforts that I find most compelling in terms of reimagining the erotics within Jewish communities. Once Plaskow starts to present examples, what was first presented as an individual opinion quickly becomes a normative assessment.

At its fullest, respect may mean regard for another as a total person; at a minimum, it may mean absence of pressure or coercion, and a commitment, in Lorde's words, not to "look away as we come together." If we need to look away, then we should walk away.[23]

So, like Borowitz, Plaskow also sets up a hierarchy. For her "fullness" is the ideal and, reformulating Lorde's statement, Plaskow makes "not turning away" into a minimal requirement. As I see it, however, Lorde's position is much more in keeping with Plaskow's initial contingency. Although there is a hierarchy in Lorde's text, it is not presented as normative. According to Lorde, each person needs to figure out what she or he values most and then act accordingly:

> Yes, there is a hierarchy. There is a difference between painting a back fence and writing a poem, but only one of quantity. And there is, for me, no difference between writing a good poem and moving into sunlight against the body of a woman I love.[24]

Lorde is clear about what she values without demanding the same assessment by others. My concern is that Plaskow's construction of a maximum and minimum standard erases this kind of contingency. By presuming that long-term monogamous relationships are a norm, Plaskow ends up demanding that others adhere to this single standard.

Again, what makes more sense to me is her initial approach, the contingent application of her criteria of respect, responsibility, and honesty within particular contexts. As I see it, these criteria could offer a more affirming strategy that would open up the possibility of different kinds of sexual expression.

In her final assessment of the erotic, Plaskow makes a direct plea for gay and lesbian relationships, but this time without appealing to her criteria. Instead, she turns to God and theology; she spiritualizes sexuality.

> If we see sexuality as part of what enables us to reach out beyond ourselves, and thus as a fundamental ingredient in our spirituality, then the issue of homosexuality must be . . . a question of the affirmation of the value to the individual and society of each of us being able to find that place within ourselves where sexuality and spirituality come together.[25]

Plaskow's justification for gay and lesbian sexuality ironically returns to a Jewish tradition. She builds on a legacy of Jewish mysticism to give weight and authority to her theological claims. Following this tradition, she writes "that sexuality can be a medium for the reunification of God."[26] (150) Her innovation is simply that this reunification need not take place in exclusively heterosexual relationships: "The reality is that for some Jews, it has been realized only in relationships with both men and women, while for others it is realized only in relationships between members of the same sex."[27] Her strategy is not to transform the tradition but to bring gay and lesbian Jews into something that already exists, making their relationships yet another means to holiness.

This theological argument further distinguishes Plaskow's efforts from Audre Lorde's work on the erotic. For Plaskow, the bonds of the erotic lead to God:

> In recognizing the continuity between our own sexual energy and the greater currents that nourish and renew it [community], we affirm our sexuality as a source of energy and power that, schooled in the values of respect and mutuality, can lead us to the related, and therefore sexual, God.[28]

This position contrasts sharply with my advocacy of her more contingent criteria of respect, responsibility, and honesty. Instead of affirming a vision of diverse and even contradictory erotic relationships, here Plaskow returns to a more unified liberal vision of community, a singular Jewish community that demands that all Jews adhere to a single sexual norm. Although Plaskow includes gay and lesbian relationships within her normative ideal, she does so only to the extent that they resemble the liberal contract of marriage. By reading against the grain of her argument for establishing this norm, I want to imagine other erotic possibilities. I want to respect and not judge the differences between different kinds of erotic relations. This is a position I believe I share with Lorde, who also does not want to tell others ultimately what kinds of erotic relationships they should have.

Despite her reliance on Lorde, I believe that Plaskow's normative claims and theological turn do not fit neatly with Lorde's depiction of the power of the erotic as a liberatory practice. By using Lorde's notion of "not turning away when we come together" as a minimal requirement for sexual relationships, Plaskow misses the power of Lorde's plea. Lorde's demand is by no means minimal, for "not turning away" is a symbol of the fullness of relating to another, an expression of radical mutuality:

> Only now, I find more and more women-identified women brave enough to risk sharing the erotic's electrical charge without having

to look away, and without distorting the enormously powerful and creative nature of that exchange.[29]

According to Lorde, "to look away" is a form of distortion that can have many manifestations. As I read it, "turning away" includes Plaskow's efforts to justify sexuality as "Godly" or "holy."[30] As Lorde writes, "These occasions are almost always characterized by a simultaneous looking away, a pretense of calling them something else, whether a *religion*, a fit, mob violence, or even playing doctor"[31] (my emphasis). These distortions, including religion, are, according to Lorde, quite dangerous. They limit one's ability to be fully present with another.

Although Lorde speaks of the erotic as spiritual, she does not want to confuse it with something outside of herself:

That deep and irreplaceable knowledge of my capacity for joy comes to demand from all of my life that it be lived within the knowledge that such satisfaction is possible, and does not have to be called *marriage*, nor *god*, nor *an afterlife*.[32](57)

Not having to attribute this experience of the erotic to something external is the challenge of "not turning away." In this way Lorde offers a way of thinking differently about an erotic self in relation to others. Lorde is concerned about living life fully:

When we begin to live from within outward, in touch with the power of the erotic within ourselves, and allowing that power to inform and illuminate our actions upon the world around us, then we begin to be responsible to ourselves in the deepest sense. For as we begin to recognize our deepest feelings, we begin to give up, of necessity, being satisfied with the suffering and self negation, and with the numbness which so often seems like their only alternative in our society. Our acts against oppression become integral with self, motivated and empowered from within.[33]

For me Lorde's construction of the erotic offers a way of thinking about relationships and selves in their complexity, over and against not only the sexual contract but also other forms of individual and social oppression, among them resignation, despair, self-effacement, depression, and self-denial. In this way she acknowledges how she herself has internalized and sustained various histories of oppression within herself, even as she works against them. In these ways Lorde's text speaks to me, invites me in. She reminds me of how and in what ways the erotic is powerful and liberatory without having to contain its powers within a framework. It is the contingent nature of Lorde's notion of the erotic that opens it up to different possibilities—in this case to two different interpretations of Plaskow's theology of sexuality.[34] It is the specificity of Lorde's account as opposed to its all-inclusiveness that appeals to me. I do not have to share Lorde's position to learn from her. I can apply her approach to my own situation and this may lead to even contradictory results.

As I read it, Lorde's notion of the erotic is at the heart of Plaskow's theology of sexuality, giving shape and texture to some of her most powerful accounts of community, relation, and belonging. In these moments, Plaskow offers an alternative to her own normative vision of liberal inclusion. I have focused on Plaskow's reading of Lorde because I see it as a promising site of contradiction within Plaskow's text where she begins to push at the seams of her own liberal feminist stance. What I have tried to demonstrate in the final sections of this chapter is that these are indeed liberating moments. Within Plaskow's reading of Lorde, she offers a more contingent feminist notion of erotic community that challenges her liberal theological vision. It is this partial vision that I carry with me out of Plaskow's text as an alternative to her liberal feminist position.

Conclusion

Throughout her feminist theology, Plaskow critiques the dynamics of domination within rabbinic Judaism. Unlike Borowitz, she adamantly resists this legacy by turning to liberalism as a feminist alternative. My disappointment is that, despite her careful critique, like Borowitz, Plaskow uses theology to legitimate and prescribe a version of the sexual contract that is offered as both Jewish and feminist. Fortunately, this is not all that is going on in her text. By turning to Audre Lorde's notion of the erotic, Plaskow gestures toward a different vision of feminist community. I want to affirm this alternative to liberalism.

By reading against the grain of Plaskow's text, I have tried to offer a vision of Jewish feminist communities, indeed Jewish feminist homes, in other than liberal terms. Building on Plaskow's criteria of respect, responsibility, and honesty, I contend that a more contingent Jewish feminist position need not presume that there is a single normative erotic ideal even for Jewish feminists. In the next section of this book, I return to feminist literary theory in order to explore other ways of imagining more complicated Jewish feminist positions.

part two

Feminist Study

Reconfiguring Jewish Identity

~

seven

Feminist Dreams of Home

At the end of the last chapter, I posited a desire for an answer to the limitation of Plaskow's theology. I dreamed of a feminist home outside of the confines of liberalism; as I returned to the texts that frame this project and all of the possibilities they have held out to me, I find myself pausing. Is feminist study a place where I can claim a Jewish feminist position? Although I have been able to embrace feminist texts like Pratt's "Identity," noting both connections and differences between our positions, I now want to ask about where I can do this kind of feminist reading and writing. Is the academic field of feminist studies a place for me to engage in this kind of critical practice? Can my work be included in this field? Is this feminist vision of an academic home open to me as a Jew?

In this chapter I want to raise some cautions about such dreams of an academic home for Jewish feminists through a reading of two feminist literary texts, Nancy K. Miller's "Dreaming, Dancing and the Changing Locations of Feminist Criticism, 1988"[1] and Teresa de Lauretis's "Feminist Studies/Critical Studies: Issues, Terms, and Contexts."[2] I begin with Miller's essay because she specifically addresses the place of Jews in feminist studies by attempting to write as a Jew. I then turn to de Lauretis's essay to show how Jews have been included in feminist study.

Dangerous Dreams

In the first section of Miller's essay—aptly titled "Whose Dream?—she juxtaposes a series of feminist and critical texts on dreaming and dancing. Through many citations of other people's writings, without any apparent intervention of her own, she demonstrates the limitations of a kind of citational inclusion within feminist writing. In the second section of her essay, "Personal Histories, Autobiographical Locations," she writes about fewer texts and positions herself as a Jew in relation to them.

Nevertheless, at the end of her essay, reflecting back on both of these experiments, her attempt to speak for others in section one and speak as a Jew in the second section, Miller writes:

> To some extent the difficulty of these two occasions was an effect of context; it was also, and more importantly, a symptom of the project of identity writing itself: impossible to elude: the co-implication, which always seems to find its borders in violence, of the "speaking as a"s and "speaking for"s. . . . It is for this reason that I have not tried, even in the space of written revision, to master the crisis by a conclusion that would put things back together again. This could only be done by a discourse of containment that depends finally on making an abstraction of that violence. (97)

Although Miller assumes an autobiographical stance, I do not believe that efforts to speak or write for others as oneself are the same as what Miller calls "the project of identity writing," which for Miller is a singular activity. It is either a writing "for others" or a writing "as something"—in this case, as a Jew. She wants to find a way to negotiate both of these moves without causing discursive violence to herself or to those others for whom she speaks. I believe that this is possible by imagining these activities as a kind of textual embrace.[3] By understanding these activities as intertwined and not solely autobiographical, I have found that I can speak, read, and write about others as myself. The question Miller's essay raises for me is the relationship between specific textual practices and the institutional practices that enable such practices. I know that feminist texts are generative of my own work but am less sure about the reception of these readings within academic feminist studies.

"Feminist Studies Reconstituting Knowledge"

According to Teresa de Lauretis, the volume *Feminist Studies/Critical Studies* and her opening essay are a record of the Feminist Studies: Reconstituting Knowledge conference held in Milwaukee in 1985. The conference and the volume were to take stock of what feminist studies had accomplished over the previous twenty years and to ask where it was heading. Conference participants were asked "what the specific concerns, values, and methods of feminist critical work are, or ought to be."[4] For this reason I have found it a helpful text in my efforts to assess the dangers involved in my own turn to feminist studies. In her account and those of others in the volume, de Lauretis both acknowledges the active role of Jewish feminists in the work of "identity politics"[5] while also carefully avoiding any mention of the specific Jewish concerns that were raised at the conference. Instead, I have come to learn about what happened at the conference from others, both Nancy K. Miller and Evelyn Beck, who offer accounts of what happened when Beck raised questions about antisemitism within feminist studies.

In Beck's essay, "The Politics of Jewish Invisibility," itself a version of the paper she presented in Milwaukee, she explains "the ways in which Jewish women's lives are left out of the feminist project and to suggest the contexts in which they should be included,"[6] using what happened in Milwaukee as an example. Moreover, "because theory builds on itself, one omission frequently prepares the way for the next,"[7] this omission was especially important in response to de Lauretis's volume which, as Beck explains, "seems likely to be a text which will, in the words of [feminist literary critic] Catherine R. Stimpson, 'do nothing less than to create the next stage of feminist thought.' If it succeeds in so doing, it will also succeed in keeping Jewish themes out of the feminist agenda."[8] She argued that "the fact that this [her] paper was not included in the body of the text, nor the episode recorded or analyzed by the editor, serve[d] to obscure the existence of anti-Semitism within contemporary feminism."[9] Although I disagree with this blanket statement, I do find it significant that Beck's work was absent from the de Lauretis volume and that this incident was not addressed.

The paper that Evelyn Beck presented in Milwaukee was about the precarious place of Jews within academic feminist studies. According to Beck, specifically Jewish concerns have often been excluded from feminist studies courses, critical texts, and conferences. In her efforts to reimagine feminist studies, Beck asked those in Milwaukee to rethink the marginal place of Jews within this academic field. Unfortunately, as Beck explains in her essay, what happened in Milwaukee reiterated the kinds of problems she had attempted to address in her paper.

Beck's version, found in an extended footnote in her essay, "The Politics of Jewish Invisibility," is an example of her larger argument:

Because such events are rarely talked about, I would like to record the basic outlines of that episode, which I am in a position to do since I was the speaker in question. First, the moderator did not allow questions in response to my talk because "time did not permit," while she allowed time for several questions for the paper following mine. When I objected to this differential treatment, one woman in the audience shouted words to the effect that "Jews control the media, which is why the Holocaust is getting so much attention, while the Middle Passage is ignored." In response to a reminder about the gassing of Jews in concentration camps in World War II, this same woman answered, "Yes, but you Jews have it so good until they come get you!" Another panel member made fun of this episode by quipping, "I can't possibly be anti-Semitic; I was married to a 'nice Jewish boy.'" Following this episode she ended her presentation by calling for solidarity with Palestinian women out of any context which would have made that appropriate. The audience, for the most part, seemed to be paralyzed and only one or two women came to the defense. By my count, about one third of the audience was Jewish.[10]

Although the tone of Nancy K. Miller's synopsis differs greatly from Beck's, her assessment of the content of Beck's remarks, as well as the outline of the incident, is quite similar.

Miller discusses this incident in "Personal Histories," the second portion of "Dreaming and Dancing." The incident is presented as one of two anecdotal accounts of her attempts to speak as a Jew in response to "identity politics within the institution."[11] Although I will return to the first of these anecdotes in the next chapter, for now I want to focus on Miller's self-consciously Jewish response to this incident.

According to Miller, the scene was dramatic;

Evelyn Beck exhorted Jewish women to identify themselves (take back their names, and their noses) and wondered out loud from the platform, aggressively, polemically, why Jewish (better yet, Yiddish), female authored texts were not taught in Women's Studies courses alongside Chicana, Native American, etc. works as "ethnic" or "minority" literature (which is a fair question).[12]

Before presenting Miller's account of the rest of the audience's reactions to this presentation, I want to look closely at Miller's description of Beck. Despite the fact that Beck, another Jewish woman, was addressing issues of Jewish inclusion in feminist studies, Miller distances herself from this discussion. She writes about Jewish women in the third person and describes Beck's plea as aggressive and polemical. Miller writes that Beck offered an inciting exhortation.[13]

Miller's use of parenthetical comments is also telling. When Beck demands that Jewish women take back what they have come to despise about themselves as Jews living in America, Miller places her comments about "taking back their [Jewish] names, and their [Jewish] noses" in parentheses, further distancing herself from these pleas. But this is only part of what is going on in her text. In a second parenthetical comment, Miller expresses her ambivalent yet guarded support for Beck's final claims by agreeing that texts by Jewish women, Yiddish texts, should be included in women's studies courses.

Having described Beck's address, Miller recounts the events that followed. She explains that Sondra O'Neale, "a black critic on the panel," quickly dismissed Beck's claims "equally polemically and upping the ante."[14] She describes O'Neale as saying "that Jews had no right to speak of oppression or marginality since, unlike blacks, they could 'choose to pass.'"[15] After this, according to Miller, the scene became increasingly charged when Blanche Gelfand, a Jewish woman in the audience, responded to these claims by "observing that six million of them [Jews] seemed to have failed to exercise that option."[16] She then explains that in response to Gelfand, Gayatri Spivak, another panelist, "urged the audience to remember their Palestinian sisters, who were not with us, and whose men were dying."[17] In response to all of this, Miller describes herself as both irritated and silent.[18] As she explains, "I sat there, in silent shock at the turn this politically correct occasion was taking, not saying anything, and waiting for it to be over. What was there, really, to say once the structure of competing oppressions had been put into place."[19] By describing this incident in terms of competing oppressions, Miller gives up the possibility of ever taking a Jewish stance. This resignation echoes Beck's critique of Jews in feminist study as well as her assessment of this particular gathering. Miller was one of "the Jewish one third of the audience" paralyzed by this incident.

From the somewhat safer distance of an endnote, Miller justifies this paralysis with an appeal to British feminist critic Jenny Bourne's contentious essay "Homelands of the Mind: Jewish Feminism and Identity Politics."[20] Bourne's essay is a telling choice, since it offers a disturbing critique of both Jewish feminism and identity politics.[21] Without going into the intricacies of Bourne's argument, in her note Miller simply states that "Bourne provides an astringent analysis of these clotted issues." This statement, albeit vague, supports Miller's claim that "once the structure of competing oppressions had been put into place,"[22] there was nothing to be done.

As I read it, both Miller and Beck describe this incident in terms of competing oppressions, a conflict between women of color and Jews. This raises additional concerns for me about the politics of feminist inclusion. Why must there be a competition between these groups of women, and whose interests does this arrangement really serve?[23] Instead of presuming this arrangement, I would have preferred to imagine the conference addressing these questions not in terms of "liberal opposition" but in terms of a critique of "horizontal violence," the in-fighting among and between oppressed groups. Despite the fact that de Lauretis gestures in this direction, she never makes the connection. Instead, she only writes about

> the constant drive on the part of institutions (in which, like it or not, feminists are also engaged) to deflect radical resistance and to recuperate it as liberal opposition. And that the proven most effective means to that end is what Flo Kennedy, speaking in Milwaukee a few months ago, called "horizontal violence," the in-fighting among members of an oppressed group.[24]

Although "horizontal violence" could have helped to explain what happened at the conference in terms of the limitations of liberal inclusion, de Lauretis does not fully challenge these liberal assumptions:

> Granted that, among women, such horizontal violence is verbal rather than physical, and that the fine line between in-fighting and critical debate is often too fine to know for sure; nevertheless, Wittig's

point on the "material oppression of individuals by discourse" must apply here, as well, and should be kept on the front burner of a feminist political consciousness as one with the issue of power.[25]

I disagree that the line between in-fighting and critical debate is that fine. As both Beck and Miller make clear in their accounts of what happened in Milwaukee, those who are oppressed by language do know when they have been violated.

Although de Lauretis gestures toward a kind of radical resistance, she insists that, even among feminists in the academy, resistance remain limited to liberal opposition. She presumes a single structure of competing oppressions and is unable to act on other possibilities she herself offers in response to this problem. As she explains, "The practice of self-consciousness—of reading, speaking, and listening to one another—is the best way we have precisely to resist horizontal violence."[26] This is a strategy very much in keeping with my notion of a kind of textual embrace where reading and writing about an interplay between self and other is both possible and positive. Although Miller opens up this possibility, she herself does not choose to engage directly in such a practice.

The rest of de Lauretis's statement on this issue of consciousness is even more telling. Having asked women to hear, read, and listen to each other "without acquiescing to institutional recuperation," de Lauretis urges it "Even as we accept, as we must, the liberal allocation of a tiny amount of 'equal' time in which to present our 'opposing viewpoint.'"[27] In this instance she is even more explicit about the fact that she accepts the terms of liberal inclusion.

Who Speaks for the Jews?

In this section I want to look carefully at what happens to Jewish voices in de Lauretis's text. Unlike Beck, I do not agree that Jewish feminists are simply absent from this essay. What is interesting to me is how and under what terms Jews are included. As if in a dream that corrects all that happened in Milwaukee, as I will demonstrate, Jews appear almost exclusively alongside women of color; the two groups are presented in solidarity.

The first place de Lauretis refers to Jewish women is in a list of specific areas of debate within feminist studies: "the attendant problems of racism and anti-Semitism."[28] Note the parenthetical point in the following passage:

> As the history of revolutionary movements in this century has shown, and as the most recent developments in feminist theory confirm beyond a doubt (developments that have been prompted by the writings of women of color, Jewish women, and lesbians, and that can be sustained only by a serious, critical, and self-critical attention to the issues they raise), consciousness is not the result of a process but the term of a process.[29]

De Lauretis presents Jewish women as key participants in this feminist revolution. Through their efforts, somehow in combination with these other women, they have helped transform feminism, demanding that feminists address issues of difference and inclusion. De Lauretis continues this line of argument by suggesting that

> consciousness of self, like class consciousness or race consciousness (e.g., my consciousness of being white), is a particular configuration of subjectivity, or subjective limits, produced at the intersection of meaning with experience. (I have never, before coming to this country, been conscious of being white; and the meaning, the sense of what it means to be white has changed for me greatly over the years.)[30]

Through her own interactions with "women of color, Jewish women, and lesbians" de Lauretis thus claims to have come to understand herself and, especially, her white skin privilege in America.

Following up on this point, she acknowledges that Jewish women were also critical to her understanding of identity as the point of departure in her own process of self-consciousness.[31] Citing *Yours in Struggle: Three Feminist Perspectives on Anti-Semitism and Racism*, de Lauretis reminds readers of the coalition between women of color and Jewish women in these efforts.[32] Thus, she credits Elly Bulkin, Minnie Bruce Pratt, and Barbara Smith, among others, for this new understanding of identity. Despite her extensive use of this particular text, however, de Lauretis does not make a connection between this book's major concerns and what happened in Milwaukee.

When she quotes from Elly Bulkin's essay, "Hard Ground: Jewish

Identity, Racism, and Anti-Semitism," de Lauretis uses Bulkin's text to support her own broad claims about multiple and contradictory identities:

> What emerges in feminist writings is . . . the concept of a multiple, shifting, and often self-contradictory identity, a subject that is not divided in, but rather at odds with, language; an identity made up of heterogeneous and heteronomous representations of gender, race, and class, and often indeed across languages and cultures; an identity that one decides to reclaim from a history of multiple assimilations, and that one insists on as a strategy: "I think," writes Elly Bulkin, "of all the women [of mixed heritage] who, told to choose between or among identities, insist on selecting them all."[33]

The specificity of Bulkin's discussion of these issues is lost here; in Bulkin's text, these words are directed to a particular group of women and are part of a specific invocation of differences. Bulkin writes these words "for the Jewish-Latina, the Arab-Jewish woman, for any Jewish woman of color who is too often, as one Jamaican-Jewish woman has said, 'a token to everybody'; for any woman of color of mixed heritage—Chinese-Korean, Native American-Black, Asian-Black, Chicana . . . Arab-American dyke . . . the Jewish lesbian."[34] By contrast, in de Lauretis's text, Bulkin's statement is used to demonstrate a radical shift in feminist thinking in general but, while there may be some truth to this claim, this is not what Bulkin says. Bulkin's is a statement about particular women of mixed heritages—heritages whose names are removed from de Lauretis's account, as is Bulkin's own lesbian Jewish feminist position.

The next place Jewish women appear in de Lauretis's text is within another broad discussion about building a more inclusive feminist frame of reference:

> We need to keep building one [feminist frame of reference], absolutely flexible and readjustable, from women's own experience of difference, differences which, as the essays by Sondra O'Neale, Sheila Radford-Hill, and Cherríe Moraga in this volume argue and document, are perceived as having as much (or more) to do with race, class, or ethnicity as with gender or sexuality per se.[35]

The long note that accompanies this statement includes a reference to Evelyn Beck's *Nice Jewish Girls: A Lesbian Anthology*.[36]—the only reference to Beck in de Lauretis's entire volume. Ironically, here again Jewish lesbians are presented alongside women of color. Even more striking is the fact that Beck's text is offered as support for the claims made by those same women of color who sat on the panel with Beck and challenged her claims about Jewish oppression. By not including Beck's paper in the volume, de Lauretis is able to make this seemingly easy reconciliation. Beck is simply able to take her place, without comment, in a note alongside various texts by women of color. Although I agree that Beck's book should have been included in this note, the tensions between O'Neale and Beck in particular also needed to be acknowledged.

Finally, I want to turn to the end of de Lauretis's essay where she presents a final passage from Bulkin's essay:

> We don't have to be the same to have a movement, but we do have to admit our fears and pain and be accountable for our ignorance. In the end, finally, we must refuse to give up on each other.[37]

The ironies are painful. This passage was also taken from Bulkin's text but was originally written by women of color to Jewish women. It was a public response to an incident of antisemitism (not unlike what Beck and Miller describe in Milwaukee) at a 1981 feminist workshop on double allegiances.[38] As Bulkin explains, "the presence of working-class Jews was ignored with remarks that 'all Jews are rich' and 'there's no such thing as a poor Jew.'"[39] The statement de Lauretis quotes was a rebuttal to these claims by Cherríe Moraga, Julia Perez, Barbara Smith, and Beverly Smith (four Third World women), whose responses was originally printed in *The Gay Community News*. As Bulkin explains, they wrote, "that the women who made these anti-Jewish remarks were not representative of all the women of color present."[40] The "we" in the passage de Lauretis cites was clearly never meant to speak to all women, as her text implies. It was a gesture of solidarity within the lesbian feminist community by women of color to Jewish women. De Lauretis does not directly present this information even as she tries to rectify, in some ways, what happened in Milwaukee with these same words.

What is disturbing about this gesture is that de Lauretis claims to have learned so much about herself from these other women: "And to the extent that I can see beyond and through that history [her own] by knowing the ways of other(s') histories, the project of this book has been empowering."[41] The question is, empowering to or for whom? At the end of her essay de Lauretis continues, "It is more than editorial correctness, therefore, that makes me end this introduction with the words of others who have enabled me to see beyond my history through them."[42] These words introduce the inclusionary statement quoted above from Bulkin's text. Unfortunately, de Lauretis does not seem to see far enough beyond her own history to address these other women in any sustained way.

Who speaks for the Jews? In this case, I hope I have made clear that de Lauretis does. She controls both who can speak and what can be said. In the first instance, Bulkin's is the only explicit Jewish voice to appear in her text but even her words are carefully edited and often taken out of context. In the one instance where Evelyn Beck is cited, she is presented as a silent supporter for the shared claims of women of color and lesbian Jewish feminists without any indication of the tensions within these alliances.

Whose Dreams?

In the beginning of the "Whose Dream?" section of Miller's essay, she cites a long passage from the prologue to Zora Neal Hurston's novel, *Their Eyes Were Watching God*:

Ships at a distance have every man's wish on board. For some they come in with the tide. For others they sail forever on the horizon, never out of sight, never landing until the Watcher turns his eyes away in resignation, his dreams mocked to death by Time. That is the life of men.

Now, women forget all those things they don't want to remember, and remember everything they don't want to forget. The dream is the truth. Then they act and do things accordingly.[43]

Hurston's words echo my reading of de Lauretis's text. Like the women Hurston writes about, de Lauretis also forgets all those things she does not want to remember and remembers what she does not want to forget. In so doing, she dreams of a reconciliation where all is made right in the space of written revision.

In Miller's text, Hurston's words and these desires serve a different purpose. They come to form a "framing puzzle" or "parable" for Miller's reflections on the question of the relationship between dreams and dreamers:

> Does it matter who dreams (or writes) the dream of Life, of Time? Man or woman? White man or black woman? Black man or black woman? Straight woman or lesbian woman? What will the gender of the dreamer, the race of the dreamer tell us about the dream? What gets left out of Black and White, Black or White? What is the relation of difference to plural? Sexism to Racism? Feminism to Racism? Race to Theory?[44]

After a long series of citations that explore these questions—lots of passages about different dreamers and their dreams—Miller concludes "Whose Dream?" by circling back to precisely these questions and Hurston's assessment: "For women, the dream is the truth, and women act and do things accordingly, then what remains to do is the work of the dream" (89). She then describes such dream work in terms of "self-consciousness" or "consciousness raising."[45] Citing de Lauretis's essay, Miller explains that such work involves "an attentiveness to experience, 'a political-personal strategy of survival and resistance that is also at the same time a critical practice and a mode of knowledge'" (89–90).

In gesturing back to this the most radical and, indeed, most hopeful aspect of de Lauretis's essay, Miller presumably alleviates certain tensions in her own text. Inclusion is made possible by linking Hurston's notion of dream work with de Lauretis's account of "self-consciousness." Citing Hurston one last time, Miller reinforces this connection. She ends "Whose Dream?" with the words of Hurston's "experienced heroine," who explains to her friend at the end of the novel that "you got tuh *go* there tuh *know* there" (90). By juxtaposing de Lauretis's account of feminist self-consciousness with this final passage from Hurston's novel, Miller presumes an equivalence between these two texts without fully articulating the specific connections she is making. Unfortunately, in the second section of her essay the weight of other possible readings collapses the delicacy of this textual strategy. As Miller comes to realize, such a use of citation to support claims of sameness or equivalence demands much more explicit explanation, something that de Lauretis herself was unable to do.[46]

In the next chapter, I return to the second half of Miller's essay in order to see how she takes up this challenge. By examining her readings of the essays on identity and home by Pratt, Mohanty, and Martin—the same feminist texts that offered me a way into feminist study—I demonstrate how specific and embodied Jewish readings can take place in feminist classrooms in other than liberal terms.

eight

~

Jews in Feminist Study

One of the things that makes feminism particular is a self-consciousness about ways of knowing and the ways in which we believe what we know. Is it possible to try and think about some kind of pedagogy or some kind of way of being that would break the cycle of trashing the predecessor, killing the mother, and instead say, "here is what this opens and now we can go on from that" or "this gives us a ground, let's then go on to do other things that they haven't dealt with."

—Nancy K. Miller, "Criticizing Feminist Criticism"

The fact ... of being both Jewish and a feminist is a crucial, even constitutive piece of my self-consciousness as a writer; and in that sense of course it is also at work—on occasion— in the style and figure of my autobiographical project.

—Nancy K. Miller, "Dreaming, Dancing"

At the end of her essay "Dreaming, Dancing," Nancy K. Miller claims that Jewishness and feminism are at work in her writing but is less clear about how these aspects of her identity are a part of her work as a feminist teacher and scholar.[1] I want to look here at "Personal Histories," the second half of her essay, and how being Jewish and a feminist are also a part of Miller's scholarly practices. I argue that Miller offers an enactment of individual self-reflection or self-consciousness as a feminist practice; I then postulate how this connects with my own efforts to claim a Jewish position within academic feminist study.[2]

"Identity" as a Way In

In "Personal Histories, Autobiographical Locations," Miller brings herself directly into a discussion of feminist inclusion. This portion of her essay, like my own feminist narrative about home, is constructed around Biddy Martin and Chandra Mohanty's "Feminist Politics: What's Home Got To Do with It?" and Minnie Bruce Pratt's "Identity: Skin Blood Heart."[3] Identifying with Martin and Mohanty,

Miller makes connections between their reading of Pratt and her own citational practice in terms of a "poetics of location." By moving between readings of Martin and Mohanty's essay and Pratt's, Miller explains her own preoccupations with other people's personal histories and autobiographical writings and also her efforts to position herself more personally. As she notes, these essays provide her with a kind of theoretical bridge between the two halves of her own essay. They allow her to make connections between a citational practice of textual inclusion and the material constraints involved in being included as a Jew in academic feminist studies. Martin and Mohanty's reading allows Miller to see Pratt's essay as "an important instance of new ways of moving 'individual self-reflection and critical practice' into the 'building of political collectivity."[4] Thus,

> a text like Pratt's would seem to embody the antithesis of deconstructive values. . . . Indeed, against the fiction of split subjects constructed by the signifiers of their own alterity, "Identity" appears as a text firmly situated in the social and whose subject emerges from its locational politics.[5]

Miller reads these essays together as an exchange between the theoretical and the personal, with Pratt's essay "undo[ing] identity on the grounds of identity itself."[6] Miller sees Pratt's essay as a dream text focusing on two specific passages about Pratt's dreams of a feminist politics, passages that "pass through the language of dreams and nightmares."[7] The first passage Miller reads as a nightmarish indictment of feminist politics, the second, as a dream of reconciliation.

Despite Pratt's often positive statements about her engagement in feminist politics, Miller points out that Pratt's first dream tells a more ambivalent story:

> I began to dream my husband was trying to kill me, that I was running away with my children on Greyhound buses through Mississippi. I began to dream that I was crossing a river with my children; women on the other side, but no welcome for me with the boys.[8]

After presenting this passage, Miller argues that "the bad dream comes true, at least in part."[9] The fact that Pratt lost custody of her children and that the courts in North Carolina did not allow her to be both a lesbian and a mother is true,[10] and yet, this is not the nightmare that Miller calls attention to.

By making this dream into a nightmare about feminist politics, Miller overlooks the initial or precipitating violence Pratt so clearly envisions: "I began to dream my husband was trying to kill me." Instead, Miller focuses on the final scene of the dream, Pratt's description of being rejected by women. She focuses on Pratt's disappointment with feminist promises of inclusion.

The only other site at which Miller addresses Pratt's struggles with men is in relation to her father. Following Martin and Mohanty, she writes:

> Pratt keeps moving forward toward that place of memory to be refound. . . with the "exhilaration" produced by the movement, by not succumbing to the inertia of old scenes, in the struggles of the experience to work through identity she is haunted by her father's claims to her.[11]

In the second dream passage, Miller presents a very different account of feminist politics. It is a hopeful dream of a feminist home in which, Miller argues, Pratt's "narrative ends with a dream of possibility."[12] Before offering Miller's account of this dream, I do want to briefly look at the passage leading up to the section Miller cites, where Pratt already explicitly expresses her belief in the possibility of feminist politics:

> And I get hopeful when I think that with this kind of work there is the possibility of friendship, and love, between me and the many other women from whom I have been separated by my culture, and by my own beliefs and actions, for so long.[13]

Although Miller does not cite this portion of the text, it supports her reading of the dream. The dream is about an uneasy reconciliation between precisely these women. The dream passage as it appears in Miller's text reads as follows:

> For years I have had a recurring dream: sleeping, I am reconciled to a woman from whom I have been parted: my mother, the Black woman who raised me, my first woman lover, a Jewish woman friend;

in the dream we embrace, with the sweetness that can come in a dream when all is made right. I catch a glimpse of this possibility in my dream; it comes, in waking life, with my friends sometimes, with my lover: not an easy reconciliation, but one that may come when I continue the struggle with myself and the world I was born in.[14]

Although this is a cautious vision, it is very much a statement about the possibility of feminist inclusion.[15]

Despite this difference, Miller very much identifies with Martin and Mohanty's close reading of Pratt's text and goes on to use it to critique her own citational practice by first criticizing Martin and Mohanty's efforts to position themselves in their text. She argues that they do not say enough about themselves and their respective backgrounds. She wants to hear more about Mohanty's background, what informs her work on the intersection of postcolonial discourses and feminism. She also wants to know more about Biddy Martin's southern upbringing and her links to Pratt as a feminist literary critic. Miller cites the following passage as evidence of this problem:

We began working on this project after visiting our respective "homes" in Lynchburg, Virginia and Bombay, India in the fall of 1984—visits fraught with conflict, loss, memories, and desires we both considered to be of central importance in thinking about our relationship to feminist politics. In spite of significant differences in our personal histories and academic backgrounds, and the displacements we both experience, the political and intellectual positions we share made it possible for us to work on, indeed to write, this essay together.[16]

This is Martin and Mohanty's only invocation of their particular homes. By calling attention to this, Miller expresses her dissatisfaction with their account of their own homes:

This is all we learn from and about the authors directly, though we are invited to find them "in the text": "Just as Pratt refuses the methodological imperative to distinguish between herself as actual biographical referent and her narrator, we have at points allowed ourselves to let our reading of the text speak for us."[17]

Miller then goes on to argue that there is no clear site of critical authority in Martin and Mohanty's essay. This becomes a crucial problem not only with their text but, as she explains, also with her own. Identifying with Martin and Mohanty, Miller continues:

> This position of identification/nonidentification,the suspension of the autobiographical referent was also a strategy that I adopted in "Whose Dream?": letting my reading of the text through the jux-taposition of quotations "at points" speak for me. But as things turned out—on the occasions in which I performed this reading—the relation of critic to text proved to be too important a matter of authority to support that degree of textual ambiguity.[18]

Miller's claim is that Martin and Mohanty's citational practice is analogous to her own and that in both cases the strategy fails. I dis-agree with this assessment.

Unlike Miller in "Whose Dream?" Martin and Mohanty present an analysis of only a single text that was prepared specifically for the de Lauretis volume *Feminist Studies/Critical Studies*.[19] In this context, although they allow Pratt's text to speak for them, they do so only on occasion; at other points, they write in their own voices. By contrast, in "Whose Dream?" Miller offers a revised version of a series of con-ference papers. The essay, "belongs in its origins to more than one occasion."[20] She offers a vast array of decontextualized voices, never self-consciously positioning herself in relation to any one of them. She describes the writing of "Whose Dream?" as a process in which the text took shape as if without her intervention: "The shape of the paper rapidly took form from the quotations which seemed to lead to each other, against each other, without me."[21] This is not Martin and Mohanty's strategy.[22]

Although Miller does not make these distinctions, in the next sec-tion of "Personal Histories" she does flesh out this powerful self-cri-tique. By recounting a failed attempt to present "Whose Dream?" to a broad audience, she indicates why she decided to relinquish the position of the straight white woman and try to write "as a Jew."[23] In what follows I look closely at one instance where I believe Miller was successful in doing this: when she offers a Jewish reading of Pratt's essay in the context of a graduate seminar.

Writing as a Jew

In her Jewish reading of Pratt's "Identity," Miller rereads Pratt's feminist dream of reconciliation. As a Jew, Miller describes what it felt like for her to read about herself— her Jewish self— in Pratt's vision of inclusion. By describing how disorienting it was for her to find herself being spoken for in the unfamiliar terms of Pratt's narrative, Miller takes a different stand. What she finds in Pratt's essay is something that approximates, but is not quite, her self. In contrast to my readings of Pratt's essay, Miller does not feel included. She comes to this essay looking for Jews, but does not find herself in the text. Despite Pratt's very careful depiction of Jews, Miller is uncomfortable with what she reads, the terms of Jewish inclusion.

In order to illustrate this problem, Miller contexualizes her reading. She describes teaching Pratt's essay in a feminist seminar at the Graduate Center of the City College of New York. Miller became increasingly uncomfortable as she and her students discussed Pratt's depiction of Jews. She focuses on the following passage from Pratt's essay:

> I had no place for Jews in the map of my thoughts . . . except that they had lived before Christ in an almost mythical Israel, and afterwards in Germany until they were killed, and that those in this country were foreign, even if they were here: they were always foreign, their place was always somewhere else.[24]

Seeing, but then again, not seeing herself reflected in this characterization of Jews, Miller describes how, in the process of teaching this piece, she suddenly realizes that she is the only Jew in the room, which makes her even more uncomfortable. She has trouble reading the phrase "my Jewish lover" embodied and fixed within Pratt's narrative. As she explains: "I didn't like reading the (negative) signifiers—Jews/foreign/somewhere else— and then feeling interpellated as "the Jewish woman" in the record of this white woman's awakening (working her anti-semitism through 'on' me)."[25]

No longer speaking from the position of the unmarked (white) feminist critic who identified with Pratt's project, here Miller finds herself in the uncomfortable position of being the one who is being spoken for. She is uneasy with the lack of fit between Pratt's description of

Jews and her own sense of Jewishness. In this way, Miller's reading of Pratt prefigures and also critiques her account of the incident in Milwaukee described in the last chapter. Here again she is isolated and fearful as a Jew, but the difference is that in this case, she does something about it. "I didn't say much, if anything, about it at the time—being the teacher—and I think now that this was an error of pedagogy."[26] In writing about this regret, she corrects the situation. As she explains, calling attention to the fact that she was the only Jew in the room might have offered her a useful way of complicating the terms of that feminist classroom discussion—a move that takes place as she writes about it in this essay.

Miller describes a central contradiction within Pratt's essay, the way in which Pratt is and is not able to celebrate others in her autobiographical narrative. According to Miller, the problem is "a failure in the writing: the shifting line between the poignancy of self-representation and the didactics of representivity."[27] It is not so clear to me that Pratt's essay is only an autobiographical account. Nor do I believe that what is at stake is merely a matter of good or bad depictions of Jews, success, or failure, since such language is dichotomizing. After all, it is only in relation to Pratt's text that Miller is able to write as a Jew. I believe that this, in and of itself, is significant, that even Miller's strong negative assessment constitutes a kind of critical engagement. I do not see this encounter as a failure precisely because Miller is able to write as a Jew about Pratt's essay.

By writing about her Jewishness in a text that also explicitly struggles with issues of identity and representation in the context of a graduate classroom, Miller not only questions what happens to Jews in Pratt's text but also begins to articulate something about the ambivalence of her own Jewish position within feminist study. In writing about what it feels like to be spoken for and the pain of finding herself at a loss for words, Miller makes explicit the disjuncture between Pratt's good intentions and her own experience of being interpellated even within this careful feminist text. She articulates the paradox of familiarity and distance that comes with finding a semblance of one's self within the text of another.

Reading Miller's account of teaching Pratt's text, I am reminded of the graduate seminar on feminist theory that I took at Emory University in the spring of 1988 in which Martin and Mohanty's essay was taught alongside Pratt's. Like Miller, I was the only Jew in that classroom, although as a graduate student and not the teacher I read these texts with a somewhat different set of desires. I was not looking for Jews. Despite Martin and Mohanty's warning, in that seminar I wanted to find my likeness in Pratt's essay and assume her position. Perhaps Miller's deep disappointment carries within it a trace of this desire for identification as well. In my graduate seminar, I believed that the vast majority of white women in that class also wanted to identify with Pratt. Given this, I hardly noticed Pratt's depictions of Jews.[28]

Part of what happened to me in that class was that I learned, despite the fact that I had found so much of myself in Pratt's essay, that there was a difference between me and Pratt and it had to do with my Jewishness. What I began to recognize was the not- quite fit between my liberal desire to be the same as Pratt and what it would mean for me to be a Jew in feminist study. In a sense this was the beginning of my letting go of liberalism. I did not have to be just like Pratt or the other white women in that classroom to be a feminist. I could voice my Jewishness as an ambivalence about letting go of the desire for identification and sameness, which was painful as well as liberating. In confronting my own disappointment in not being just like Pratt—what I imagined as a communal desire for a liberal feminism—I began to notice how, in lots of different ways I found myself in a similar position. This is how I began to reimagine my relationship to liberalism as partial. I wanted an emancipatory vision, but I also came to realize that the universal, inclusive claims of liberalism's vision were not quite what I had imagined them to be. By realizing that I was almost, but not quite able to be just like Pratt, I began to let go of liberalism's demand for a universal sameness as a basis for liberation.[29] I began to recognize my ongoing investment in a liberal vision of feminism that required a kind of sameness between women. By giving up this requirement, I began to imagine other ways of imagining liberation as specific and local.

It is in owning these conflicting desires that I have come to identify most strongly with Miller. Although we both have responded to different aspects of Pratt's text, we also have both expressed an ambivalence in reading this essay in the context of feminist study. Like Miller, I have wanted to both identify and distinguish myself from Pratt.[30] Thus, although I was initially disappointed about not being able to claim Pratt's story as my own, I have come to find this distinction liberating. "Liberating" is perhaps too strong a claim because it obscures the pain, disappointment, and frustration I felt in that classroom, but there is an elation and freedom I associate with letting go of that need that has ironically allowed me to feel more at home in feminist study.[31]

Although the tones of our accounts are different, a thwarted liberal desire for identification with Pratt connects me to Miller. It also helps explain why Miller argues that Pratt's narrative was a failure.

Occasioned Jewish Positions

As I see it, issues of inclusion and identity are always already imbricated in a feminist project of self-consciousness. They operate in tension: doing one does not preclude the possibility of doing the other. When we write about or "for" others, we already do so from somewhere "as" lots of contradictory things. The danger is in losing sight of this interrelationship, of trying to do one without taking the other seriously.

What continues to draw me to Miller's essay is her complicated presence in this writing. In watching her move between the stance of a feminist critic whose whiteness and Jewishness are present but unmarked, and her attempts to position herself as a Jew at various moments in her essay, I have come to recognize crucial things about my own Jewish position. Like Miller, I too have wanted to pass into feminist study unmarked as just another white woman. I have wanted to be like the vast majority of students in that graduate classroom in Atlanta. And, like Miller, I have found it impossible to do that. I could not lose my Jewish self in that graduate classroom, nor can I do so now as a professor in Philadelphia teaching some of these same feminist texts to graduate students. At Temple University, I remain one of very few Jews in my classrooms.[32]

In a letter she wrote to Peggy Kamuf in the summer of 1989 for the volume *Conflicts in Feminism*, Miller revisits the 1985 conference in Milwaukee.[33] She uses the conference as a way of talking about how feminist criticism had changed since her very public debate with Kamuf in 1981:[34]

My sense of the development of feminist theory since 1981, and in particular since 1985, is that it has been one of intense dislocation. I pick 1985, which I see as a kind of radical turning point, because of two events, two conferences on feminist theory that took place within months of each other that year; both of which have now become books edited by their organizers: *Feminist Studies/Critical Studies*, Teresa de Lauretis (1986) and *Coming to Terms: Feminism, Theory, Politics*, by Elizabeth Weed (1989). At both conferences, but most dramatically at the first in Milwaukee, where the effects of polarization were intense and explicit, the splits and fractures within feminisms, and the violence with which they are *lived*, especially around issues of race were painfully in evidence.[35]

By returning to this scene in the context of this exchange—a series of letters with an old sparring partner—Miller calls attention to how her own position has changed. She writes about her sense of dislocation by describing the pain and violence of these academic occasions:

> Since then—though I take this moment as an archival mark, rather than an originary occasion, because the elements of the struggle have been in place for at least a decade—feminism has been traversed by currents impossible to elude. The blindness of a feminist "we" to its own exclusions has continued to complicate and deeply trouble the relations within feminism—manifested by an acute self-consciousness about the deployment of pronouns; and tempered, if not transformed by the grounding assumptions of feminist theory. (I am thinking in particular of the powerful fiction of universal female subject.) (124)

Miller then uses this moment not to give up on feminist criticism, as she did in "Dreaming, Dancing," but rather to argue for a feminist politics in the academy. She continues: "This is not to say that I think 'we' should give up on feminism, or its institutionalization as a project for cultural and social change. But it does mean that the moment of a certain jubilation about 'identity politics' has passed" (124). Although Miller goes on to say that she is not clear about the language of this ongoing struggle, she is optimistic.

In this more hopeful light, I reread Miller's resignation in Milwaukee as itself a product of a particular moment, a moment when the tides shifted and she lost her bearing. In this sense, the conference opened her eyes to dangers she had not seen, difficulties that were always there but that she had failed to fully consider. I too believe it would "be more fruitful to rethink strategies together (the eternal, canonical feminist belief in coalition, a term more bandied about than enacted, however)" (124). As I have argued, by locating and relocating our readings within the particular social contexts in which we live—in our case, feminist classrooms and academic conferences—we can move beyond not only the identificatory logic of sameness within liberalism but also its oppositional logic. In other words, by locating feminist critical practices within specific social locations, it is possible not only to claim a nonuniversal local and specific feminist position but also to engage in acts of radical resistance from that place. I believe it is possible not to reduce and contain these differences within an oppositional logic: There need not be only two opposing sides to any issue.[36]

By contrast, a self-conscious feminist practice is, I believe, what Miller herself refers to in the passage I cite at the beginning of this chapter. Taken from another exchange, this time a conversation among Nancy K. Miller, Marianne Hirsch, and Jane Gallop that is also included in the *Conflicts in Feminism* volume, Miller again demands that feminists take these insights with us into our classrooms.[37] In this respect, I have tried to show what Miller's own writing has opened up and to suggest where we can go from here.

In the chapters that follow, which comprise part 3 of this book, I build on this notion of social location in order to expand my purview beyond the question of Jewish inclusion in feminist study. I turn to a consideration of the place of Jewish feminists within an American dream of home. In these chapters, I offer a self-conscious embrace of two contemporary Jewish feminist literary texts about being at home in America as a way of making connections between these texts and my relationship to specific places in America that have been my homes.

part three

Ambivalent Embraces

nine

∼

Returning to Atlanta

i can't go back
where i came from was
burned off the map

i'm a jew
anywhere is someone else's land

—Melanie Kaye/Kantrowitz,
"Notes of an Immigrant Daughter, Atlanta"

All of my homes have been in America. These homes, including my place in feminist study, have been informed by a particular set of immigrant desires. America offered my Eastern European Jewish grandparents the promise of a better life, the promise of stability and political agency as citizens of the United States. They could belong. I have often taken for granted my own deep commitment to this promise. Most of my life I have hardly been able to imagine my relationship to this country in other than these terms.

As in my ambivalent embrace of the emancipatory dreams of liberalism, liberal Jewish theology, and feminist study, in this the final section of this book I question my place within an explicitly American dream of home by pushing hard against my own loyalties to this country.

In order to get at these issues, in this chapter I offer a selected reading of Melanie Kaye/Kantrowitz's poem "Notes of an Immigrant Daughter; Atlanta."[1] Through my reading of this poem, I return not only to the textual Atlanta of Kaye/Kantrowitz's poem, but also as an immigrant granddaughter, to the city that was the first home of this book, the place where I became an academic, and the place where I was raped. I return to this particularly ambivalent American home in order to raise questions about my own faith in this country's liberal vision of emancipation for Jews and for women.

In many ways this chapter is an expression of my disappointment, not because I don't feel bound to this country, but because, especially in my Jewish family, such criticism has been carefully avoided. Ironically, precisely because of all that has happened to me, I have come to feel safe enough to articulate these disappointments.

Notes

I begin my reading of Kaye/Kantrowitz's poem by focusing on its title. It offers me a way of addressing how Jewish immigration to the United State from Europe continues to shape the contingencies of being at home in America. In part, the precariousness of this situation is signified by the first term in the poem's title, "notes." In thinking about the ephemeral quality of notes, I return to Nancy K. Miller's essay "Dreaming, Dancing."[2] In the opening of her essay, Miller explains why she decided to write in the form of "notes." Like me and Kaye/Kantrowitz, Miller was also concerned about a legacy of immigration; Miller wrote the final version of her essay in America for a European audience. She was uncomfortable with what it meant for her to move between these two continents. In order to deal with this discomfort, Miller found comfort in citation. She quotes a long passage from poet Adrienne Rich's essay "Notes Towards a Politics of Location," an essay that was also originally intended for a European audience.[3] Miller uses Rich's text to make certain distinctions about feminist criticism at the end of the 1980s in the United States for a European audience.

For location is not incidental. To Miller and Rich, the site of critical inquiry, where we do our work, is crucial. Location shapes what we can say. Rich makes this point explicitly in her essay. Instead of writing broad generalizations about women or feminists, she writes from "'the geography closest in—the body,' 'a North American Jew, born and raised three thousand miles from the war in Europe'; 'whiteness as a point of location for which I need to take responsibility.'"[4] In this way, Rich foregrounds certain crucial aspects of her identity as they inform her work. For Rich, Jewishness is crucial in relation to location: had she not been born in North America but in Europe, she might not have survived the war, much less been able ever to return to Europe.

Being born in North America, however, has come with other complicated burdens. For Rich these include the privileges and responsibilities of being marked as white. As I have already explained, Miller, like Rich, also had to come to terms with this legacy. But, in the opening section of her essay, Miller lets Rich's words speak for her without comment.

Moved by Rich's "mode of enunciation," Miller addresses only the question of writing. She cites the following passage from Rich's essay in order to explain her own strategy: "I come here with notes but without absolute conclusions. This is not a sign of loss of faith or hope. These notes are the marks of a struggle to keep moving, a struggle for accountability" (74). Writing in relation to Rich, Miller continues:

> The choice to have the essay take the form of notes characterizes a mode of theorization and self-inscription that I call a "poetics of location." In this shift of emphasis from an account of a feminist struggle in the world to an attention to the struggle as a resistance in form, I also produce a translation from Rich's activist positionality as a "radical feminist" to the less glamorous and much maligned posture of my own, an academic "bourgeois feminist." From within the university—where she is also some of the time— I read Rich reading the world. In a way, my paper is an embodiment of that double move; it is also about the extreme difficulty of continuing thus located. (74)

Again, I identify with Miller's desire to read Rich from her position in the academy and to enact a kind of double move, and I am still not convinced of the impossibility of such moves. Although it is difficult, Miller builds on Rich's work, claiming an academic position alongside Rich.

Although Miller does not say that, like Rich, she is also a North American Jew, born here and not in Europe, the resonances are there. Miller wants both politics and writing even as she expresses her discomfort at putting these things together in her own writing. Although she explicitly wants to move from politics to writing, she cannot sustain any neat opposition between these engagements. Rich's position disrupts this desire. Although Miller wants to let Rich do the political work so that she can read "Rich reading the world" from the shelter of the university, she recognizes the impossibility of such a move.[5]

Even though Rich is a "radical feminist," she also resides in the academy, at least on occasion. Thus, even as Miller tries to claim the position of the "bourgeois feminist" in opposition to Rich, she already knows that this distinction is tenuous.

The question of "glamor" is also relevant to this dilemma because it reiterates Miller's ambivalence toward Rich, for Miller describes radical feminists as "glamorous" and those in the academy as much maligned. And yet these assertions are by no means self-evident. By 1988, Adrienne Rich was actually a much maligned figure in academic feminist criticism precisely because she was considered a "radical feminist."[6] Although I have reservations about this characterization of Rich's work, it is important to this discussion. Thus, the reversal of this seemingly obvious account from the academy repeats Miller's earlier ambivalence. It is a telling reminder of Miller's admiration and indebtedness to Rich in an academic feminist criticism, where it has become increasingly difficult to claim such loyalties.

Like Rich and Miller, Kaye/Kantrowitz also offers "notes" as opposed to "absolute conclusions"[7] about what it means to be an immigrant Jewish daughter in Atlanta in 1981.[8] This contingency is also evident in each of the other images in the poem's title: "immigrant," "daughter," and even "Atlanta." Although an immigrant leaves one country to settle permanently in another, permanence is itself a tenuous proposition. This realization is a part of what it means to be a daughter. A daughter is one's female child, a female descendant, or one who is considered "as if" in a relationship of child to parent. The example given to illustrate this less biological reading of daughterhood in my *American Heritage Dictionary* is about national identity: "a daughter of the nation." This example describes well the desire to belong as if it is somehow natural even when it is not.

Finally, the reference to "Atlanta" in the title of Kaye/Kantrowitz's poem reinforces this reading. As a major urban center of the South in a once-divided United States, a center that burned to the ground, it too is a transitory place. And, yet, unlike the European centers of Jewish life that were burned off the map, in the case of Atlanta, victims and perpetrators of the crimes of slavery both returned to claim very different relationships to this past.[9] In this sense, Atlanta remains a site of ongoing struggle, a place haunted by its past. Given this complicated legacy, "Atlanta" also disrupts Kaye/Kantrowitz's immigrant vision of a mythic, single, unified America. By placing herself in

Atlanta, like Rich, Kaye/Kantrowitz confronts the brutal legacy of American racism by making tentative connections between this history and the legacy of European antisemitism for Jews. For Kaye/Kantrowitz and, in different ways, for me, Atlanta embodies a disappointment and a betrayal. The violence that built, destroyed, and rebuilt Atlanta—much less the ongoing violence of that place have become for me a graphic reminder of all that America cannot be. The confluence of these histories, histories of both Europe and America in this poem, make visceral the precariousness of being at home in America.

In what follows, I offer a reading of selected pieces of Kaye/Kantrowitz's poem. I move back and forth between the poem and a series of family narratives in order to, in a sense, return to Atlanta. Instead of reconfiguring the space of my apartment, I now return to Atlanta in the space of writing. By reading this poem in pieces, I focus on those places in the text that speak to me in order to tell a different version of my family's story. In this way, Kaye/Kantrowitz's words accompany my own. Through this selected reading of the poem, sometimes full sections, at others, simply pieces, I demonstrate how it is possible to return to a lost home.[10]

"Notes of an Immigrant Daughter, Atlanta"

> you dream
> of what it looked like
> before the europeans came, before
> they brought the africans, chained—
> when native peoples rode hunted grew corn
> & sang   all over the many-nation's face:
> cheyenne   sioux   cherokee   pontiac   comanche
> winnebago   passamaquoddy   navajo   mohican
> apache   kiowa   hopi   chickasaw
>
> too many to name[11]

This is the beginning of "Notes of an Immigrant Daughter, Atlanta." The poem opens with a dream about the past, a dream about what America looked like "before the europeans came, before / they brought the africans, chained—." The scene is idyllic. America is filled with native peoples riding, singing, hunting, and growing corn. These are images taken primarily from childhood textbooks, Hollywood movies, the names of trailers and cars, yet a few of them remain unfamiliar to me. This naming offers me a reminder of all that I do not know about the past, all that I have little or no access to about what it once meant to be an American. Before the burning, Atlanta, like the rest of this country, was already a site of terrible violence, loss, and displacement.

> 1. a movie, BIRTH OF A NATION, called
> "a classic." black women
> **having rolling eyewhites;**[12] **white women**
> are blond and rapeable
> by black men. the ku klux klan
> is the hero (124)

In the first numbered section of the poem, Kaye/Kantrowitz shifts from the tragic history of Native Americans to a discussion of slavery. She uses the classic racist film *Birth of a Nation* to tell this story in detail. Although Kaye/Kantrowitz questions the film's demeaning depictions of African Americans and its justification of the klan as protectors of southern white womanhood, she insists on confronting the ongoing implications of this mythic narrative, a vindication of white supremacy. As in Pratt's essay, for Kaye/Kantrowitz the klan remains a haunting presence.[13] As she explains, it was a screening of this film in Greensboro, North Carolina, in 1978 that precipitated the antiklan demonstration in which five protesters were killed (the same incident that Pratt writes about in her essay).

> when they show this movie in greensboro, north carolina
> people—black & white—gather
> to protest; five are shot dead
> by local nazis
> & the hero klan (124)

Kaye/Kantrowitz points to the interrelationship between local nazis and the klan. They are not the same, but they are related in their belief that what it means to be an American is to be white. As she has already explained, there was no nation before the Europeans came, and for this to happen, other peoples had to be enslaved and/or destroyed.

From here, Kaye/Kantrowitz focuses more sharply on Atlanta and the South.

> the one time i was in atlanta
> some rich white woman told us, don't
> go downtown at night
> so we go downtown—
> it's alive with black people, women, men
> out on the streets after the movies or a concert—
> something to fear? (124)

There is danger in Atlanta, but Kaye/Kantrowitz questions who should be afraid of whom. Despite the fact that historically "death's face is white," she describes a white woman who is afraid.

I too learned to be afraid in Atlanta, but my fear was not primarily about race. Nightly, the eleven o'clock news was filled with reports of women killed, maimed, or missing in and around Atlanta. More often than not those women who were reported as missing were eventually found dead. As a woman living alone, I became increasingly fearful. The high rate of these violent crimes against women was alarming, but what frightened me most was how little was being done to address this problem.

I became increasingly suspicious of those in charge, those who were suppose to protect me. More than once, Atlanta police officers told me to get a gun. They told my friend who later became my roommate not only to get a gun but also what to do after using it: if the perpetrator was not in the house, he was told to drag him in.

In Kaye/Kantrowitz's poem the image of black people in downtown Atlanta out on the streets is set in sharp contrast to the dead protesters in Greensboro.

> klansmen on trial right now in greensboro
> claiming self-defense (125)

As in Pratt's reading of this same incident, here again the klan's claim to self-defense rings hollow. According to Kaye/Kantrowitz, as power dynamics begin to shift, the loss of white privilege is necessarily remythologized as a justification for violence in *Birth of a Nation*. By repeating the klan's victory over the forces of change, each new screening of this "classic" racist film naturalizes this particular configuration of the nation.

> 2. in france they're bombing synagogues
> this country   concerned as usual when
> jews get killed says
> nothing (125)

Section two of Kaye/Kantrowitz's poem is about Europe, that other continent, where Jews are still in danger, which means that she cannot escape the legacy of racism in America by going back to Europe. Even in France, whose government was the first to grant Jews citizenship, Jews are still at risk. And despite all that has happened, especially in the last fifty years, no one seems to care. There is no place for American Jews to return to, "i can't go back."

When I consider these questions in relation to my own immigrant family, I am struck by how and under what conditions my family, has returned to Europe. I think about my father's tour of duty between 1944 and 1945. The first in his family to return to Europe, he did so as an American soldier with an "h" on his dog tag, for "Hebrew." And, yet, when I speak to him about this voyage he does not, even now, see the irony. My father, an immigrant son, returned to Europe but as an American first and foremost. Although relieved not to have been sent to a more foreign place in the Pacific, he refused to consider the complications of his Jewishness in making this journey back across the Atlantic.

When I persisted and asked again if my father thought it at all strange to be returning to Europe as a Jew at the same time that Jews were being systematically tortured and killed in this not-so-long-lost place of family origin, or the fact that his own government had marked him as a Jew, he still could only see himself as an American soldier fighting for his country. Trying to jolt his memory, I asked if he had any relatives still in Europe; I have asked this question many times before and always received the same answer: "We had no relatives left in Europe." This time, however, the story changed, he had more to say.

Nonchalantly, he told me and my mother about an uncle, his mother's brother, who remained in Europe. He told us that this uncle survived a concentration camp, that the uncle had been married before the war but that his wife died in a camp. We were then told that in 1947 or 1948, this man contacted his siblings in the United States, he was still alive and needed their help in securing passage to this country.

By 1947, however, the ties between members of my father's family in America were already frayed. Time, poverty, and the Depression had all taken their toll on these relations. My grandmother, this man's sister, had already been dead for ten years. Nevertheless, another sibling secured passage for this uncle and his new wife to come to America. She was, also, according to my father, a survivor.

I still do not understand my father's emotional distance from this story. I tried to ask what it felt like, any of it. He was blank. The story had no drama, no emotional edge. My mother thinks he should be ashamed of this; I just don't understand. My grandmother's brother was in a concentration camp and I learn about this fifty years later without emotion? Although, as I was to learn, the details of my father's version of this story are not quite accurate, I have been able to verify that this uncle did remain in Europe after his siblings came to America and that he did survive the war—just not in a concentration camp. Before the war he had lived in Lithuania, in what was to become disputed territory. When the territory was taken over by Hitler, he escaped to the Soviet Union where he joined the army and successfully fought in numerous battles. I am told that he became some kind of a war hero. It was only after the war that he defected from the Soviet army and renewed contact with his siblings in the United States.[14] Why had my father never thought to tell me about this uncle before, and why had he gotten the story so terribly wrong when he did? I do not have a firm answer to these questions, but I want to believe that for my father forgetting was comforting and that, when he finally did begin to remember, thinking the worst possible scenario made the forgetting seem more plausible.[15]

This particular discussion continued as my mother tried to figure out who these relatives were. Did she know them? Why weren't they invited to their wedding—or were they? And then she too remembered something. "Didn't they live near Muriel?" These relatives lived down the street from my father's sister? He said these things matter-of-factly, again with no affect. Perhaps he learned early on not to show his emotions as a form of self-protection, but he could not tell me this.

This uncle died in the 1950s—young, like his sister. What my father recalled was that, once in America, this uncle and his new family "did well." I wonder what my father means by this. Like most of my father's family, this uncle also settled in Albany, New York. Here they were all poor, but my father's immediate family was more so. This may explain why, according to my father, some of these other relatives seemed to have prospered. It may simply be that they were better off than his family. By all accounts, no one in this extended family did particularly well.[16]

As I understand it, these stories and, more specifically, my father's ways of dealing with old fears, trauma, and loss are some of the secrets so close to his heart that I will never fully understand them. These scars and my father's ways of attending to them are so old, so thick, and so far away that they frighten me. Like my mother, sometimes I want to just shake my father and ask if he feels anything, but I have learned that I cannot get him to say more about these things or how they shaped his return to Europe.

> 3. i dream: i'm climbing a ladder behind a young woman, blond,
> dressed punk style; stitched on the leg of her jeans, in green &
> pink letters, the words: *how will you die, who will you kill.* (125)

Section three of Kaye/Kantrowitz's poem begins with a dream about a blond woman. It is a dream about the struggle to resist and survive. Following this blond woman up a ladder, the trek is precarious. She is unsteady, and so am I. I am reminded of other blonds. I think again about my parents. This time I think about passing, about being blond and surviving in America.

In Army basic training in Arkansas my father insisted that despite his dog tags, no one knew that he was Jewish.[17] Although decidedly not blond, my father believes that he was able to pass. He is sincere in this belief even now, and yet it strikes me as completely unfounded. I see no correlation between my father's sense of Jewish invisibility and how others saw him, especially at that time and in that place. Even then he took pains not to call attention to himself, keeping quiet and showing no emotion. Unlike his "kinky haired" friend stationed in Georgia, my father did not make the mistake of talking about racial politics with his fellow recruits. He is relieved, even now, that he was able to pass unnoticed as a northern Jew stationed in Arkansas in 1944.

Unlike my father, however, my mother was quite decidedly blond. In our family it was understood that my mother was "an Aryan child." I cannot remember a time when I did not know this about my mother. Ten years younger than my father, during the war she was a chubby, fair-skinned child with braids. She could have been one of those children depicted on Nazi posters. I've seen pictures. It was important that my mother could have been mistaken for one of the enemy's own. In the excess of this eerie "Aryan" desire, I now see that this was more than just a pride in passing. My grandparents' investment in my mother's looks was also about fear and a strong desire for her safety. As I now understand it, being an "Aryan child" was a way of imagining how my mother could have survived the war not only had her family not left Europe, but even in America. With her blond hair in braids, my mother was safe.

When I recently asked my mother about these things, she told me about living in a German neighborhood in Queens. She remembered the taunts of neighborhood children who were angry to discover that she was not one of them. But mostly my mother talked about the larger political climate in New York in 1944. She told me about Nazis on Long Island, describing Lindenhurst, New York, as an important site for Nazi organizing. Both of my parents explained that it was a well-known fact that the Germans had contacts there and that patrols around Long Island were especially fierce because of this. I suppose this made it all the more important that my mother could pass when her family moved to Long Island.

Section three of the poem continues:

> in the morning i read the news—in atlanta
> black children
> are being killed
>
> a daycare center blows up
>
> children go out to play or to the store &
> disappear: fifteen missing or found
> strangled, shot, or drowned or
> dead—cause undetermined
>
>> for months they say these deaths
>> are not related (125)

In the light of day, Kaye/Kantrowitz reads in the paper about the deaths of poor black children in Atlanta, children who cannot pass, children in imminent danger in Atlanta in 1981. Despite mounting evidence, the papers continue to insist that these deaths are unrelated. Months go by and the number of children found dead or missing continues to increase and still no connections are made. There are no suspects.

There are crucial differences between my parents and these children. Although there are costs to passing or pretending to pass, the ability to do any of these things distinguishes immigrant sons and daughters from the children at risk in Atlanta in 1981—but it also connects them.

> 4. all over the nation is someone else's land
> for example, the whole state of maine might have been
> passamaquoddy nation, had the treaty
> saved by a woman in a shoebox been honored
> as written; had the people risked
> everything   on the young ones' faith
>
> they won millions of acres anyhow
> and dollars, and the children
> can all go to college
> but first they learn their language
> and their people's ways (126)

In section four of the poem, Kaye/Kantrowitz questions white ownership of American soil. Having sat for years in a shoebox in a woman's closet, a treaty is eventually revived; when the case comes to court millions of acres are returned to the Passamaquoddy. According to the settlement, in order for this to happen, however, Passamaquoddy children must first "learn their language/and their people's ways" (126). Whose language, whose ways, are not so clear.

In section five, the longest segment of the poem, the situation in Atlanta worsens.

> 5. a mother's voice booming across the TV miles
> how many children going to lose their
> lives mr mayor before you
> do something (126)

Mothers cry out publicly, demanding that the mayor of Atlanta do something to protect their children. How many must die before action is taken? Even as these women cry out, the papers say they "just / don't take care."[18] The mothers keep pleading. They did not know, they were never told about the danger, "if / i'd known, i'd never have / let him out, my / baby be alive." Despite the fact that these mothers are themselves cruelly blamed, they continue to demand justice. They call on their mayor to do something to stop the killing. They demand a face-to-face meeting.

There is a desperation in this telling. The mothers are exasperated. They cannot believe that their mayor does not care. They try to confront the powers that be, but there is no relief for their fear and their pain. They cry out in vain.

In order to make explicit the pain of this situation, Kaye/Kantrowitz becomes increasingly specific. She focuses on a single mother, Camille Bell, who has lost one child and worries about her other three. She asks, what "if they were white children. . ." would this make a difference? This question is interrupted almost immediately by a reporter, perhaps one of those who had already blamed these mothers for their children's deaths, who reminds Ms. Bell that the mayor and the chief of police are black. Does this mean that they care about her children? Camille Bell responds that this is not just about race. The children who are dying and missing are also poor. The text breaks off here, shifting focus from Atlanta back to the larger context of white supremacy.

The poem continues with accounts of newspaper stories about the klan, reports that have been clipped and saved by the narrator in her own shoebox. These are stories about their guerrilla activities all across the country: Atlanta, Nashville, Houston, Dallas, Buffalo, Kingston, Portland, Oregon, and Youngstown, Ohio. In all of these places the klan gathers. In response to this mounting evidence, Kaye/Kantrowitz returns to the questions of survival and resistance. She now changes the narrator's voice, away from the second person to the first person plural, asking questions about dying and killing: *"how will we die / who will we kill"*? She explains that klan activity demands our attention, yet when we try to seek justice, like Camille Bell our voices are not heard.

Kaye/Kantrowitz then reports that the verdict in Greensboro was not guilty and asks: if commies, Jews, and black people hadn't been killed, would this have been the verdict? Back in Atlanta, what if the mayor were on welfare or if the governor got pregnant, would that make a difference? In this way section five continues.

Reading this text in 1996, I have come to see that such simple readings of identity have not translated into useful political positions. Not all poor people or all women or all black people share any single stance. If elected officials were mothers, would it make a difference? The answer is not nearly as clear as, perhaps, Camille Bell or Melanie Kaye/Kantrowitz had hoped. These questions raise concerns about priorities, about the investment in armaments as opposed to children. If only the mothers in Atlanta were running things, Kaye/Kantrowitz asks, wouldn't the world be a better place? I am not so sure. And yet I continue to believe that it is important to try to imagine alternatives.

Not long after I was raped in Atlanta in 1989, I also cried out to the mayor for help. At that time Atlanta had one of the highest crime rates in the nation. A front-page newspaper article on the 911 system in Atlanta opened with an account of my rape. I allowed my name and the story of my rape to be used as an example of the failures of that system to respond to violent crime and I asked that the system be reassessed.[19] The report described my landlady's failed attempts to reach 911 as I called out for help as well as my own difficulties in reaching the police after the rape. My case was an example of the larger failings of Atlanta's 911 system.

The author gave me editorial control over the content of the article. It was my decision to end on a hopeful note with me asking the mayor to change the system.[20] I wanted the article to offer a partial solution to the larger issue of violence in Atlanta. Suffice it to say, however, there was no response. As far as I know the system never changed, and the crime rate in Atlanta has not decreased in any significant way since then.[21]

Section five of Kaye/Kantrowitz's poem continues by describing what it means to teach children to survive nonetheless. She describes this as an awesome physical and spiritual task. It is about church values, "God loving the little children of the world," as well as about not getting into a stranger's car. Despite the fact that the mayor, the press, and the chief of police did not seem to care, to these mothers in Atlanta in 1981, poor black children remained precious.

Rereading this section of the poem I am still struck by how much has not changed since 1981. If anything, the situation of poor black children has grown even more desperate.[22] Nevertheless the response remains the same. Poor single mothers continue to be blamed.

> 6. don't   say it's
> over   they
> caught   the killer
> one   black   man
>
> the white south stands on corners
> with bibles
> shaking hands
>
> why whistle dixie
> unless you like the tune
>
> why call a restaurant "plantation house" unless
> you mourn the demise
>
> why move the people from their land
> unless you want it (128)

In section six, the final section of the poem, Kaye/Kantrowitz raises questions about the resolution of the 1981 crisis in Atlanta. She asks if the situation is really over when a single black man is offered up as the culprit. Perhaps for some of the city's white citizens this is the case. They can once again stand on corners with bibles and shake hands, whistle Dixie in public, express their love of the South as it once was—before the flames, before the Civil War.[23] They can find relief in white men once again restoring order.

"Why move the people from their land / unless you want it"? By raising this question Kaye/Kantrowitz brings the poem full circle. She returns to the history of violence that brutally displaced all those native peoples who once inhabited this land.

> at a house named for plantations
> i cannot eat
>
> nor can i go back
> my people were burned off the map

the flames still crackle
on crosses
in buffalo
portland
atlanta

all over the nation
our children are watching
to see
who we become
                              December 1981 (128)

Along with Kaye/Kantrowitz, I also cannot avoid living on someone else's land in America, nor can I go back to Europe. Instead, I have come to see that I too must make my home in America alongside others who have been displaced. Having left Atlanta in 1992, like Kaye/Kantrowitz, I continue this struggle elsewhere without guarantees.

ten

Claiming America

America is not my chosen home, not even the place of my birth. Just a spot where it seemed safe to go to escape certain dangers. But safety, I discover, is only temporary. No place guarantees it to anyone forever. I have stayed because there is no other place to go.

—Irena Klepfisz, *"Bashert"*

Awakening from my immigrant Jewish family's dreams of America, I have had to reconfigure my own sense of home. I was introduced to Irena Klepfisz's poem *"Bashert"*[1] in the same graduate seminar in feminist theory in Atlanta where I first read the essays by Pratt, Mohanty, and Martin. Unlike those texts, however, this poem did not offer me a way into feminist study. Instead it offered a different way into a more familiar place. As an uncanny account of America as a Jewish home, it helped me reimagine my relationship to the promises of this place. It provided a way of imagining home on different grounds.

This text shares much with my reading of Kaye/Kantrowitz's poem. In this poem America is also located within what Klepfisz has described as "Inhospitable Soil," also the title of the series of poems of which *"Bashert"* is a part.[2] This series opens with the Kaye/Kantrowitz passage from her poem about being a Jew and not being able to go home.[3] Both literally and figuratively, in these poems and particularly in *"Bashert,"* Klepfisz struggles with the difficulty of claiming specific places in America as her home. In what follows I offer a reading of a single prose section of *"Bashert,"* "3. Brooklyn, 1971: I am almost equidistant from two continents," where Klepfisz reluctantly claims this country as her home.

Part of what has drawn me to her account of America is its stark-

ness. Klepfisz does not share with either Kaye/Kantrowitz or with me
a belief in the promises of immigration. She presents America as just
a place on the map that seemed to be safe for a while. After I was
raped, when I too became convinced that "there was no other place
to go," to move to in Atlanta, it was these words that helped me
decide literally to stay in my home.[4]

As in each of the texts I examined in the last chapter, "3. Brooklyn,
1971" highlights the relationship between past and present in terms of
a contrast between Europe and America. Here Klepfisz struggles to
make a life that neither denies the past nor ignores the present. Unlike
Kaye/Kantrowitz, Rich, Miller, and me, she was born in Europe. She
is an immigrant who has spent most of her life in America.

In Brooklyn in 1971, she is at a critical juncture. She is about to
turn thirty, the age of her father when he died in the Warsaw Ghetto
Uprising, the age of her mother when they were in hiding together in
Poland.[5]

> I am almost equidistant from two continents. I look back towards
> one, then forward towards the other. The moment is approaching
> when I will be equidistant from both and will have to choose.
> Maintaining equidistance is not a choice (82).

In many ways this whole section of *"Bashert"* is about a choice.[6] It
acknowledges that Klepfisz has already made a life for herself in this
country, but there is no neat symmetry between past and future,
Europe and America, those who died and those who survived as in
some of the other sections of this poem.[7] America has been chosen,
but it is an ambivalent choice, made in the passive voice. Klepfisz is
uncertain about her ability to choose. She knows that she cannot and
does not live in between these continents. She must take her life into
her own hands, but doing so is difficult. She is unsteady.

In response to this uncertainty, like Pratt, Klepfisz also returns to
the past and offers a retelling of her life story that highlights her relationship with her father, who died in Europe. She writes about their
shared birthday and about his death in terms of "one of those minor
and peculiar coincidences that permanently shape and give texture to
our lives" (82). Two years after she was born, he was dead, and by
the end of the war his grave in what was once the brush factory dis-
trict of the Warsaw Ghetto had been lost within the midst of the

rubble that was postwar Warsaw. This is the legacy of her father's continent, her birth, his death, the uprising, and his burial.

The narrative then returns to Brooklyn in 1971.

> In one of the classes that I teach, all of the students are Black and Puerto Rican. I am the only white. Initially, the students are nervous, wondering if I will be a hard task master. I am nervous too, though I do not yet have a name for it. After a few months together, we grow accustomed to each other. I am trying to understand my role here. This is the heritage of the other continent. (82)

In this account, like me and Miller, Klepfisz is also a university instructor. She is the sole "white" woman and the only Jew in this college classroom and not sure what to make of these differences. The students are concerned about how difficult the course will be, and she is trying to understand her role here as a white person with power over others. She is nervous and has no language to express what it feels like to be in this position of authority.

Approaching her thirtieth birthday, she writes:

> The moment [in time] when I will be equidistant from two land masses, I feel some kind of cellular breakdown in my body, a sudden surging inside me, as if flesh and muscle and bone were losing definition. Everything in me yearns to become transparent to be everywhere, to become like the water between two vast land masses that will never touch. I desire to become salt water, to establish the connection. (82)

This passage captures so eloquently the struggle of this entire section of "Bashert." In each of the narrative sections of the poem, Klepfisz expresses such ambivalences viscerally, as within her body and tearing her apart. Even as Europe grows distant, she wants to hold on to her father's legacy.

> April 17, 1955. I have been asked to light one of the six candles [for the six million Jews who had died]. I stand on the stage in the large, darkened auditorium, wait to be called, wait to accept the flame, to pass it on like a memory. I am numb with terror at the spectacle around me. I fear these people with blue numbers on their arms,

people who are disfigured and scarred, who have missing limbs and uneasy walks, people whose histories repel me. Here in this auditorium, they abandon all inhibitions, they transform themselves into pure sound, the sound of irretrievable loss, of wild pain and sorrow. Then they become all flesh, wringing their hands and covering their swollen eyes and flushed faces. They call out to me and I feel myself dissolving. (82–83)

In this passage the horrors of Europe come into focus in the context of a Holocaust commemoration in New York. The narrator stands on a stage, a lone child. She will light the final candle, the one for the children who were lost. In this context she is called to stand in for all of those other children who did not make it out of Europe, those who died. In this gathering of tortured adults, she comes to embody a lost hope but cannot carry the weight of their pain and anguish. Their bodies bear the scars of that other continent and she is fearful of losing herself in their loss. She already feels herself dissolving as they call out to her. They become a part of her.

When it is time for me to come forward, to light the candle for those children who were burned, who were shot, who were stomped to death, I move without feeling. And as I near the candelabra, I hear them call out common Yiddish names: *Surele. Moyshele. Channele. Rivkele. Yankele. Shayndele. Rayzl. Benyomin. Chavele. Miriam. Chaim.* (83)

The narrative continues with a more elaborate description of these proceedings. As she is accosted by the names of dead children, common Yiddish names one after another, "the names brush against my face, invade my ears, my mouth. I breathe them into my lungs, into my bones" (83). She is fourteen years old.

This scene is then juxtaposed to that other time and place, the classroom in Brooklyn.

March, 1971. There are twenty-eight people in the class. Eighteen women, ten men. Some married. Some single. Alone. With children. With parents and grandparents. Nieces. Nephews. They are here because they have not met the minimum standards of this college. This class is their special chance to catch up. Subject and verb agreement. Sentence fragments. Pronoun reference. Vocabulary building. Paragraph organization. Topic sentence. Reading comprehension. Study skills. Discipline. All this to catch up, as one student said to me, his eyes earnest: "I want to write so that when I go for a job they won't think I'm lazy." (83)

The students in this classroom also struggle. They are part of a remedial program designed to give them a chance to catch up.

I am required to take attendance. I check through the names, call them out each morning: *James. Reggie. Marie. Simone. Joy. Christine. Alvarez. Ashcroft. Basile. Colon. Corbett. White. Raphael. Dennis. Juan. Carissa. Lamont. Andrea.* Fragments of their lives fall before me. The chaos and disorganization. (83)

As the teacher, the narrator is required to take attendance. She looks out to confirm who is and is not there. This recitation of the names of those sitting in her classroom echoes the common Yiddish names of all those children who died in the Holocaust. By reciting these different and unfamiliar names, Klepfisz begins to make sense of her student's lives. The material difficulties of their daily struggles also become palpable.[8]

"A mother needing help filling out forms in English. A sick child" (83). These images could have been out of the narrator's own life; a desperate mother isolated and fearful, a sick child.[9] Despite the gulf between these two groups of people, European Jews and African and Latin Americans, the juxtaposition draws a connection between these struggles. She now lives in a place where other people struggle, "the daily grind interrupting their catching up, and the increasing sense that with each day missed, they will fall further behind" (83). These insights into their lives both connect and separate her from them. The contrasts between these desperate peoples are real and painful.

I am almost equidistant from two continents. I look back towards one, then forward towards the other. There is a need in me to become transparent like water, to become the salt water which is their only connection. (84)

She repeats her refrain. She wants to be like the salt water that connects them, to become one with this ocean of tears. The sorrow and loss offer a link even if the names and legacies are by no means equivalent. The point is not to compare dead children to those who are alive and struggling, for there is no comparison on that level; but, as in Kaye/Kantrowitz's poem, here again connections need to be made in order to live as a Jew in America.

> March, 1971. Marie wants to study medicine. She concedes it's a long haul, but, as she says, "It's only time. What difference does it make?" Slightly older than the others, she lives alone with her daughter. To some of the women's horror, she refuses to have a telephone, does not like to be intruded upon. When necessary, she can always be reached through a neighbor. She rarely misses class, on a few occasions brings her daughter with her who sits serenely drawing pictures. Facing Marie, I sometimes do not know who I am and wonder how she perceives me. She seems oblivious to my discomfort. She is only focused on the class, always reworking her assignments, reading everything twice, asking endless questions to make sure she really understands. One day, at the end of the hour, when we are alone, she asks: "What are you?" I am caught off guard, know the meaning of the question, but feel the resistance in me. I break it down and answer quietly: "A Jew." She nods and in that moment two vast land masses touch. (84)

In this final scene in that Brooklyn classroom the text becomes quite specific. Like Camille Bell in "Notes of an Immigrant Daughter, Atlanta," here again a single mother comes into focus, Marie. Marie knows that she is in for a long struggle but persists. It is in her relationship with this familiar and yet deeply unfamiliar woman that Klepfisz comes to make a decision about herself. When Marie asks her what she is, she is able to make a connection. Despite old fears and resistances to such questions, in that classroom, she is able to answer honestly. She tells Marie that she is a Jew and in that moment she is able to bring together the most disparate parts of her life, "in that moment two vast last masses touch." (84)

The final passage in this section of the poem is the one that I have taken as an opening quote for this chapter. As the narrator passes the age of thirty, that ever so brief moment in time when she is equidistant from these two continents and their legacies, "everything in me becomes defined again. I am once again muscle, flesh, bone" (84). At that moment she regains self-definition and claims her home in America.

In this account, the legacies of various pasts are embodied in what Adrienne Rich has called the geography closest in, one's own body.[10] They remain with Klepfisz wherever she lives. Since they are a part of her muscle, flesh, and bone, they are not bound by a specific place or time. Given the contingencies of her particular history, America has offered her a place to make a life, at least for a time.

What America can and cannot offer its people, those who came here from various other continents more and less willingly, those who were forcefully brought here in chains, those who came by choice, or those who already lived here, is not necessarily unlimited. Safety, let alone dreams, cannot be taken for granted. "No place guarantees it to anyone forever."

I no longer feel bound by a desire for guarantees or permanence. By simply feeling safe enough, I have come to appreciate the ambivalences within my own position. As much as I love this country, and I do love this country, it continues to disappoint me.

Holding on to Klepfisz's words, I have been able to embrace some of these disappointments. I have been able to let go of some of the excesses in my immigrant Jewish family's dreams of America as a promised land. Mine is a more ambivalent embrace not because I have given up on this country, but because I can no longer pretend simply to be at home in America. I have let go of this fantasy in order to imagine a somewhat safer and more liberating America for myself and others.

eleven

~

What's in a Name?

i can't go back
where i came from was
burned off the map

i'm a jew
anywhere is someone else's land

—Melanie Kaye, "Notes of an
Immigrant Daughter, Atlanta"

(think about asking every Jew you know: what *was* your name?)
—Melanie Kaye/Kantrowitz,
"Some Notes on Jewish Lesbian Identity"

In 1982 when Irena Klepfisz first attributed the passage from "Notes of an Immigrant Daughter, Atlanta" to Melanie Kaye,[1] permission had been granted by *Nice Jewish Girls: A Lesbian Anthology*.[2] In 1984, when the second edition of *Nice Jewish Girls* was published, some but not all pieces previously attributed to Melanie Kaye were reattributed to Melanie Kaye/Kantrowitz, but, all the permissions to publish these works were still attributed to Melanie Kaye.[3] When the third edition of *Nice Jewish Girls* was published in 1989, however, all remaining references to Melanie Kaye were changed to Melanie Kaye/Kantrowitz.[4]

In reflecting on these changes, I was struck by a lack of explanation. Since I know of few other instances of retroactively attributing previously published works to an author under her or his new name, I went in search of clues.[5] I was interested in the politics of changing one's name in print.[6] In Melanie Kaye's essay "Some Notes on Jewish Lesbian Identity," which also appears in all editions of *Nice Jewish Girls*, I found some answers.[7]

This essay was written in Santa Fe, New Mexico, between the summer of 1980 and the winter of 1981 for *Nice Jewish Girls*. In it, Melanie Kaye reflects on, among other things, a desire to change her name and what such a change might mean. The essay is divided into eight sections: "Jewish Tradition," "Jewish Identity," "Jewish Names," "Looking Like a Jew," "Sounding Like a (Low Class) Jew," "Acting Like a Jewish Woman," "Jewish Women," and "Jewish Fore-mothers." Each section deals with aspects of the author's American Jewish lesbian identity. Names are crucial, intersecting with all these other concerns. Thus, the section on Jewish identity concludes with a passage from Primo Levi on the loss of Jewish names in the Holocaust:

> Nothing belongs to us anymore; they have taken away our clothes, our shoes, even our hair; if we speak, they will not listen to us, and if they listen, they will not understand. They will even take away our name: and if we want to keep it, we will have to find in our-selves the strength to do so, to manage somehow so that behind the name something of us, of us as we were, still remains.[8]

Levi's powerful statement speaks to the importance of keeping a Jewish name. What is interesting is that this citation, located so clearly within the context of Europe and the Holocaust, leads Melanie Kaye directly into a discussion of Jewish names, primarily as they appear in America: "In the new world too, many of us, like other immigrants, lost our names or heard them mutilated, out of gentile ignorance, laziness, or hostility. Some of us shed our names like a ragged coat" (38). In this way she figures immigration to America also in terms of loss.

For her "Kaye" is a new name. "Kantrowitz" is her father's lost name, "Wolfgang," her mother's. In this account, she focuses on "Kantrowitz," the family name that marks her own identity. Not a long-lost name, her parents had to decide whether to pass it on to her. Her mother pushed for the change to Kaye before she and her sister were born. Her mother threatened an absurd first name, Forsythia, for her sister, the couple's first child, if her father did not legally change their last name. Thus, in 1942, with the birth of the author's sister, her father changed the family's name from Kantrowitz to Kaye.[9]

Reading about the frightful Forsythia Kantrowitz, I think about my own mother's name. She was born Phyllis Bialostofsky in New

York in 1935. As she likes to explain, she has no middle name because this name was just too long. In 1941, however, my grandfather's extended family, his parents, his brothers, and all of their wives and children changed the family name to Bialow. A note added to my grandmother's New York state pharmacy license describes this change. Next to Blanche Bialostofsky[10] (the name on the license), the following handwritten note appears:

Name changed to Blanche Bialow at a Special Term of the City Court of the City of New York held in and for the County of Queens at the Courthouse there of 88–11 Sutphin Boulevard in the Borough of Queens, City of New York on January 10, 1941 to take effect on February 19, 1941. Albany N.Y., May 8, 1941

The note is signed by Ernest E. Cole, the Commissioner of Education for the State of New York. This official record of the change in my mother's family's name took place only a year before the Kantrowitzes changed their name.

I have always liked the sound of the name Bialow—billowy, light, airy. My cousin hates it. She prefers Bialostofsky and writes semiautobiographical short stories about characters with this and other once-changed names. Everyone called Melanie Kaye's father Mr. K; anyway, he says, Kantrowitz was just too hard.

Before changing her name to Kaye/Kantrowitz,[11] Melanie Kaye considered taking back her mother's maiden names—as far back as she could go. Or, perhaps, her father's. Or both. What she came to realize in considering all of these different options, however, was that despite the fact that Kaye is a made up name, it too has a history, a history of assimilation. As she explains, Kaye is both history and closet, the history of a kind of closet. She decided she does not want to erase this history either by getting rid of this name.

In reaching her decision, Melanie Kaye asks the parenthetical question I cite at the opening of this chapter, "(think about asking every Jew you know: what *was* your name?)" (39).[12] In response to this question, I think about Levitt, my father's name, which is also a construct. It was once Schimshelevich, or something like that, but there is no official record of this change.

Even where there are records, as in my mother's family, there are other complications. The name Bialostofsky was itself an American

immigration mistake. It was the name of the place that my grandfather's parents came from, and not their family name. That name, I
believe, was Saperstein. Ironically, this mistake is one of the few connections I had been able to make between continents in my entire
extended family until, of course, my father's recent revelations about
his uncle. For a long time, Bialostofsky connected me to Europe and
to the Shoah. It was my link to that other continent. It connected me
to those who resisted and those who died in the Bialystock ghetto.[13]

In the last portion of her description of "Jewish Names," Melanie
Kaye, like Evelyn Beck in Milwaukee, describes the discomfort of
immigrant daughters becoming American. She writes about those
names she learned to ridicule, old-world names, Yiddish names, as
well as carefully crafted American names like "Susan, Ellen, and
Judy." As she points out, even these supposedly American names have
become Jewish, the names of a generation of immigrant daughters.

Recounting the impressions names give or do not give, Melanie
Kaye writes about being known by this name. "I recently met a woman
who knew me through my written work. 'Oh,' she said, 'I expected you
to be tall and blond.'"[14] As she explains, often those who did not know
her expected her to be tall and blond, decidedly not Jewish. Uncomfortable with this confusion, she begins experimenting with other options
and eventually hits upon Kaye/Kantrowitz as an effective strategy of
maintaining continuity as well as the history of change.

As I read it, the construct Kaye/Kantrowitz, the doubling and the
slash, enact a move both to re/member a series of histories but also
to disrupt present practices of naming.[15] The fact that this change was
not only enacted by the author but also both supported and reenacted
within a series of Jewish and feminist publications is also significant.
For this was not a legal enactment like marriage or like those efforts
of a previous generation to change their names. In this case, Melanie
Kaye/Kantrowitz self-consciously changed her own name as a way of
demonstrating a different kind of commitment to the past and the
present. Her Jewish and feminist commitments to this change do not
appeal to the authority of the law as a guarantee for inclusion.
Rather, this informal change, its reproduction and circulation within
a series of Jewish and feminist publications, holds out a less-grand
promise of acceptance. It offers an ambivalent embrace of a particular American Jewish feminist legacy.

conclusion

∼

Writing Home

Everything is poised. Everything is waiting for the emptiness to be filled up, for the filling-up that can never replace, that can only take over. Like time itself. Or history.

—Irena Klepfisz, *"Bashert"*

Change . . . is not a simple escape from constraint to liberation. There is no shedding the literal fear and figurative law of the father, and no reaching a final realm of freedom . . . the past, home, and the father leave traces that are constantly reabsorbed into a shifting vision.

—Biddy Martin and Chandra Mohanty,
"Feminist Politics: What's Home Got to Do with It?"

The ambivalent desires that inform my embrace of each of the specific sites and individual texts that I have claimed in this book (America, liberalism, rabbinic Judaism, liberal Jewish theology, and feminist study) remain a part of me. But to embrace them has also meant learning how to let go. Ambivalence marks not only the interrelationship between these various traditions in my life and the contradictions between them, but also my interactions with each of them separately. Each relationship has also been marked by an ambivalence—the desire to hold on and the desire to let go.

As I contemplate letting go of this book, I find myself returning to the photograph of my grandmother in front of the dome of the United States Capitol, but this time I notice other things about the image. I begin to see some of my grandmother's ambivalences in her body. She is tired, a bit weary; the weight of gravity pulls against the frailty of her arms. They hang a bit too low despite her efforts to extend them. They remain quite close to her body. And, yet she remains poised, balancing perhaps her own ambivalences about her place in this country.

When this photograph was taken she did not know what the future would bring. I know this stance. I know it well.

My grandmother died in 1980, not long after this photograph was taken. She died while I was away at college. It was the spring semester of my sophomore year. She died just as I was beginning my journey out of my parent's home. She and I did not know then that the academy was going to be my way out.

Despite my ongoing desire for a sense of permanence, at this moment I again find myself moving on. I leave this particular journey knowing that I can write home. Although I have discovered that the realm that once seemed strange and distant has become more familiar and that what was once familiar has become more strange, I know that I can locate myself in writing.

Irena Klepfisz ends section two of *"Bashert,"* "Chicago, 1964: I am walking home alone at midnight,"[1] with the passage that opens this conclusion. Klepfisz writes about leaving her mother's home for the first time to attend graduate school in the middle of America. In this unfamiliar place she begins to figure out her own position in this strange land that was becoming her home. Although I also find myself poised, at this point, I am no longer waiting for history to happen to me. I am not waiting for a future that will fill me up anew. Nor am I looking for something to replace all that has come before. Although I have moved on, I do not believe that it is possible to leave the past behind. Instead, I find myself already living within an ever-changing present, a present already formed by the history of my immigrant Jewish family's settlement in this country. For me, this remains a strangely familiar territory.

Although the present never replaces the past, I do not mourn the loss of permanence, a permanence that time and again has proven to be more illusive than I could have dreamed. By writing about my desires for home as well as my many disappointments, I have come to appreciate a different sense of security. I have learned that, although nothing is permanent, traces of the past remain with us as part of a shifting vision. It is this partial, ironically still immigrant vision of home that I embrace as I journey out into an uncertain future.

Notes

Preface

1. It was only after writing this preface that I realized why this title seemed so familiar. It is part of the title of Irena Klepfisz's poem *"Di rayze aheym*/The journey home." Irena Klepfisz, *A Few Words in the Mother Tongue: Poems Selected and New (1971–1990)* (Portland, OR: Eighth Mountain Press, 1990), 216–224.

2. *American Heritage Dictionary of the English Language*, 3d ed. s.v. "permanent."

3. Is it really that different from the German verb, *bleiben*, to stay, to remain to endure? With some of these thoughts in mind I gave this German name *Bleiben* to my dog when I adopted him from a shelter in Atlanta. He came to live with me in November of 1989.

4. The note is a **Word History**, an innovation of the *American Heritage Dictionary*, that is included after the definition as a separate entry.

Introduction

1. Gayatri Chakravorty Spivak, "French Feminism Revisited," *Outside in the Teaching Machine* (New York: Routledge, 1993), 141.

2. These texts include: Minnie Bruce Pratt, "Identity: Skin Blood Heart," in *Yours in Struggle: Three Feminist Perspectives on Anti-Semitism and Racism*, Elly Bulkin, Minnie Bruce Pratt, and Barbara Smith (Brooklyn: Long Haul Press, 1984), 11–63; Biddy Martin and Chandra Mohanty, "Feminist Politics: What's Home Got to Do With It?" in *Feminist Studies/Critical Studies*, ed., Teresa de Lauretis (Bloomington: Indiana University Press, 1986), 191–212 and Nancy K. Miller, "Dreaming, Dancing and the Changing Locations of Feminist Criticism, 1988," in *Getting Personal: Feminist Occasions and Other Autobiographical Acts* (New York: Routledge, 1991), 72–100.

3. I use the term "America" here and at various points throughout this book

because the desires I am interested in exploring, the longing evoked by the dream of this country, are configured as "America" and not the United States. As this dream connects to Jews especially in the twentieth century, see such titles as: Deborah Dash Moore, *At Home In America: Second Generation New York Jews* (New York: Columbia University Press, 1981) and Jenna Weissman Joselit, *The Wonders of America: Reinventing Jewish Culture 1880–1950* (New York: Hill and Wang 1994).

4. Teresa de Lauretis, "Feminist Studies, Critical Studies: Issues, Terms, Contexts," *Feminist Studies/Critical Studies*, 8.

5. On this point see chapter 3 and my reading of the questions Napoleon posed to the Jewish notables as a prerequisite to emancipation. See also Pierre Birnbaum and Ira Katznelson, ed., *Paths of Emancipation: Jews, States, and Citizenship* (Princeton: Princeton University Press, 1995), and Benjamin Ginsberg, *The Fatal Embrace: Jews and the State* (Chicago: University of Chicago Press, 1993).

6. On this point see Barbara A. Scheier, *Becoming American Women: Clothing and the Jewish Immigrant Experience* (Chicago: Chicago Historical Society, 1994).

7. Robert Morris was an American revolutionary politician and financier as well as a signer of the Declaration of Independence. Like Salomon, he raised money for the Continental Army.

8. I use the single term "antisemitism" throughout this book because I do not want to reify Jewishness. The notion of "Semitism" with a capital "S" is marked by a disturbing history of racializing otherness within a European imaginary. When I quote other texts that use this term, I will follow their usage.

9. *Hadassah*, (August/September, 1994), 58. I thank Susan E. Shapiro for this reference and for her description of this image in a telephone conversation, September 25, 1994.

10. In this respect my work is different from much of Jewish feminist scholarship in both feminist studies and in Jewish studies and religion. I engage with theory in explicit ways. Although texts like those of Evelyn Torton Beck, ed., *Nice Jewish Girls: A Lesbian Anthology* (Boston: Beacon Press, 1989) and Melanie Kaye Kantrowitz and Irena Klepfisz, ed., *Tribe of Dina: A Jewish Women's Anthology* (Boston: Beacon, 1989) offer powerful personal narratives, they do not necessarily theorize out of these works. This is especially important in articulating a notion of subjectivity that is both constructed and shifting. I assume that identities are not fixed, but the notion of a fixed identity remains steadfast even within these rich anthologies. It also remains true for much Jewish feminist scholarship in the fields of Jewish studies and religion where often important resources from the past and present are gathered but often left untheorized. For examples of this kind of work see: Judith Plaskow, *Standing Again at Sinai: Judaism for a Feminist Perspective* (San Francisco: HarperCollins, 1990); Judith Baskin, ed., *Jewish*

Women in Historical Perspective (Detroit: Wayne State University Press, 1991); Rachel Biale, *Women and Jewish Law: An Exploration of Women's Issues in Halakhic Sources* (New York: Schocken, 1984); and Susannah Heschel, ed., *On Being A Jewish Feminist: A Reader* (New York: Schocken, 1995, 1983). In these ways, liberal enlightenment assumptions about identities remain unchallenged.

By way of contrast, see the various essays in Miriam Peskowitz and Laura Levitt, ed., *Judaism Since Gender* (New York: Routledge, 1997) as well as both the essays and reviews of recent works across various disciplines of Jewish study in Laura Levitt and Miriam Peskowitz, eds., "Engendering Jewish Knowledges," a special issue of *Shofar: An Interdisciplinary Journal For Jewish Studies*, 14.1(Fall 1995).

11. For work of postcolonial criticism on issues of gender see Spivak, *Outside in the Teaching Machine*, and Rajeswari Sunder Rajan, *Real and Imagined Women: Gender, Culture and Postcolonialism* (New York: Routledge, 1993). More generally, see my references to Homi Bhabha below. On Jewishness and these questions, see Jonathan Boyarin, "The Other Within, the Other Without," in *Storm from Paradise: The Politics of Jewish Memory* (Minneapolis: University of Minnesota Press, 1992), 77–98.

12. On colonialism as a discursive configuration see David Spurr, *The Rhetoric of Empire: Colonial Discourse in Journalism, Travel Writing and Imperial Administration* (Durham: Duke University Press, 1993).

13. Homi Bhabha, "Of Mimicry and Man: The Ambivalence of Colonial Discourse," *October* 28(1984): 127.

14. I use the term "people of color" here to refer to the various diasporic communities of colonial peoples living in the West. The term "black" could also have been used here since, as Andrée Nicola McLaughlin has explained, outside of the United States, "black" carries these broader connotations. Andrée Nicola McLaughlin, "Black Women, Identity, and the Quest for Humanhood and Wholeness: Wild Women in the Whirlwind," in *Wild Women in the Whirlwind: Afra-American Culture and the Contemporary Literary Renaissance,* Joanne M. Braxton and Andrée Nicola McLaughlin, ed., (New Brunswick: Rutgers University Press, 1990), 147–180. Writing within the United States, however, I did not want to erase these other meanings. Moreover, since references to black people living in the United States are now more often made in terms of African Americans, I wanted to indicate that I am speaking about more than just the United States.

15. See for example, Adrienne Rich's account of her father's efforts to fit in, to be an American, in "Split at the Root: An Essay on Jewish Identity (1982)," *Blood, Bread, and Poetry: Selected Prose 1979–1985* (New York: W.W. Norton, 1986), 100–123. For an excellent account of these kinds of complicated excesses and the ambivalence of Jewishness, see Linda Nochlin and Tamar Garb, eds., *The Jew in the Text: Modernity and the Construction of Identity* (New York: Thames and Hudson, 1995).

16. Although I have chosen to discuss these gaps here in terms of Jewishness, they are also evident in terms of gender. In chapter 4 I discuss how the experience of Jewish women combines these critiques. For now, however, I simply want to make clear how the kinds of colonial dynamics Bhabha writes about operate within the liberal West. For a series of nuanced accounts of the problematics of Jewish assimilation in the nineteenth century, see Jonathan Frankel and Steven Zipperstein, ed., *Assimilation and Community: The Jews in Nineteenth-Century Europe* (Cambridge: Cambridge University Press, 1992).

17. Marianna Torgovnick, "The Politics of the 'We'," in *Eloquent Obsessions: Writing Cultural Criticism*, Marianna Torgovnick, ed. (Durham: Duke University Press, 1994), 267. For another more recent example of this kind of complicated relationship to the Western canon see Adam Begley, "Colossus Among Critics: Alan Bloom," *New York Times Magazine*, November 25, 1994.

18. Torgovnick, 266. For more on Trilling, see also Susanne Klingenstein *Jews in the American Academy 1900–1940: The Dynamics of Intellectual Assimilation* (New Haven: Yale University Press, 1991), chapter 5, "A Professor of Literature," 137–198.

19. See, for example, Klingenstein, *Jews in the American Academy 1900–1940*; Marcia Graham Synott, *The Half-Opened Door: Discrimination and Admissions at Harvard, Yale and Princeton, 1890–1970* (Westport, CT: Greenwood Press, 1979), Dan Orren, *Joining the Club: A History of Jews and Yale* (New Haven: Yale University Press, 1985).

20. Trilling taught at Columbia from the 1930s to the 1970s.

21. At that time, Emory's graduate program in religion was one of very few where it was possible to work with a tenured Jewish feminist scholar in theology. It was the only place where I could work on these kinds of questions. Ellen Umansky had been recently tenured at Emory. For more on her work see: Ellen Umansky, *Lily Montagu and the Advancement of Liberal Judaism: From Vision to Vocation* (New York: Edwin Mellen Press, 1983), *Lily Montagu, Sermons, Addresses, Letters and Prayers* (New York: Edwin Mellen Press, 1985); "Piety, Persuasion, and Friendship: Female Leadership in Modern Times," in *Embodied Love, Sensuality and Relationship as Feminist Values*, ed. P. Cooey, S. Farmer, and M. Ross, ed. (San Francisco: Harper & Row, 1987), 171–87. Umansky's work of recovery and construction continues to be at the forefront of Jewish feminist scholarship in religion. Her work unearths the voices of liberal Jewish women who served as religious leaders in various Jewish communities in the United States and Great Britain from the late nineteenth through to the middle of the twentieth century. Umansky writes from a contemporary liberal Jewish feminist position. My work builds directly on Umansky's important efforts.

22. This engagement was greatly enhanced by the fact that Emory University has one of the oldest interdisciplinary graduate programs in the United

States, the Institute for the Liberal Arts (the ILA) where I did a great deal of my graduate work.

23. Elsewhere I discuss these differences in terms of the interplay between the material differences articulated within feminist identity politics, on the one hand, and the discursive play of différance in critical theory, on the other. For this more detailed account of the interplay between difference and différance in feminist literary theory and how it might be used in thinking about Jewish feminist identity/ies see, Laura Levitt, "Rethinking Jewish Feminist Identity/ies: What Difference Can Feminist Theory Make?" in *Interpreting Judaism in a Postmodern Age*, ed. Steven Kepnes (New York: NYU Press, 1996), 361–77.

24. As Martin and Mohanty explain:

> It is noteworthy that some of the American feminist texts and arguments that have been set up as targets to be taken apart by deconstructive moves are texts and arguments that have been critiqued from within "American" feminist communities for their homogenizing, even colonialist gestures; they have been critiqued in fact, by those most directly affected by the exclusions that have made possible certain radical and cultural feminist generalizations. (194)

25. Martin and Mohanty write:

> Antihumanist attacks on "feminism" usually set up "American Feminism" as a "straw man" and so contribute to the production—or, at the very least, the reproduction—of an image of "Western feminism" as conceptually and politically unified in its monolithically imperialist moves. (194)

26. This double notion of partiality parallels that offered by Bhabha in his reading of mimicry.

27. On my use of "identity/ies" in this way see my "Rethinking Jewish Feminist Identity/ies"; "Reconfiguring Home: Jewish Feminist Identity/ies," in *Gender and Judaism: The Transformation of Tradition*, ed. Tamar Rudavsky (New York: NYU Press, 1995), 39–49.

28. Carole Pateman, *The Sexual Contract* (Stanford, CA: Stanford University Press, 1988).

29. Irena Klepfisz, "*Bashert*," in *Keeper of Accounts* (Watertown, MA: Persephone Press, 1982), 74–87, reprinted in Klepfisz, *A Few Words in the Mother Tongue, Poems Selected and New (1997–1990)*, (Portland, OR: Eighth Mountain Press, 1990), 183–200.

Chapter One

1. Angelika Bammer, ILA 751W, "Feminist Theory and Literary Criticism," course at Emory University, Atlanta, GA, Spring, 1988.

2. Biddy Martin and Chandra Mohanty, "Feminist Politics: What's Home Got To Do with It?" in *Feminist Studies/Critical Studies*, Teresa de Lauretis, ed., (Bloomington: Indiana University Press, 1986), 191–212; Minnie Bruce

Pratt "Identity: Skin Blood, Heart," in *Yours in Struggle: Three Feminist Perspectives on Anti-Semitism and Racism*, Elly Bulkin, Minnie Bruce Pratt and Barbara Smith, (Brooklyn: Long Haul Press, 1984), "Feminist Politics," 9–63.

3. Martin and Mohanty, 210.

4. On this issue of embrace as a feminist practice see Laura Levitt, "(The Problem with) Embraces," in *Judaism Since Gender*, Miriam Peskowitz and Laura Levitt, ed., (New York: Routledge, 1997).

5. For example an *Atlanta Journal/Constitution* article from December 29, 1989, notes the following: "A letter claiming responsibility for two recent fatal bombings and threatening more assassinations in retaliation for black men raping white women contains the same identifying code as follow-up letters sent to some of the bomb targets. . . ." Gail Epstein and Bill Montgomery, "More bombings threatened, Code appears to link writer to 2 slayings," *Atlanta Journal/Constitution*, 12/21/89. Although later coverage of these bombings led to the capture of a lone "crazy man," these initial stories remained with me. I thank Betsy White for her help in locating this article.

6. See Laura Levitt, "Speaking Out of the Silence Around Rape: A Personal Account," *Fireweed*, 41 (Fall 1993): 20–31.

7. Referring to my rape is difficult. For the first few years I spoke about it in terms of "the rape." I have since worked against reifying this experience while also claiming it as my own. The next permutation was "my rape." This construction "my being raped" is new. I thank David Watt for pushing me to reconsider once again how I refer to having been raped. For more on this question of the difficulty of speaking about rape, see Levitt, "Speaking Out."

8. This question is even more striking to me in retrospect. In rereading those initial accounts, other ironies have emerged. As the Epstein and Montgomery article of 12/29/89 explained in regard to one of the initial letters sent, "It referred specifically to the case of Julie Love, an Atlanta woman whose 1988 kidnapping, rape and slaying was blamed on two black men, stating 'She is only one of thousands of innocent white women who have been raped and murdered by inhuman black barbarians.'" What is striking about this reference is that Julie Love was a Jewish woman. Although this is not acknowledged by the bombers, I know a great deal about this particular case. I lived in Atlanta in 1988 and remember quite vividly the numerous flyers posted all around Atlanta asking if any one had seen Julie Love. At the time I worked as a religious school teacher at the Temple, the first reform congregation in Atlanta. Ms. Love had grown up in this congregation, and the Temple was very much involved in efforts to find her. For months, the doors of the Temple were plastered with these flyers. This was one of the first of many cases of violence against women that was heavily covered by local media and it is one of the first that I remembered.

9. On this point see most recent statistics on abuse. See also Susan Estrich, *Real Rape: How the Legal System Victimizes Women Who Say No* (Cambridge: Harvard University Press, 1987). For more on the problematics of rape and marriage, see chapter 3.

10. Although recent efforts to take more seriously the threat to women and children in their homes have resulted in new legislation that allows police to intervene more easily in domestic disputes, these remain thorny issues. The propriety of government or legal intervention into domestic affairs remains heavily skewed in favor of husbands and fathers. Prosecution of husbands who beat or rape their wives remains difficult. These points will all be developed in much more detail in chapter 4.

11. See Laura Levitt, "Reconfiguring Home: Jewish Feminist Identity/ies," Ph.D. diss., Emory University, Atlanta, GA 1993.

12. On these struggles, see Minnie Bruce Pratt, *Rebellion: Essays 1980–1991* (Ithaca: Firebrand, 1991) and *Crimes Against Nature* (Ithaca: Firebrand, 1990).

13. On this point, see chapter 2 for an interrogation of rabbinic rape and marriage laws through a close reading of the *ketubbah*, the rabbinic marriage contract, and a specific talmudic text on rape.

14. In a similar kind of move, Lawrence D. Kritzman writes about his complicated relationship to French culture as a Jew:

    I have now come to realize, in incarnating my parents' "otherness," that it is that same culture that has seduced and at times betrayed me, French culture, whose intellectual traditions have nurtured me since I was eighteen, that I still love (although somewhat less naively), and which sustains me every day of my life. It is indeed because of my more authentic and somewhat less phantasmic relationship to those traditions that I have finally been able to reflect more critically on the "Jewish Question" in France, and publish this volume.

    Lawrence D. Kritzman, "Introduction," in *Auschwitz and After: Race, Culture, and "the Jewish Question" in France*, Lawrence D. Kritzman, ed. (New York: Routledge, 1995), 10. See also, Alice Kaplan, *French Lessons: A Memoir* (Chicago: Univeristy of Chicago Press, 1993).

15. In addition to Pratt, recent scholarship on Poe has raised similar issues about the complicated relationship between the legacy of slavery and issues of gender in Poe's work, especially the work of Joan Dayan. For example, Dayan writes:

    for Poe the cultivation of romance and the facts of slavery are inextricably linked.... It is perhaps not surprising that some of Poe's critics—the founding fathers of the Poe Society, for example—sound rather like the proslavery ideologues who promoted the ideal of the lady as elegant, white, and delicate. Poe's ladies, those dream-dimmed, ethereal living dead of his poems, have been taken as exemplars of what Poe called "supernal Beauty"—an entitlement that he would degrade again and again. Think about Lady Madeline Usher returning from the grave as a brute and bloodied thing, reduced from a woman of beauty to the frenzied iterated *"it"* of her brother Roderick. Many of the dissolutions and decays so marked in Poe's tales about women subvert the status of the women as a saving ideal, thus undermining his own "Philosophy of Composition": the "death of a beautiful woman is, unquestionably, the most poetic topic in the world." No longer pure or passive, she returns as an earthy—and very unpoetical—subject.

Joan Dayan, "Amorous Bondage: Poe, Ladies, and Slaves," *American Literature*, 66.2 (June 1994): 240. See also Dayan "Romance and Race," in *The Columbia History of The American Novel*, Emory Elliot, ed. (New York: Columbia University Press, 1991), 94–102. I thank Janet Jakobsen for calling my attention to Dayan's work.

16. In fact, in "Amorous Bondage," Dayan makes a strong case for "a rereading of Poe that depends absolutely on what has so often been cut out of his work: the institution of slavery, Poe's troubled sense of himself as a southern aristocrat, and, finally, the precise and methodical transactions in which he reveals the threshold separating humanity from animality. As [she] will demonstrate, his most unnatural fictions are bound to the works of natural history that are so much a part of their origination. Read in this way, Poe's sometimes inexplicable fantasies become intelligible. Poe's gothic is crucial to our understanding of the entangled metaphysics of romance and servitude. What might have remained local historiography becomes a harrowing myth of the Americas" (241).

17. For a similar take on this issue of the loss of Eastern European Jewish culture and specifically Yiddish in America, see Ellen Rifkin, "*Fun di oysyes koyekh shepn*/Drawing Strength from Letters: Language and Land in the Diaspora," *Bridges* 5.2 (Winter 5756), 20–30.

18. Sigmund Freud, "The 'Uncanny'(1919)," in *Studies in Parapsychology* (New York: Collier Books, 1963), 19–60. I thank Susan E. Shapiro for helping me see the uncanny elements in my project about home. I am especially grateful to Susan for a series of engaging conversations about the uncanny in my home in the summer and fall of 1992. It was with Susan that I reread my marked up copy of Freud's essay. For a complicated analysis of the uncanny, Jews, and the feminine, see Susan Shapiro's work on the "Jewish Uncanny," "Troping Jews," Modern Language Association, Chicago, December 1995; "The Uncanny Jew: A Brief History of an Image," *Judaism*, 46.1 (Winter 1997), forthcoming; "Uncanny Jews: The History of an Image and Its Consequences," The Francis Thau Memorial Lecture, The Jewish Theological Seminary, October 17, 1996. See also Susan E. Shapiro, *Écriture judaïque*: Where Are the Jews in Western Discourse? " in *Displacements: Cultural Identities in Question*, Angelika Bammer, ed. (Bloomington: Indiana University Press, 1994), 182–201.

19. In many respects it is chapters 3 and 4, the chapters on liberalism, that I

understand most clearly as my father's legacy to me and not the chapters on rabbinic or liberal Judaism.

Chapter Two

1. I am using the spelling most commonly used in reference works such as *The Encyclopedia Judaica*, "Ketubbah." I will use other spellings only when quoting other sources.

2. See for example Richard Siegel, Sharon Strassfeld, and Michael Strassfeld, *The First Jewish Catalog* (Philadelphia: Jewish Publication Society, 1973); and Anita Diamant, *The New Jewish Wedding* (New York: Fireside, 1985). More recent examples of this desire to reclaim the ketubbah include Sally A. Downey, "A decorative contract seals Jewish nuptials," *Philadelphia Inquirer*, June, 7, 1996. This article from the home-and-design section of the paper describes various styles of ketubbot as well as information on where to buy them and how much they cost. In a recent (June 1996) ad in a Washington lesbian and gay newspaper, "Israeli Accents" of Rockville, Maryland, advertised "Gay & Lesbian Ketubahs/Commitment Documents." I thank Miriam Peskowitz for this reference.

3. I found a few beautifully wrought picture books. The best examples of these are David Davidovich, *The Ketuba: Jewish Marriage Contracts Through the Ages* (Jerusalem/New York: Adama Books, 1968, 1985); and Shalom Sabar, *Ketubbah: Jewish Marriage Contracts of Hebrew Union College Skirball Museum and Klau Library* (Philadelphia; Jewish Publication Society [JPS], 1990). Davidovich's text is interested in issues of artistic nuance vis-à-vis historical ketubbot from various locations around the world. It offers beautiful color reproductions of a full range of historical documents. As Cecil Roth writes in his foreword to Davidovich's text, "Slowly the categories of Jewish art are at last being established and investigated. Among them the illuminated ketuba or marriage contract is one of the most significant as well as one of the most charming." The Sabar volume is described in the JPS catalogue as follows: "The illustrated ketubbah is a unique artifact of Judaica. It is, first of all, a legal document virtually unchanged since talmudic times. It is also an artistic expression of aesthetic tastes and social mores from centuries of Jewish wandering." See also the reissue of Moses Gaster's 1923 volume on these documents. Moses Gaster, *The Ketubah* (New York: Hermon, 1974).

4. For some examples of these texts see: Leo Jung, "The Jewish Way to Married Happiness" *The Jewish Forum*, 1930; Sidney Goldstein, *Meaning of Marriage and Foundations of the Family: A Jewish Interpretation* (New York: Bloch, 1942); Hayyim Scheid, ed., *Marriage* (Philadelphia: Jewish Publication Society, 1973); Maurice Lamm, *The Jewish Way in Love and Marriage* (San Francisco: Harper and Row, 1980); Aryeh Kaplan, *Made in Heaven, A Jewish Wedding Guide* (New York: Moznaim, 1983); Reuven

Bulka, *Jewish Marriage: A Halakhic Ethic* (New York: Ktav, 1986); Michael Kaufman, *Love, Marriage and Family in Jewish Law and Tradition* (Northvale, NJ: Jason Aronson, 1992).

5. For examples of some of these new ketubbot and some explanation of them see Diamant, *The Jewish Wedding*, 71–91.

6. For a scholarly account of these questions in relation to a particular set of ketubbah documents see S.D. Goiten, *A Mediterranean Society: The Jewish Communities of the Arab World as Portrayed in the Documents of the Cairo Geniza, Volume 3, The Family* (Berkeley: University of California Press, 1978). On the question of ornamentation, see 110–113.

7. These documents have also been altered to reflect not only egalitarian concerns but also, particularly in the conservative movement, the problem of Jewish divorce and the husband's control over divorce.

8. I thank Angelika Bammer for helping me begin to think about these issues. After reading an early draft of this chapter she told me that she would never look the same way at a beautiful ketubbah prominently displayed in a colleague's home. On this issue of display see Diamant, *The New Jewish Wedding*. As she explains, "Many couples frame and hang their *ketubot* in special places in their homes. If you share the same bed before marriage, hanging the *ketubah* over it affirms the change in your relationship" (82). By contrast to this recent desire to display these documents, Goiten explains how and why the ketubbot fragments found within the Cairo Geniza ended up there. See Goiten, 3: 113–14. As he explains, "The ketubba was given to and kept by the wife, since it spelled out the financial and other obligations of her husband towards her. For reasons of safety she would deposit it somewhere else" (113).

9. Goiten, volume 3, 104.

10. Kaplan, *Made in Heaven*, 105.

11. See Mordechai Akiva Friedman, *The Jewish Marriage in Palestine, A Cairo Geniza Study, Volume 1, The Ketubba Traditions* (New York: The Jewish Theological Seminary of America, 1980), 7–8.

12. The Tannaitic period usually refers to the first century or so after the destruction of Jerusalem. Tannaitic sources include the Mishnah, the Tosefta, and various early midrashic texts. The term comes from *Tanna*, Aramaic, repeater which is especially interesting given the importance of these documents in the construction of gender. On this point see Miriam Peskowitz, *Spinning Fantasies, Rabbis, Gender and History,* (Berkeley: University of California Press, 1997). In this study, Peskowitz shows how gender is constructed within daily life through repetitive acts. Instead of using the language of later rabbinic sources to define this period, Peskowitz locates these texts within the aegis of Roman rule. By contrast, later sources define the period through the "Tannaim" as those early rabbinic authorities who put together the Mishnah. See, for example, Robert Goldenberg, "Talmud," in *Back to the Sources. Reading the Classic Jewish*

Texts, Jewish Marriage in Palestine, Barry W. Holtz, ed. (New York: Summit Books, 1984), 129–75.

13. Friedman, *Jewish Marriage in Palestine,* 1; 4.

14. To help account for this lack, Mordechai Friedman suggests that the ketubbah was a part of a lay legal literature that was concerned with common practice and, therefore, never a part of the rabbinic canon. Instead, he argues, it was distinguished from canonical rabbinic literature by both its form and language, which he calls *leshon hedyot*—literally, the language or formulary of laymen. They were written by local scribes through whose efforts ketubbot became standardized. See Friedman, *Jewish Marriage in Palestine,* 1; 4–8.

15. See Friedman's introduction for a more complete discussion of this history. Friedman, *Jewish Marriage in Palestine,* 1; 1–47.

16. See Friedman, *Jewish Marriage in Palestine,* volumes 1 and 2, for a thorough discussion of these documents. See volume 2 for full editions of the texts with translations and commentaries. For further discussion about what the Geniza documents tell us about the institution marriage in the Arab world at this time, see Goiten, *A Mediterranean Society,* 3: 47–159; and Judith Baskin, "Jewish Women in the Middle Ages," in *Jewish Women in Historical Perspective,* Judith Baskin, ed. (Detroit: Wayne State University Press, 1991) 96–102.

17. For more on these variations, see the discussions in both Friedman and Goiten. On the specific issue of the problematics of divorce within the Babylonian tradition and contemporary practice, especially the issue of the *agunah,* the chained wife who can not initiate a divorce—see Laura Levitt, "Reconfiguring Home: Jewish Feminist Identity/ies," Ph.D., diss. Emory University, Atlanta, GA 1993, chapter 1, for a fuller discussion. See also the discussion of divorce in Rachel Biale, *Women and Jewish Law: An Exploration of Women's Issues in Halakhic Sources* (New York: Schocken, 1984).

18. For a more concise reading of this kind see Levitt, "Reconfiguring Home: Jewish Feminist Identity/ies," in *Gender and Judaism: The Transformation of Tradition,* Tamar Rudavsky, ed. (New York: NYU Press, 1995), 39–49.

19. Kaplan, *Made in Heaven.* For more specific information about this particular text see Kaplan, 104, n. 1. I use this particular version of the ketubbah text because Kaplan's book was virtually the only source I found that included in its guide to marriage a full ketubbah text in English and in Aramaic. All subsequent references to this ketubbah document will be from Kaplan's text, with page numbers presented in parentheses in the text. For a slightly different English translation, see Mendell Lewittes, *Jewish Marriage: Rabbinic Law, Legend, and Custom* (Northvale, NJ: Jason Aronson, 1994), 60–61.

20. For a more complicated account of virginity, marriage, and remarriage within the Arab world of the Geniza fragments, see Goiten, *A Mediterranean Society,* 3: 100–102.

21. Kaplan notes that if the bride is not a virgin other specific words to describe her status must be inscribed in the ketubbah. These include divorcee, widow, and convert. See especially Kaplan, *Made in Heaven,* 109–110, n. 16.

22. There are numerous reasons why a text, particularly a legal document, may be repetitive, but my reading is very much about the naturalization of the kind of power relationship inscribed in the ketubbah text.

23. See Exodus 22:15–16, *Tanakh* (Philadelphia: Jewish Publication Society, 1985), 119.

24. See Miriam Peskowitz's *Spinning Fantasies* on these conflations of early rabbinic, biblical, and other legal authorities. See especially chapter 6.

25. Another question worth asking is why these two are separated. Are we to assume that sex is not a necessity for women? This seems to reinforce my argument that the specification of sexuality parallels the reference to virginity that precedes it.

26. "The burden of domination is hard to bear. Dominators have, first, to establish their position, then to safeguard it. Subsequently, they must make both the dominated *and* themselves believe in it." Mieke Bal, *Lethal Love, Feminist Literary Readings of Biblical Love Stories*, (Bloomington: Indiana University Press, 1987), 110.

27. For a different account of wives contracting into a marriage see Friedman, *Jewish Marriage in Palestine*, 1: 181–88. Despite the seeming equality of the Palestinian documents Friedman examines, in most cases the bride agreed to "serve," "attend," "esteem," and "honor" her husband (182). See also Goiten, volume 3.

28. Although this notion of women retaining rights to their own property is often presented in contemporary apologetic literature as a sign of the Rabbis' better treatment of women, this is not necessarily the case. For a more complete reading of these sources see Levitt, "Reconfiguring Home: Jewish Feminist Identity/ies," chapter 1. For a powerful account of tensions within early rabbinic sources around questions of who controls a woman's property—not only the property she brings with her into a marriage but also the "works of her hands"—see Miriam Peskowitz's nuanced account of these enactments within the fictions of early rabbinic texts. See *Spinning Fantasies*, especially chapter 1.

29. Judith Baskin argues in her essay, "Jewish Women in the Middle Ages" (in *Jewish Women in Historical Perspective*, ed. Judith Baskin [Detroit: Wayne State University Press, 1991]) that the documents from the Cairo Geniza suggest that the property women brought into marriage was considerable; "The bride brought property into the marriage in the form of her dowry. This was generally worth many times more than the husband's marriage gift." (99). By contrast, Kaplan explains that this fixed sum was usually set at more than the value of those named assets in the previous clause and offers a paternalistic explanation about how this was done in order to protect those women who came from poor families.

30. When I write about ancient Rabbis, those referred to in the classic rabbinic sources, I follow the scholarly practice that capitalizes this term as opposed to references to contemporary rabbis, leaders, and teachers in specific Jewish communities.

31. Kaplan, *Made in Heaven*, 121. On this issue of strictness, Goiten has a somewhat different stance on the texts that he examines, because these were not found in the majority of these texts. He writes, "Some groups of Gianuzzi ketubbas contain the assurances normally found in legal documents, namely, that the parties were in full command of their physical and mental faculties, that they acted out of free will, were not coerced or in error, that the document was executed in accordance with the strictest provisions of Jewish (and gentile) law, and so on; others the majority, do not" (100).

32. Marcus Jastrow, *Dictionary of the Targumim, Talmud Babli, Yerushalmi and Midrashic Literature* (New York: Judaica Press, 1982), 1391.

33. Kaplan, *Made in Heaven*, 101–102.

34. "*Kinyan*" comes from the Hebrew root of the verb to take. The notion of acquisition in relation to this term comes from the biblical text. The proof texts are multiple. See full discussion of this issue and the relevant halakhic text, Kiddushin 2a in Rachel Biale, *Women and Jewish Law, An Exploration of Women's Issues in Halakhic Sources* (New York: Schocken, 1984), chapter 2, 44–69. Biale included a translation of the Kiddushin text as well as an extended discussion about its implications for Jewish women. My approach to this topic is more narrowly focused than Biale's. I am looking only at the ketubbah and its implications. I raise the question of "kinyan" or acquisition only in relation to how this process comes into play in the signing of the ketubbah.

35. As Biale suggests, within rabbinic Judaism the kinyan of marriage was enacted through a monetary exchange. In so doing, the rabbis linked these biblical traditions to explain how a man should go about "taking a wife." See Biale, *Women and Jewish Law*, 44–45.

36. In the marriage ceremony, an additional two witnesses must make sure that the groom gives the bride a ring, a parallel exchange or an act of kinyan that makes the transaction binding. For more on this exchange, see the discussion in *The Encyclopedia Judaica* (Jerusalem: Macmillan, 1971), vol. 11, entry "Marriage," subsection, 'The Ring,' 1043–44. All subsequent references will be presented as *EJ*, volume, entry, and column numbers.

37. Kaplan, *Made in Heaven*, 102. See also *EJ*, vol. 11, "Marriage," 1036.

38. Kaplan, *Made in Heaven*, 106.

39. According to Friedman, "The few *ketubbot* which omit it [kinyan] may reflect the older Palestinian traditions. In these documents the affirmation of the mutual agreement of the parties was apparently adequate to establish the obligations undertaken in the *ketubba* ('they took upon themselves the stipulations . . . from beginning to end'), and it was not necessary to perform the symbolic *qinyan*" (466–67). Friedman then goes on to say that "a noteworthy feature in the *qinyan* formula where it does appear is that

more frequently than not 'we performed the *qinyan* with *them*' is used rather than ' . . . with the groom'" (467). See Friedman, *Jewish Marriage in Palestine*, vol. 1, 465–67 for a more complete discussion of this matter of kinyan in the Palestinian tradition.

40. This issue of the bride's absence is less clear in many of the Geniza documents that Goiten and Friedman examine. On the issue of who signs and represents whom in these texts see Goiten, *A Mediterranean Society*, vol. 3. As Goiten explains, "In many marriage contracts, especially the more ancient ones, which are executed according to the Palestinian rite, and in all the Karaite ketubbas the bride appoints a representative, and his name and those of the two persons witnessing the appointment are mentioned" (103).

41. Kaplan, *Made in Heaven*, 180.

42. On the evolution of this ritual, see Biale, *Women and Jewish Law*, 56–59.

43. The ketubbah as protection for the woman is a common assumption of virtually all secondary sources with the exception of recent works by Peskowitz, *(Spinning Fantasies)* and Daniel Boyarin, *Unheroic Conduct*, (Berkeley: University of California Press, 1997). For a critique of these other secondary sources on this question see Levitt "Reconfiguring Home: Jewish Feminist Identity/ies," chapter 1.

44. In a very different context, Ann Clark makes a similar argument. "It seems to be a fact of life that the fear of rape imposes a curfew on our movements; a fact that if we stay at home we will be safe, but if we venture out alone we face the strange rapist in the dark alley. . . . These fears and restrictions, however, do not derive from common-sense caution. By limiting our own freedom, we obey the dictates of a myth— a myth which overtly warns us that rapists punish women who stray from the proper place" (1). Clark traces this myth to the late eighteenth and early nineteenth centuries in England. What I am suggesting is that this myth, the need for protection as it relates to the control of women's agency, has much earlier antecedents. The mechanism seems to be at work in the rabbinic material I have presented in this chapter. See Ann Clark, *Women's Silence, Men's Violence: Sexual Assault in England 1770–1845* (New York: Pandora, 1987). For a similar account of these dynamics in early rabbinic sources, see Peskowitz, *Spinning Fantasies*, chapter 6.

45. Biale, *Women and Jewish Law*, 59.

46. I use the term "consent" here as a legal term that defines an agreement or assent that is binding. As will become clear in what follows, there is a tension between such legally binding agreements and who may have such "consent" in relation to a women's body, and the issues of a woman's sexual volition. Although her desires are imagined to have an effect on her experience of intercourse, they are by no means the same as "consent." Within the talmudic discussion of the pain of rape that follows, rabbinic fantasies about how women experience even desired intercourse are presented within an economy of pain. The question of a woman's sexual

desire is placed outside of the legal framework of "consent." It is made to explain issues of pain and the relative merits of compensation for such pain.

47. These discussions are a part of both the Palestinian and the Babylonian Talmuds. Because the Babylonian Talmud became authoritative, I focus on its discussion of these matters in what follows. For more on these sources and the differences between these texts, see Goldenberg, "Talmud," in *Back to the Sources*.

48. This particular use of silence as consent can be traced back to a rabbinic reading of Deuteronomy 22:23–27. The logic was that if it was possible for a woman to scream and be heard, she was required to cry out. If she did not, she was deemed guilty of a major offense. On these issues see Biale, *Women and Jewish Law*, 240–243.

49. At that time, I read both the Palestinian and the Babylonian Talmud texts. In the reading that follows, I look only at a translation of the Babylonian text again because it became authoritative.

50. There is no ketubbah text given within the Talmud. This added to the mystification of this contract and its origins. Moreover, following this precedent, the *Encyclopedia Judaica* also does not provide a copy of a ketubbah in either its entry under "ketubbah" or "marriage."

51. I have chosen to focus on the discussion in the Babylonian version of this tractate not only because it is more extensive but also because the Babylonian tradition became normative. It has set the terms for the rabbinic tradition.

52. Tractate Ketubbot, chapter 3, Mishnah 4, 39a. All references to this text, unless otherwise specified, come from Samuel Daiches, Israel W. Slotki, and I. Epstein, *Babylonian Talmud, Tractate Kethuboth* [Hebrew-English Edition] (London: Soncino Press, 1971).

53. Tractate Ketubbot, Chapter 3, Mishnah 4, Gemara, 39a–39b. For a somewhat different interpretation of this text see Biale, *Women and Jewish Law*, 243–245. I also want to thank Daniel Boyarin for sharing with me his reading of this text. Private correspondence, summer 1995.

54. For feminist readings of some of these efforts at legal reform see: Susan Estrich, *Real Rape, How the Legal System Victimizes Women Who Say No* (Cambridge: Harvard University Press, 1987); Carol Smart, *Feminism and the Power of Law* (New York: Routledge, 1989), especially chapter 2, "Rape: Law and the Disqualification of Women's Sexuality" and Vikki Bell, "'Beyond the "Thorny Question": Feminism, Foucault and the Desexualisation of Rape," *The International Journal of the Sociology of Law* 19 (1991); 83–100.

55. A *baraita* is usually a legal text not included in the Mishnah but attributed to an early Rabbi as an authoritative source. For more on these early sources see Peskowitz, *Spinning Fantasies* and Goldenberg, "Talmud," in *Back to the Sources*.

56. According to Daniel Boyarin, "From this baraita we learn that the pain of which the Mishna speaks and for which the rapist is liable is not the incidental pain caused by the violence pursuant to the rape [since her husband will presumably not throw her onto the ground], but is, in fact, the pain of unwilled intercourse itself for which the rapist is held liable." Private correspondence, summer 1995.

57. The *naharah*, or young virgin referred to in the Mishnah text, seems to be the subject of the opening section of the Gemara, but then the text turns into a discussion about married women. Given this, as I read it, this discussion of pain is not just about virgins.

58. Boyarin writes that the majority opinion is in total disagreement with R. Simeon. As he explains, "the pain of forced intercourse is much greater than the pain of desired (first) intercourse, . . . therefore he [the rapist] is liable." Private correspondence, summer 1995.

59. Moshe Halbertal and Avishai Margalit, *Idolatry*, trans., Naomi Goldblum (Cambridge: Harvard University Press, 1992), 11.

60. Actually, the Ezekiel text is much more complicated. God is not only the husband to "Jerusalem" in the language of the text, He (*sic*) is also her adopted father. The relationship is both as father and husband. On this relationship see Halbertal and Margalit, *Idolatry*, chapter 1, 11–36. Also on this complicated relationship see Moshe Greenberg, *Ezekiel 1–20, The Anchor Bible*. (New York: Doubleday, 1983), 270–306. Although these texts do describe this relationship in incestuous terms, neither critically assess the implications of a God who is both father (*sic*) and husband (*sic*). Instead, each seems to take a kind of paternalistic stand. The questions of possible abuse, especially the abuse of power on the part of God in this troubling relationship, is never raised. Instead they each focus on the faults of the woman. She must be disciplined, shamed, put back in right relation to God, a relationship of "subordination." For more on this relationship see chapter 4.

61. I use the masculine possessive pronoun "His" because I read this construction of gender as critical to the Ezekiel text.

62. Ketubbot, chapter 3, Mishnah 3, Gemara, 38a. Biale argues that not only does the father receive compensation for the loss of his daughter's virginity, but also the "pain" inflicted is also his. Here pain is a measure of shame. "While the fine paid by the man to compensate the father for the financial loss is set at fifty silver shekels, the fines for the indignity, blemish, and the pain are determined by the father himself" (245).

63. Mishnah 4, Gemara, 39a.

64. Daniel Boyarin suggests that "clever women" were probably midwives. Private correspondence, summer 1995.

65. Boyarin suggests the following translation of this passage's reference to desired intercourse: "A virgin having sex willingly does not feel pain on first intercourse." This reading is in keeping with a desire to keep heterosex

carefully contained within the confines of marriage. I thank Daniel Boyarin for sharing this reading with me. Private correspondence, summer 1995.

66. Soncino, *Babylonian Talmud, Tractate Kethuboth*, note d:13, 39a.

67. Here I do not agree with the commentator who states in relation to the first of these analogies, hot water to a bald head, that this refers to "slight but pleasurable pain." (*Babylonian Talmud, Tractate Kethuboth*, note a:4, 39b) . It is not clear to me that this or any of these examples are particularly pleasurable.

68. The voyeurism and invasiveness of this whole discussion was brought home to me in rereading Steinsaltz. In a "background" note on the question of the pain referred to in the Mishnah, the text reads, "Such pain results from insufficient moistening of the vagina, or from contraction of the vaginal muscles (these problems generally do not exist when a woman has intercourse of her own free will)" (182). There is no evidence given for this assertion and, to make matters worse, this commentary continues as follows: "Moreover, a woman who was raped usually finds even minor pain intolerable, since she did not want to have intercourse (which might even cause physical injury) in the first place. The Gemara is apparently not referring to the pain caused by the rupture of the hymen, which is generally minimal, and no worse than that of a minor wound in a sensitive area, as the Gemara states" (182). Here again no evidence is given for these claims and, in so doing, the contemporary commentary perpetuates the problem of men talking to men about women's bodies that is at the heart of this entire Gemara. *The Talmud: The Steinsaltz Edition*, vol. 9, Tractate Ketubot, part 3 (New York: Random House, 1993).

Chapter Three

1. "Emancipation" in this sense refers specifically to the legal granting of citizenship to Jews, but even this usage is complicated. First, the term itself is used somewhat anachronistically in this context, on this issue, see Jacob Katz, "The Term *Jewish Emancipation*: Its Origin and Historical Impact," in *Studies in Nineteenth-Century Jewish Intellectual History*, ed. Alexander Altmann (Cambridge: Harvard University Press, 1964), 1–25. Second, legal, social, and cultural integration were already a part of what it meant to grant Jews citizenship. These processes all went together. Thus, other accounts of this process use terms like Jewish "regeneration," "naturalization," "amelioration," "acculturation," "assimilation," and/or "betterment." For more on these imbrications, see Amos Funkenstein, *Perceptions of Jewish History* (Berkeley: University of California Press), 1993, 220–56; Jonathan Frankel and Steven Zipperstein, ed., *Assimilation and Community: The Jews in Nineteenth-Century Europe* (New York: Cambridge University Press, 1992); Jay R. Berkovitz, "The French Revolution and the Jews: Assessing the Cultural Impact," *AJS Review* 20.1 (1995): 25–86; and Pierre Birnbaum and Ira Katznelson, ed., *Paths of Emancipation: Jews,*

States, and Citizenship (Princeton: Princeton University Press, 1995).

2. For an excellent discussion of some of these issues, see Linda Nochlin and Tamar Garb, eds., *The Jew in the Text: Modernity and the Construction of Jewish Identity* (New York: Thames and Hudson, 1995).

3. Paula Hyman, *From Dreyfus to Vichy, The Remaking of French Jewry, 1906–1939* (New York: Columbia University Press, 1979), 22.

4. Christian Wilhelm Dohm, "Concerning the Amelioration of the Civil Status of the Jews," in *Modern Jewish History: A Source Book*, Robert Chazan and Marc Lee Raphael, ed. (New York: Schocken, 1969), 1–13. All subsequent references to this work will be from this text, unless otherwise noted. For more on the innovations of Dohm's approach to the Jewish problem, and particularly his move from theology to politics and philosophy, see Katz, "The Term *Jewish Emancipation,*" 12–16.

5. The texts I will examine include Napoleon Bonaparte, "Imperial Decree Calling for an Assembly of Jewish Notables (May 30, 1806)"; Count Molé, "Napoleon's Instructions to the Assembly of Jewish Notables (July 29, 1806)"; Abraham Furtado, "Reply on Behalf of the Assembly to Count Molé"; and The Assembly of Jewish Notables' "Answers to Napoleon." Translations of all of these texts are to be found in Paul R. Mendes-Flohr and Jehuda Reinharz, ed., *The Jew in the Modern World: A Documentary History* (New York: Oxford, 1980), 112–120. See also, Diogene Tama, "The Emancipation of French Jewry: The act of the Israelitish Deputies of France and Italy," in Chazan and Raphael, ed. *Jewish History: A Source Reader* (New York: Schocklen, 1969), 14–31.

6. For more on Jews in France during the period leading up to the French Revolution see Arthur Hertzberg, *The French Enlightenment and the Jews* (New York: Columbia University Press, 1968).

7. Chazan and Raphael, *Modern Jewish History*, 10.

8. For more on these efforts see documents included in Mendes-Flohr and Reinharz, *The Jew in the Modern World*, 103–139.

9. A 1787 essay contest in France asking, "Are there means of making the Jews happier and more successful in France?" came up with a similar strategy. In his winning essay, Adolphe Thie'ry, like Dohm, argued that "we can make of the Jews what we want them to become, for their faults and vices derive from our institutions." Hyman, *From Dreyfus to Vichy*, 4.

10. Hyman, *From Dreyfus to Vichy*, 3.

11. Ibid., 4.

12. Ibid., 5. For an extended account, see Mendes-Flohr and Reinharz, *The Jew in the Modern World*, 103–105.

13. Homi Bhabha, "Of Mimicry and Man: The Ambivalence of Colonial Discourse," *October* 28 (1984), 127.

14. See Mendes-Flohr and Reinharz, *The Jew in the Modern World*, 103–111.

15. For a careful account of Napoleon's various encounters with the Jews of France and more specifically the relationship between the Assembly of

Notables and the Great Sanhedrin, see Simon Schwarzfuchs, *Napoleon, The Jews and the Sanhedrin* (London: Routledge & Kegan Paul, 1979).

16. Chazan and Raphael, *Modern Jewish History*, 15.

17. Ibid.

18. Ibid., 16.

19. Despite the gains French Jews made during the revolution, their status remained precarious both socially and politically. See Schwarzfuchs, *Napoleon*, 1–45; and Berkovitz, "The French Revolution," especially 78–86.

20. Chazan and Raphael, *Modern Jewish History*, 16–17.

21. Ibid., 18–19.

22. For an account of how the dynamics within the assembly of Jewish notables were not so much about class differences as about rabbinic versus enlightenment philosophical authority, see Schwarzfuchs, *Napoleon*, 64–87.

23. This was true in relation to the leaders of the revolution who granted Jews citizenship in 1789; and again in 1806, when Napoleon, the restored monarch, needed to assert his own authority over the Jews of France, whom he could deem worthy of French citizenship. For a more extensive series of classic texts of Jewish emancipation throughout western Europe, see Mendes-Flohr and Reinharz, *The Jew in the Modern World*, 103–139.

24. Chazan and Raphael, *Modern Jewish History*, 19.

25. These were in fact the first of the questions to be answered and came to model the answers for all of the other questions. Here the important role of the rabbis in framing the answers to these and then all of the other questions became apparent. See Schwarzfuch, *Napoleon*, 66–71.

26. For a more recent account of this ambivalence in France, see Susan Rubin Suleiman, "The Jew in Sartre's *Réflexions sur la question juive*: Exercise in Historical Reading," in Nochlin and Garb, *The Jew in the Text*, 201–218.

27. For more on the issue of "assimilation" in France, see Phyllis Cohen Albert, "Israelite and Jew: How Did Nineteenth-Century French Jews Understand Assimilation?" in Frankel and Zipperstein, *Assimilation and Community*, 88–109.

28. This renunciation of difference around sexual practices was an important form of social control not only at home in France but in the colonies as well. In both instances "others" were required to conform to "civilizing" dominant practices.

I am indebted to the excellent analysis of this dynamic in the colonial context presented by M. Jacqui Alexander in "Redrafting Morality; The Postcolonial State and the Sexual Offenses Bill of Trinidad and Tobago," in *Third World Women and The Politics of Feminism*, ed. Chandra Talpade Mohanty, Ann Russo, and Lourdes Torres, (Bloomington: Indiana University Press, 1991), 133–52. In a lecture at Temple University (Philadelphia, PA: April 30, 1992), Homi Bhabha also helped clarify for me this connection between colonialism and liberalism.

On the relationship between Jewish and postcolonial discourse see Jonathan Boyarin, *Storm from Paradise: The Politics of Jewish Memory* (Minneapolis: University of Minnesota Press, 1992).

29. Here the law of Moses seems to refer to rabbinic practices. See Schwarz-fuchs, *Napoleon*, 64–87.

30. Chazan and Raphael, *Modern Jewish History*, 19.

31. Ibid., 20.

32. Ibid.

33. Chazan and Raphael, *Modern Jewish History*, 14. See also Schwarzfuchs, *Napoleon*, 69–71.

34. The standard translation of these transactions from the French were done in London in 1807 by F. D. Kirwan. This translation is in both the Mendes-Flohr and Reinharz and the Chazan and Raphael collections. M. Diogene Tama, *Transactions of the Parisian Sanhedrin or Acts of the Assembly of Israelitish Deputies of France and Italy*, trans. F. D. Kirwan (London: C. Taylor, 1807). In this translation, this reference is to a Jewish woman in the singular, "the Jewess." For an account of various uses of this term and the problematics of its usage, see A. J. Levine "A Jewess, More and/or Less, " in *Judaism Since Gender*, Miriam Peskowitz and Laura Levitt, ed. (New York: Routledge, 1997). It is striking that in Levine's essay Jewesses often occupy border positions not unlike that in this case, where the issue is "intermarriage."

35. This is where the Jewish experience differs most radically from the experience of the colonial subjects Alexander writes about. At issue are constructions of racial differences and their relation to accumulation of wealth. As Alexander explains, in the colonial Caribbean, "conjugal marriage was actively encouraged among slaves but was actively discouraged between white men and colored women because it interrupted the accumulation of private property and wealth by the white father and his 'natural' heirs. According to the planter class, 'free coloreds were acquiring property and wealth by inheriting land from their natural white fathers,' so active measures were put in place to discourage it" (134). Up until the late nineteenth-century, Jewish difference was not understood as "racial" in this sense. Given this, it was considered possible for Jews to intermarry into the dominant culture. See Alexander, "Redrafting Morality."

36. Chazan and Raphael, *Modern Jewish History*, 21.

37. Ibid.

38. Again, on these tensions between rabbis and philosophers among those assembled, see Schwarzfuchs, *Napoleon*, 64–87.

39. This open embrace of Jews, the dream of assimilation, was to be superseded in the twentieth century by a much more virulent ideology of racial antisemitism, which no longer understood this to be possible. For more on these later developments in France, see Hyman, *From Dreyfus to Vichy*.

40. Carole Pateman, *The Sexual Contract* (Stanford, CA: Stanford University Press, 1988).

Chapter Four

1. Carole Pateman, *The Sexual Contract* (Stanford, CA: Stanford University Press, 1988). In retelling the conjectural history of the social contract in terms of "the freedom won by sons who cast off their natural subjection to their fathers and replace paternal rule by civil government" (2), she goes on to describe this masculine exchange of power in terms of how these same sons also gain sexual rights:

   > The sons overturn paternal rule not merely to gain their liberty but to secure women for themselves. Their success in this endeavor is chronicled in the story of the sexual contract. The original pact is a sexual as well as a social contract: it is sexual in the sense of patriarchal—that is, the contract establishes men's political right over women—and also sexual in the sense of establishing orderly access by men to women's bodies. . . . Contract is far from being opposed to patriarchy; contract is the means through which modern patriarchy is constituted. (2)

   For more on the question of contract as a form of patriarchy, see Pateman, *Sexual Contract,* chapter 2, "Patriarchal Confusions," 19–38.

2. Although there are contemporary Jewish feminists who offer different approaches to these questions—secular Jewish feminists (such as those I discuss in chapters 9 and 10)—Jewish feminists working out of religious Jewish communities and the study of Judaism continue to define liberalism and rabbinic Judaism as the two main poles within their efforts to reimagine a feminist Judaism. See, for example, my reading of Judith Plaskow's work in chapter 6, this volume.

3. Pateman, *Sexual Contract,* chapter 6, "Feminism and the Marriage Contract," 154–88.

4. On the gains of Jewish women within and pushing against the rigid boundaries of liberal inclusion see Paula Hyman, *Gender and Assimilation in Modern Jewish History: The Roles and Representation of Women* (Seattle: University of Washington Press, 1995); Beth Wenger, "Jewish Women and Voluntarism: Beyond the Myth of Enablers," *American Jewish History* 79.1(Autumn 1989); 16–36; Linda Gordon Kuzmack, *Women's Cause, The Jewish Woman's Movement in England and the United States, 1881–1933* (Columbus: Ohio State University Press, 1990); Marion Kaplan, *The Making of the Jewish Middle Classes: Women, Family, and Identity in Imperial Germany* (New York: Oxford University Press, 1991), and *The Jewish Feminist Movement in Germany: The Campaigns of the Jüdisher Frauenbund, 1904–1938* (Westport, CT: Greenwood, 1979).

   For a critical assessment of the limitations and possibilities the liberalism of the French Revolution posed for women more generally, see Joan Landes, *Women and the Public Sphere in the Age of the French Revolution* (Ithaca: Cornell University Press, 1988); Madelyn Gutwirth, *The Twilight of the God-*

desses: Women and Representation in the French Revolutionary Era (New Brunswick, NJ: Rutgers University Press, 1992); Christine Fauré, *Democracy Without Women: Feminism and the Rise of Liberal Individualism in France* (Bloomington: Indiana University Press, 1991); Sami I. Spencer, ed., *French Women and the Age of Enlightenment* (Bloomington: Indiana University Press, 1984); Nancy K. Miller, *French Dressing: Women, Men and Ancien Régime Fiction* (New York: Routledge, 1995); Joan Scott, "Universalism and the History of Feminism," *Differences: A Journal of Feminist Cultural Studies* 7.1(1995); 1–14; Rachel M. Brownstein, *Tragic Muse: Rachel of the Comédie-Française* (Durham, NC: Duke University Press, 1995).

5. *The American Heritage Dictionary of the English Language*, 3d. ed., s.v. "consent."

6. John Locke's *Two Treatises of Government* was originally published in 1698. For a powerful feminist critique of Locke, see Linda J. Nicholson, *Gender and History: The Limits of Social Theory in the Age of the Family* (New York: Columbia University Press, 1986), especially chapter 5. See also Zillah Eisenstein, *The Radical Future of Liberal Feminism* (New York: Longman, 1981), especially chapter 3, "John Locke: Patriarchal Antipatriarchalism," 33–54.

7. This phrase comes from an advertising campaign run by the U.S. army following the war in Persian Gulf. I thank Janet Jakobsen for making me aware of this campaign.

8. Pateman, "Women and Consent," in *The Disorder of Women: Democracy, Feminism and Political Theory* (Stanford, CA: Stanford University Press, 1989) 71.

9. Ibid. See also Carole Pateman, *The Problem of Political Obligation, A Critique of Liberal Theory* (Berkeley: University of California Press, 1979).

10. Pateman, *The Disorder of Women*, 71.

11. Pateman, *Sexual Contract*, 159.

12. These infringements include not only rape but also assault. For an excellent analysis of the problem of wife-beating see, Anna Clark, "Humanity or Justice? Wifebeating and the Law in the Eighteenth and Nineteenth Centuries," in *Regulating Womanhood: Historical Essays on Marriage, Motherhood and Sexuality*, ed. Carol Smart (New York: Routledge, 1992), 197–206.

13. "Equal protection" in the United States refers to the fourteenth amendment of the U.S. constitution. The argument here is that married women are not equally protected from sexual assault. See "To Have and To Hold: The Marital Rape Exemption and the Fourteenth Ammedment," *Harvard Law Review* 99.6(April 1986): 1255–73; and Robin West, "Equality Theory, Marital Rape, and the Promise of the Fourteenth Amendment," *Florida Law Review* 42.1(January 1990); 45–79.

14. Pateman, *Sexual Contract*, 154.

15. The text referred to here is Shouler's 1874, *A Treatise on the Law of the Domestic Relations* as cited by Pateman, *Sexual Contract*, 155.

16. "If very large amounts of property are involved in a marriage today, a contract will sometimes be drawn up that resembles much older documents, common when marriage was a matter for fathers of families and not free choice of two individuals," Pateman, *Sexual Contract* (164). These documents, prenuptial agreements in the present, do in fact resemble the ketubbah text in their enumeration of property and, in the case of divorce, of who gets what. The point is that having a document in the liberal arrangement is quite rare. The contract is generally unwritten, in sharp contrast to the ketubbah. On this point see Pateman, *Sexual Contract*, 163–164.

17. The submission in this case is to the institution of marriage. Within the terms of the institution, a wife submits to her husband. The language of consent obscures this power differential.

18. Pateman, *Sexual Contract*, 164.

19. See Adrienne Rich, "Compulsory Heterosexuality and Lesbian Existence," in *Blood, Bread, and Poetry: Selected Prose 1979–1985* (New York: Norton) 23–75. For another reading of the compulsory nature of this contract, see Teresa de Lauretis's notion of the "heterosexual contract," which she develops in *Technologies of Gender: Essays on Theory, Film, and Fiction* (Bloomington: Indiana University Press, 1987). The "heterosexual contract" is especially useful in that it makes clear the problematics of contract. For an excellent use of this term in the context of a critique of modern political theory, see Christine Di Stefano, *Configurations of Masculinity, A Feminist Perspective on Modern Political Theory* (Ithaca: Cornell University Press, 1991). These works and this argument are all in keeping with recent efforts to deny state recognition of gay and lesbian marriages in the United States.

20. Here I have in mind the tremendous resistance to gay and lesbian marriages, especially in the United States. For a powerful discussion of the legal connections made between gay and lesbian sexualities and marital rape in a postcolonial context, see M. Jacqui Alexander, "Redrafting Morality; The Postcolonial State and the Sexual Offenses Bill of Trinidad and Tobago," in *Third World Women and the Politics of Feminism*, ed. Chandra Talpade Mohanty, Ann Russo, and Lourde Torres (Bloomington: Indiana Univeristy Press, 1991), 133–52. On this question Alexander writes, "The potentialities of women's agency get collapsed into 'wives' and ultimately into a subordinated position. The importance, therefore of examining both elements of the discourse on morality (rape and marriage and lesbian sex) was to demonstrate the complex way in which women's agency is being recast when morality is predicated on women as 'wives.' It is only in their capacity as 'wives' that women can make certain claims of the state. Nonwives, prostitutes, lesbians can make no such claims" (147).

21. Coverture is ironically a rather revealing term. It is derived from the term "covert." It is defined first as "the state of being concealed; disguised" and only then as "the status of a married woman under common law." Under the definition for "covert," the legal entry reads: "Being married and there-

fore protected by one's husband." Protection is therefore offered as a form of disguised or concealment. *American Heritage Dictionary of the English Language*, 3d ed., s.v. "coverture."

22. Pateman, *Sexual Contract*, 155–56.
23. See discussion of marital rape laws below. For a more elaborate discussion, see chapter 2 of Laura Levitt, "Reconfiguring Home: Jewish Feminist Identity/ies," Ph.D. diss., Emory University, Atlanta, GA, 1993.
24. For more on the specific problems posed by French law, see Fauré, *Democracy Without Women*.
25. *American Heritage Dictionary*, 3d ed., s.v. "rape."
26. Susan Estrich, *Real Rape: How the Legal System Victimizes Women* (Cambridge: Harvard University Press, 1987), 8.
27. Ibid., 5.
28. Pateman, *The Disorder of Women*, 79. For more on this trope of women making false accusations or recounting their testimony, see Helena Michie, "The Greatest Story (N)Ever Told: The Spectacle of Recantation," in *Tatoo, Torture, Mutilation, and Adornment: The Denaturalization of the Body in Culture and Text*, ed. Frances E. Mascia-Lees and Patricia Sharpe (Albany: State University of New York Press, 1992), 10–29.
29. Chances are women are revictimized by the legal system. In *Real Rape*, Estrich argues that the United States legal system has no way of dealing with cases of acquaintance rape. Moreover, she shows how this same legal system does little to address cases of what she calls "real rape," cases in which a woman is sexually assaulted by a stranger.
30. For more on this legislation, see Levitt, "Reconfiguring Home," chapter 2.
31. On the problem of acquaintance rape, see Susan Estrich, *Real Rape*. See also Peggy Reeves Sanday, *A Woman Scorned: Acquaintance Rape on Trial* (New York: Doubleday, 1996).
32. This is still true in most places in the United States as well as elsewhere in the world. On this problem in Great Britain, Australia, New Zealand, and Canada as well as the United States, see Pateman, "Women and Consent." For a complete analysis of the marital rape exemption in the United States and each of its individual states, see Diana E.H. Russell, *Rape in Marriage* (Bloomington: Indiana University Press, 1990). This is also a problem in terms of cases of various kinds of domestic abuse as well.
33. This appears to be a mistake in the original text, since Hale wrote this exemption in 1778, M. Hale, *The History of the Pleas of the Crown 629*, ed. S. Emlyn (1778). See "To Have and To Hold," 1256, n.6.
34. "To Have and to Hold," 1255–56.
35. "To Have and to Hold," 1255. See also Helena Michie, "The Greatest Story."

Chapter Five

1. These conversations took place during the 1982–83 academic year in Jerusalem. I thank Moshe Re'em for his ongoing critical engagement with

me on this and many other issues. For an example of Borowitz's critical reading and appropriation of modern Jewish thought, see Eugene Borowitz, *Choices in Modern Jewish Thought: A Partisan Guide*, 2d ed. (West Orange, NJ: Behrman House, 1995). For a more general account of his position, see Eugene Borowitz, *Liberal Judaism* (New York: Union of American Hebrew Congregations, 1984).

2. On the centrality of Borowitz's position in this movement, see Eugene Borowitz, *Reform Judaism Today*, vols. 1–3 (New York: Behrman House, 1978).

3. During the 1984–85 academic year, I was a graduate student at Hebrew Union College–Jewish Institute of Religion in New York City. During that year I worked extensively with Eugene Borowitz. At that time he helped me move from a vision of Jewishness as only rabbinic to a liberal Jewish position. I am very much indebted to him for this even now having already let go of this vision of my own Jewishness.

4. Eugene Borowitz, "When is It Moral to Have Intercourse?" in *Exploring Jewish Ethics: Papers on Covenant Responsibility* (Detroit: Wayne State University Press, 1990), 256.

5. On the internalization of liberal values among early liberal theologians, especially Reform Jews, see Israel Jacobson, "A Dedication Address," "The Association for the Reform of Judaism," and Abraham Geiger, "Prefaces to the Frankfort Prayerbook," in *Modern Jewish History, A Source Reader*, Robert Chazan and Marc Lee Raphael, ed. (New York: Schocken, 1969), 45–62. See also, "IV Emerging Patterns of Religious Adjustment: Reform, Conservative and Neo-Orthodox" of *The Jew in the Modern World: A Documentary History*, Paul R. Mendes-Flohr and Jehuda Reinharz, ed. (New York: Oxford, 1980), 145–81; and Michael Meyer, *The Origins of the Modern Jew, Jewish Identity and European Culture in Germany, 1749–1824* (Detroit: Wayne State University Press, 1979).

6. In this chapter I offer a reading of Eugene Borowitz's *Renewing the Covenant, A Theology for the Postmodern Jew* (Philadelphia: Jewish Publication Society, 1991). In chapter 6 I offer a similar reading of Judith Plaskow's *Standing Again at Sinai, Judaism From a Feminist Perspective* (San Francisco: HarperCollins, 1990). As I will argue, Borowitz explicitly advocates an overtly heterosexual contract, while Plaskow argues for a more inclusive contract. Despite the centrality of the marriage contract, even when these authors present readings of rabbinic sources, neither ever refers explicitly to the terms of the ketubbah. In both, the sexual contract is normative.

7. Borowitz, "On Homosexuality," 277. Here Borowitz highlights certain aspects of the rabbinic tradition and not others. What the rabbis actually believed is not the issue; what is important is how Borowitz claims traditional authority for his own positions. For a reading of Borowitz and other contemporary Jewish theologians on issues of sexuality see David Biale,

"Eros and the Jews," *Tikkun* 7.5 (Sept/Oct 1992); 49–52, 78–79. Biale's position is that "in a kind of modern apology, writers such as the Orthodox Rabbi Norman Lamm, the Conservative Rabbi Robert Gordis, and the Reform Rabbi Eugene Borowitz all lay aside their other differences to agree that the Jewish tradition has a healthier attitude towards the erotic than does Christianity. No neurosis is to be found here, but rather an affirmation of the 'joy of sex' within the framework of traditional marriage. . . . Thus even though these theologians claim to represent the historical Jewish tradition, they have reframed it according to a singular American ethos, and as such, their writing is an attempt to negotiate the assimilation of Judaism to American culture: the Jews have the most authentically "American" version of sexuality" (49). This is not unlike my reading of the centrality of "proper" sexuality in the negotiations for Jewish emancipation. What is striking about Biale's piece is the absence of Jewish feminist voices in his discussion. Despite the fact that Judith Plaskow, as we shall soon see, devotes a large section of her *Standing Again at Sinai* to the issue of sexuality, she is neither cited nor is her position addressed.

8. Martin Buber, *I and Thou* (New York: Charles Scribner and Sons, 1958). The book first appeared in German in 1923 and in English in 1937.

9. Borowitz, *Renewing the Covenant*, 2. Again, he never refers to this relationship in terms of a ketubbah in this text.

10. Ibid. What is striking is that, despite the centrality of covenant in Borowitz's work, the nature of the covenant with Abraham—the ritual act of circumcision—is never addressed. Instead, the *brit*, the Hebrew covenant, is separated from this enactment. Borowitz translates the covenant with Abraham into the language of loving relationships and, more specifically, into the language of heterosexual marriage. For a more extensive analysis of this problem, see Laura Levitt "Reconfiguring Home: Jewish Feminist Identity/ies," Ph.D. diss., Emory Univeristy, Atlanta, GA, 1993, chapter 3.

11. See, for example, the promise God made to Abraham in *Genesis* 17 as a result of circumcision: "Behold, my covenant is with you, and you shall be a father of a multitude of nations. . . . I will make you exceedingly fruitful; and I will make nations of you, and kings shall come forth from you. And I will establish my covenant between me and you and your descendants after you throughout their generations for an everlasting covenant" (*Genesis* 17:4–7). Note the promise is made solely to Abraham's male descendants. *The New Oxford Annotated Bible, The Holy Bible., Revised Standard Version Containing the Old and New Testaments*, ed. Herbert G. May and Bruce M. Metzger (New York: Oxford University Press, 1973), 19. See also Gerda Lerner, *The Creation of Patriarchy* (New York: Oxford, 1987). As Lerner explains:

> What is more logical and appropriate than to use as the leading symbol of the covenant the organ which produces this "seed" and

which "plants" it in the female womb? Nothing could better serve
to impress man with the vulnerability of this organ and with his
dependence on God for his fertility (immortality). The offering of no
other part of the body could have sent so vivid and descriptive a
message to man of the connection between his reproductive capacity and the grace of God. Since Abraham and the men of his house-
hold underwent the rite of circumcision, as adults, the act itself,
which must have been painful, bespoke their trust and faith in God
and their submission to His will. (192)

For more on these issues, see Levitt, "Reconfiguring Home," chapter 3.

12. As cited by Carole Pateman, *Sexual Contract* (Stanford, CA: Stanford University Press, 1988), 155.

13. When I was a student at HUC–JIR in New York, I wrote a paper for
Borowitz on this dynamic, but not in terms of his own work. At that time
I had not made these connections to Borowitz's own work. Laura Levitt,
"To Be Worthy of God's Love: Sin and Atonement in Franz Rosenzweig's
The Star of Redemption," unpublished manuscript, February 1985. At the
end of that paper I call for rethinking the human-divine relationship in
nonhierarchical terms, challenging the abusiveness of the metaphor of the
lover and the beloved in Rosenzweig's text. A mark of how distant this
argument was for me from Borowitz's own work is the fact that I made it
in relation to Rosenzweig and not in relation to Buber. In the final sentence
of that paper I ask: "Need we hit ourselves to be worthy of love?" I thank
Susan E. Shapiro for rereading this paper with me and helping me see the
connections between that early argument and my critique of Borowitz's
covenantal theology.

14. Pateman, *Sexual Contract*, 15.

15. Ibid., 159.

16. Ibid., 188

17. Ibid., 8.

18. Borowitz, *Renewing the Covenant*, 31.

19. This image of submission or sacrifice is especially disturbing in a theological interpretation of the Holocaust, because it denies the human horror
experienced by those who were tortured and killed. This problem is
inscribed in the term "Holocaust." It associates the mass destruction of
European Jewry with ritual conflagrations, or burnt offerings. The shift in
terminology from "Holocaust" to the Hebrew term "Shoah" is, in part a
response to this problem. I thank Susan E. Shapiro for originally suggesting these connections to me. See also the discussion of these terms in James
Young, *Writing and Rewriting the Holocaust: Narrative and the Consequences of Interpretation* (Bloomington: Indiana University Press, 1988).

20. Borowitz, "When is It Moral to Have Intercourse?" 256.

21. Although I will move between the terms "queer" and "gay and lesbian"
throughout this and the following chapter, when possible I try to use the
term "queer" in the ways it has been used in recent works in queer theory.

See, for example, Judith Butler, ed., "More Gender Trouble: Feminism Meets Queer Theory," a special double issue of *Differences: A Journal of Feminist Cultural Studies* 6.2,3 (Summer–Fall 1994). I thank Claudia Schippert for pushing me on this question.

22. Borowitz, "Reading the Jewish Tradition on Marital Sexuality," in *Exploring Jewish Ethics*, 258–69.

23. For Ellen Umansky's use of a similar strategy, see Ellen Umansky's classic essay "The Liberal Jew and Sex," *Response* 10:4, 15:4 (Winter 1976–77), 71–74 (Winter 1976–77). Even in her more recent work, Umansky builds this model, specifically as laid out in Borowitz's *Choosing a Sex Ethic, A Jewish Inquiry* (New York: Schocken, 1969).

24. Borowitz, "When is It Moral to Have Intercourse?" 246. Borowitz continues this argument by noting that his position is modeled on a logic similar to that of the rabbis. His major concern here is not different sexualities but, rather, premarital intercourse; nevertheless, the argument is the same. His hierarchical assessment of different approaches to this issue is attributed to the rabbis. He notes:

> I am thinking of something like the rabbis' multileveled judgement of what constitutes sexual misbehavior. Some acts, like intercourse with one's betrothed, are forbidden, but once committed, the couple marries without penalty or official stigma. Some acts, like adultery, are within human jurisdiction to punish, but others, like incest, are left to God's own justice. Other acts, like rape or seduction, are matters of community concern, while still others, such as intercourse between consenting unmarried adults, are left to the domain of conscience. The Rabbis, though they sought to serve God in their legal and moral teaching, accepted a multiplicity of values in the variety of human behavior they knew people faced. This commends itself to me as a model for working out an approach to premarital intercourse that is not overly simplistic. (246)

Despite his use of the Rabbis to justify his hierarchical approach to difference, no specific texts are ever cited. For a more detailed account of the problems with this approach see Levitt, "Reconfiguring Home," chapter 3.

25. See Wayne Booth, *Critical Understanding, The Powers and Limits of Pluralism* (Chicago: University of Chicago Press, 1979). I thank Susan E. Shapiro for bringing this text to my attention. As Booth argues, this kind of position is not so much a form of liberal pluralism but a comprehensive monism.

26. In Borowitz, *Exploring Jewish Ethics*, 270–86. This essay is a continuation of his earlier writing on sexuality. By offering a unified hierarchical position he presumes that he is open to positions that are different from his own. In a sense, he tolerates them as inferior. See for example his essay, "When is It Moral to Have Intercourse? A Personal Summary," in *Exploring Jewish Ethics*, 244–57. The quotation from Borowitz that opens this chapter was taken from this particular essay.

27. Given this, it is not clear why Borowitz is not more adamant in denying the ordination of single Jewish men and women. If they are supposed to be role models, then it would follow that being single should prohibit one from being ordained. I thank Ellen Umansky for reminding me of this problem. It is part of her ongoing argument with Borowitz about why it is that he singles out gay, lesbian, and bisexual Jews for exclusion from ordination. Telephone conversation with Ellen Umansky, July 1992.

28. Although Borowitz attempts to position himself as open to change, this does not appear likely:

> In sum, I find our community continues to reflect a Covenantal concern, theological and prudential, in denying the equivalence of the faithful homosexual Jewish family to its heterosexual counterpart. I hasten to add that this is my present understanding of the case. Our community has shown its capacity to change its standards with regard to sexual standards, as the general acceptance of certain kinds of nonmarital intercourse indicates. Perhaps it will do the same with regard to homosexuality and the homosexual family. But I do not now see any such significant shift of attitude under way with regard to homosexuality. ("On Homosexuality," 280)

Even in the best-case scenario, lesbian and gay families would be tolerated only under certain prescribed conditions. The best they can hope for is to be treated like those who participate in "certain kinds of nonmarital intercourse." This does not say that they can be rabbis. Moreover, Borowitz ends this discussion by not taking full responsibility for his position. He argues that he is compelled to follow the attitudes of the Jewish community although not absolutely but this is exactly what he does. His text continues:

> Again as a liberal Jew I do not feel bound by what the Jewish community is saying on this issue, as best I understand it. But as one who shares the community's covenant, I give its attitude very serious consideration. (280)

29. This is a reference to the U.S. military's position on gay and lesbians serving their country in the armed forces.

30. This is the policy of the Reconstructionist Rabbinical College, as Borowitz notes ("On Homosexuality," 283). What is most telling about this entire essay is the fact that he does not really know the policy of Hebrew Union College–Jewish Institute of Religion. As he notes, in his correction, HUC–JIR no longer screens gay and lesbian candidates from admission. Nor does it deny them ordination. He goes on to make clear that he supports the reinstitution of these policies:

> My view of our Jewish religious obligations in this area requires me to dissent from the College's present policy, one I would characterize as passive permissiveness. I would instead urge the Conference [The Central Conference of American Rabbis, CCAR] to use its good office with the College to get it to return to its earlier practice as I and others understood and experienced it. (284)

31. This is itself a strange statement, because it says that it is all right, once ordained, for a rabbi to be gay or lesbian; they just cannot be "out" at the college, so that Borowitz himself will not have to condone their lifestyle. I thank Aaron Taub for pointing out this contradiction.

32. When compared with his final comments on the subject where he calls for the reinstitution of blatantly discriminatory policies, this is, in fact, the best he can do. Nevertheless, I find this position both disrespectful and paternalistic. Even Borowitz's paternalism and good will are offered indirectly in the name of other students and not those with institutional power.

33. This appeal to biology or race is especially striking, because Borowitz uses the Holocaust as a justification. This is for many a counterintuitive move since it was precisely arguments that pinned Jewish identity to notions of biology and race that were used to justify genocide. He notes, for example, that, "the imperiled situation of the Jewish community as a minority makes family *unity* a particularly important instrument of our survival." ("On Homosexuality," 279) (my emphasis).

Chapter Six

1. Judith Plaskow, *Standing Again at Sinai: Judaism From a Feminist Perspective* (San Francisco: HarperCollins, 1990). On the significance of Plaskow's work, see Laura Levitt, "Review Essay: '*Standing Again at Sinai: Judaism from a Feminist Perspective*,'" *Religious Studies Review* 20.1 (January 1994): 16–20.

2. Returning to Sinai, Plaskow asks the question, "Where were Jewish women?"

   Entry into the covenant at Sinai is the root experience of Judaism, the central event that established the Jewish people. Given the importance of this event, there can be no verse in the Torah more disturbing to the feminist than Moses's warning to his people in Exodus 19:15, "Be ready for the third day; do not go near a woman." For here, at the very moment that the Jewish people stands at Sinai ready to receive the covenant—not now the covenant with individual patriarchs but with the people as a whole—at the very moment when Israel stands trembling waiting for God's presence to descend upon the mountain, Moses addresses the community only as men. The specific issue at stake is ritual impurity: An emission of semen renders both the man and his female partner temporarily unfit to approach the sacred (Lev. 15:16–18). (25)

3. Miriam Peskowitz, "Engendering Jewish Religious History," in *Judaism Since Gender*, ed. Miriam Peskowitz and Laura Levitt (New York: Routledge, 1997).

4. Carole Pateman, *The Sexual Contract* (Stanford, CA: Stanford University Press, 1988), 39.

5. Wayne Booth, *Critical Understanding, The Power and Limits of Pluralism* (Chicago: University of Chicago Press, 1979). In Plaskow's text, each of the

major aspects of her theology—God, Torah, and Israel—are organized around the same pattern of inclusion.

6. In this way she goes on to explain that monotheism "may be thought of in terms of the same part/whole analogy that I used to characterize differences within community. Just as the subgroups within a community are all part of a larger unity, so any individual image of God is part of the divine totality that in its totality embraces the diversity of an infinite community" (151).

7. My argument here is very similar to that presented by Ellen Umansky. See Ellen Umansky, "Review of *Standing Again at Sinai: Judaism From A Feminist Perspective,*" *Sh'ma, a journal of Jewish responsibility* 20/390 (March 16, 1990): 78–79. Umansky argues that if Plaskow truly intends to argue for pluralism, her monotheism is a problem:

   > While she identifies her defense of monotheism not as a boundary issue but as one that maintains the "vision of a unity that embraces diversity," it seems to me that a feminist Judaism freed from boundaries might make an equally strong case for the worship of many deities, insisting, for example, that polytheism reflects the vibrant diversity of creation. (78)

   Plaskow does not fully account for this problem. Her inclusive liberal monotheism denies precisely the kinds of diversity Umansky suggests exist among Jewish feminists. "If we as feminists truly respect one another as unique, why insist on an underlying unity?" (78).

8. Audre Lorde, "Uses of the Erotic: The Erotic as Power," *Sister Outsider* (Trumansburg, NY: Crossing Press, 1984), 53–59.

9. Plaskow, *Standing Again at Sinai,* 196.

10. On this ambivalence, see Plaskow, *Standing Again at Sinai,* 185–91.

11. Judith Plaskow, "Towards a New Theology of Sexuality," in *Twice Blessed: On Being Lesbian, Gay, and Jewish,* ed. Christie Balka and Andy Rose (Boston: Beacon Press, 1989), 141.

12. Ibid., 142. See also Ezekiel 16:62–63.

13. Plaskow, *Standing Again at Sinai,* 157.

14. Plaskow, "Towards a New Theology of Sexuality," 144.

15. In this account, like Borowitz, Plaskow does not directly refer to the ketubbah.

16. Plaskow, "Towards a New Theology of Sexuality," 144.

17. Ibid., 145.

18. Ibid.

19. Ibid.

20. Ibid., 149.

21. Ibid.

22. Ibid.

23. Ibid., 149–50.

24. Lorde, "Uses of the Erotic," 58.

25. Plaskow, "Towards a New Theology of Sexuality," 150.

26. Ibid.
27. Ibid.
28. Ibid., 151.
29. Lorde, "Uses of the Erotic," 59.
30. It is interesting to note that, using a radically different framework, conservative Jewish ethicist David Novak also writes about the power of the erotic and the problem of "turning away." See David Novak, *Jewish Social Ethics* (New York: Oxford University Press, 1992). In his chapter, "Sex, Society and God in Judaism," Novak writes about sexual love:

> It is mistaken, it seems to me, to consider the essence of sexual love to be pleasure, although it is certainly a *sine qua non* of it, for in all other bodily pleasures, such as eating, drinking, bathing, we seek a heightened sense of awareness of our bodies. Our pleasure is essentially a taking-in, that is, our desire is to make our world around us an extension of our own bodies. In heterosexual love, on the other hand, we seek ecstacy, which comes from two Greek words, *ex histemi* meaning "to stand out." In other words, our sexuality intends transcendence. Eros seeks spirit. It seems that in true eros we seek to *go beyond our bodies through them.* For a moment we experience a going beyond the body, which is ordinarily the limit of the soul. Nevertheless, sexual love in itself lasts only for a moment before the body, the ever-present finite, mortal vessel, claims the soul once again. (96–97)

Unlike Audre Lorde who offers an embodied *eros*, in Novak's account eros flees the body. It strikes me that this particularly narrow reading of orgasm begs the question of whose orgasm is being talked about. His notion of eros is particularly phallic, especially when read in conjunction with Lorde's lesbian feminist account.

To back up his position, Novak cites a rabbinic narrative that may be more to Lorde's point. It suggests that in turning away from one another in an erotic encounter, God is no longer present:

> David said before God, "My father Jesse did not intend to sire me, but intended only his own pleasure. You know that this is so because after the parents satisfied themselves, *he turned his face away and she turned her face away* and You joined the drops." (Vayiqra Rabbah 14.5, ed. Margoles, 2:308) (97) (my emphasis)

A final powerful connection in this regard is Buber's notion of "God turning his [sic] face away" from Israel. See my analysis of this concept as it appears in Borowitz's *Renewing the Covenant* in chapter 5.

31. Lorde, "Uses of the Erotic," 59.
32. Ibid., 57.
33. Ibid., 58.
34. Lorde herself writes about these connections in Audre Lorde, "Age, Race, Class, and Sex: Women Redefining Difference," in *Out There: Marginalization and Contemporary Cultures*, ed. Russell Ferguson, Martha Gever,

Trinh T. Minh-ha, and Cornel West (Cambridge: MIT Press, 1990), 281–88.

Lorde writes:

> Black women and white women are not the same. For example, it is easy for Black women to be used by the power structure against Black men, not because they are men, but because they are Black. Therefore, for Black women, it is necessary at all times to separate the needs of the oppressor from our own legitimate conflicts within our communities. This same problem does not exist for white women. Black women and men have shared racist oppression and still share it, although in different ways. Out of that shared oppression we have developed joint defenses and joint vulnerabilities to each other that are not duplicated in the white community, with the exception of the relationship between Jewish women and Jewish men. (284)

In a panel on cultural appropriation sponsored by the Women's Section of the American Academy of Religion (AAR), Kansas City, November 1991, Plaskow critically assessed her "appropriation" of Lorde's text. For this discussion see, "Special Section: Appropriation and Reciprocity," *Journal of Feminist Studies in Religion* 8:2 (Fall 1992): 91–122, especially 109–110.

Chapter Seven

1. Nancy K. Miller, "Dreaming, Dancing and the Changing Locations of Feminist Criticism, 1988," *Getting Personal: Feminist Occasions and Other Autobiographical Acts* (New York: Routledge, 1991), 72–100. In this essay Miller italicizes her own words and uses regular typeface to cite other people's texts. For the sake of clarity, when I cite Miller in this chapter and those that follow, I use regular typeface throughout. When Miller cites another text I use quotation marks to distinguish between her words and those of others.
2. Teresa de Lauretis, "Feminist Studies/Critical Studies: Issues, Terms, and Contexts," in *Feminist Studies/Critical Studies*, ed. Teresa de Lauretis (Bloomington: University of Indiana Press, 1986), 1–19.
3. For a more detailed account of this problem as posed by Miller, see Laura Levitt, "(The Problem with) Embraces," in *Judaism Since Gender*, Miriam Peskowitz and Laura Levitt, ed. (New York: Routledge, 1997). See chapter 1 for my reading of Pratt's essay as a kind of textual embrace.
4. de Lauretis, "Feminist Studies," 2.
5. de Lauretis claims that they raised questions about antisemitism "in the representation and definition of feminism" (7).
6. Evelyn Torton Beck, "The Politics of Jewish Invisibility," *NWSA Journal* 1.1 (1988): 93–102; 99.
7. Ibid, 99.
8. Ibid., 100–101.
9. Ibid., 100.

10. Ibid., 100–101, n. 21.

11. See also Nancy K. Miller, "Hadassah Arms," in *People of the Book: Thirty Scholars Reflect on Their Jewish Identity*, Jeffrey Rubin-Dorsky and Shelley Fisher Fishkin, ed. (Madison: University Of Wisconsin Press, 1996), 161. For another account of Miller's response to this incident, see my discussion of Miller's work in chapter 8.

12. Miller, *Dreaming*, 96.

13. "Exhortation-speech or discourse intended to advise, incite, or encourage." *American Heritage Dictionary*, 3d ed. s.v. "exhortation."

14. Miller, "Dreaming," 96.

15. Ibid.

16. Ibid.

17. Ibid.

18. These too are presented parenthetically. See Miller, "Dreaming," 95.

19. Ibid., 96.

20. Jenny Bourne, "Homelands of the Mind: Jewish Feminism and Identity Politics," *Race and Class* 29.1 (Summer 1987); 1–24.

21. By appealing to Bourne, Miller returns to her position in "Whose Dream?" She writes: "Jenny Bourne provides an astringent analysis of these clotted issues" (100). On the problematics of citing Bourne in this context see Laura Levitt, "Rethinking Jewish Feminist Identity/ies: What Difference Can Feminist Theory Make?" in *Interpreting Judaism in a Postmodern Era*, ed. Steven Kepnes (New York: NYU Press, 1996), 361–377.

22. Miller, "Dreaming," 96.

23. These are significant questions that I will not be able to fully address in this chapter. In what follows I suggest that the work of self-consciousness offers a radical alternative to liberal opposition. In chapter 9 I return to issues of American Jewish whiteness, especially in the context of racially charged Atlanta, through a reading of Melanie Kaye/Kantrowitz's poem "Notes of an Immigrant Daughter, Atlanta." For an early piece of my next project on issues of Jews and race, see Laura Levitt, "Race, Gender and Jewish Excess: Rereading Jewish Cinematic Difference," Conference paper, The American Academy of Religion, Philadelphia, November 1995.

24. de Lauretis, "Feminist Studies," 7.

25. Ibid.

26. Ibid., 8.

27. Ibid.

28. Ibid., 7.

29. Ibid.

30. Ibid.

31. Ibid., 9.

32. Elly Bulkin, Minnie Bruce Pratt and Barbara Smith, *Yours in Struggle: Three Feminist Perspectives on Anti-Semitism and Racism* (Brooklyn, NY: Long Haul Press, 1984).

33. de Lauretis, "Feminist Studies," 9.

34. Bulkin, Pratt, and Smith, *Yours in Struggle*, 106.

35. de Lauretis, "Feminist Studies,"14.

36. Evelyn Torton Beck, ed., *Nice Jewish Girls: A Lesbian Anthology*, (Trumansburg, New York: Crossing Press, 1982). See de Lauretis, "Feminist Studies," 19, n. 16.

37. de Lauretis, "Feminist Studies," 18.

38. On this point, see Bulkin's note, which cites the context of the full statement. It reads as follows, "Cherríe Moraga, Julia Perez, Barbara Smith, Beverly Smith, 'Racism and Anti-Semitism" (letter), *Gay Community News*, March 7, 1981, 4. See also Rosario Morales' article on the workshop, 'Double Allegiance: Jewish Women and Women of Color,' *A Working Conference on Women and Racism: New England Women's Studies Association Newsletter* (May 1981)." Bulkin, Pratt, and Smith, *Yours in Struggle*, 216, n. 29.

39. Bulkin, Pratt, and Smith, *Yours in Struggle*, 150.

40. Ibid.

41. de Lauretis, "Feminist Studies," 18.

42. Ibid.

43. Zora Neal Hurston, *Their Eyes Were Watching God* (Chicago: University Of Illinois Press, 1978), as quoted in Miller, "Dreaming," 77.

44. Miller, "Dreaming," 77.

45. In a different reading of Hurston and Their Eyes Were Watching God, Andrew Lakritiz examines a moment of self-consciousness, the narrator's painful coming to consciousness about her blackness: "In part Janie's reason for returning to Eatonville, like Hurston's own reasons for returning to her village, is to tell that story, a story about the ambiguity of an individual's sense of social and racial identity poised right at the very origins of her emerging self-consciousness. She comes to know who she is at the very moment when she recognizes that she had been mistaken or ignorant." Andrew Lakritiz, "Identification and Difference: Structures of Privilege in Cultural Criticism," in *Who Can Speak? Authority and Critical Identity*, ed. Judith Roof and Robyn Wiegman (Urbana and Chicago: University of Illinois Press, 1995), 3–29; 21.

46. For a similar critique of Miller, see Dympna Callaghan's reading of the introduction to *Getting Personal* in "The Vicar and Virago: Feminism and the Problem of Identity," in Roof and Wiegman, *Who Can Speak?*

Chapter Eight

1. Nancy K. Miller, "Dreaming, Dancing, and the Changing Locations of Feminist Criticism, 1988," in *Getting Personal: Feminist Occasions and Other Autobiographical Acts* (New York: Routledge, 1991), 72–100. Miller who teaches literature and feminist theory at Lehman College and the Graduate Center at the City University of New York

2. For a more complete account of how this works, see Laura Levitt, "(The Problem with) Embraces," in *Judaism Since Gender*, ed. Miriam Peskowitz and Laura Levitt, (New York: Routledge, 1997).

3. Biddy Martin and Chandra Mohanty, "Feminist Politics, What's Home Got to Do with It?" in *Feminist Studies/Critical Studies*, ed. Teresa de Lauretis (Bloomington: Indiana University Press, 1986), 191–212; Minnie Bruce Pratt, "Identity; Skin Blood Heart," in *Yours in Struggle: Three Feminist Perspectives on Anti-Semitism and Racism*, Elly Bulkin, Minnie Bruce Pratt and Barbara Smith, (Brooklyn, NY: Long Haul Press, 1984), 9–63.

4. Miller, "Dreaming," 90.

5. Ibid., 91.

6. Ibid.

7. Ibid., 92.

8. Ibid.

9. Ibid.

10. Pratt has written powerfully about this painful and disturbing experience, especially in her poetry. See Minnie Bruce Pratt, *Crimes Against Nature*, (Ithaca: Firebrand, 1990)

11. Miller, "Dreaming," 92.

12. Ibid.

13. Bulkin, Pratt, and Smith, *Yours in Struggle*, 57.

14. Miller, "Dreaming," 92.

15. When I first read this passage I thought they all embraced together, and only later did I begin to notice the singularity of this embrace. In the dream this reconciliation is presented in the singular and not the plural.

16. Miller, "Dreaming," 92–3.

17. Ibid.

18. Ibid.

19. At the beginning of her essay, "Feminist Studies/Critical Studies: Issues, Terms and Contexts," in *Feminist Studies/Critical Studies*, de Lauretis writes: "All the contributions to this volume are revised and/or expanded versions of papers presented at the conference, with the exception of the essays by Modleski, Moraga, and Martin and Mohanty. These contributors, however, were also invited to participate, and, but for Moraga, who was unable to attend due to prior commitments, did take part in the conference" (1).

20. Miller, "Dreaming," 72. As Miller explains, these occasions include, "the conference "Feminism and the Dream of a Plural Culture" (Queens College) and the colloquium at the School of Criticism and Theory (Dartmouth College), both held in 1988. In its final revised form here, however, the essay reflects my efforts to make the problems of a North American criticism meaningful (less local) to a European audience at two subsequent destinations: the first in Paris at a conference on "Cultural Translation" (November 1988); the second, for a new graduate program in Women's Studies at the University of Utrecht (November 1988)" (72).

21. Ibid., 76.

22. Actually her reading of their text alongside Pratt's is much closer to their strategy since here, in contrast to "Whose Dream?" Miller is much more focused. She addresses only two interrelated texts and allows her own voice to appear much more directly in her own text.

23. On this incident see Laura Levitt, "Rethinking Jewish Feminist Identity/ies: What Difference Can Feminist Theory Make?" in *Interpreting Judaism in a Postmodern Era*, Steven Kepnes, ed. (New York: NYU Press, 1996), 361–77. In the transcript from a discussion between Miller, Jane Gallop, and Marianne Hirsch, Miller writes about the process of writing "Dreaming, Dancing": "I was working on 'Dreaming, Dancing, and the Changing Locations of Feminist Criticism,' my piece on the conflicts within feminism, including the question of race. When I finished (and gave!) the piece 'on race'—let's just say it created more problems than it solved—I began to wonder whether there was any position from which a white middle-class feminist could say anything on the subject without sounding exactly like that. . . . The rhetorical predictability of it all. The political correctness. Just like 'men in feminism.' In which case it might be better not to say anything. I had tried to circumvent the problem by a kind of montage of quotations. That didn't work any better. So now I'm thinking: just do the work—the reading, the institutional politics—forget the rhetoric *about* doing it" (Gallop, Hirsch, Miller "Criticism," 364). Jane Gallop, Marianne Hirsch, Nancy K. Miller, "Criticizing Feminist Criticism," in *Conflicts in Feminism* Marianne Hirsch and Evelyn Fox Keller, ed., (New York: Routledge, 1990), 349–369.

24. Miller, "Dreaming," 95; Prett, "Identity," 31.

25. Miller, "Dreaming," 95.

26. Ibid.

27. Ibid.

28. For more on what bothered me at that time, see my discussion of these texts in the introduction and chapter 1 of this book.

29. See the introduction to my dissertation for a less worked-through account of this disappointment. Laura Levitt, "Reconfiguring Home: Jewish Feminist Identity/ies," Ph.D. diss., Emory University, Atlanta, GA, 1993. On this issue of wanting to be like everyone else only more so, see also Adrienne Rich, "Split at the Root," in *Nice Jewish Girls: A Lesbian Anthology*, ed. Evelyn Beck (Boston: Beacon Press, 1989), 73–90.

30. On identification as an ambivalent desire, see Dianne Fuss, *Identification Papers* (New York: Routledge, 1995).

31. Ironically, in this case, I wanted to be at-home within a stance of "not being home." In the graduate seminar at Emory, being in constant motion appeared to be a feminist answer to stable hegemonic notions of identity. The problem was that this too was not a resting place although I had wanted it to be one. Mohanty and Martin had set "not being home" in

opposition to Pratt's father's fixed position, and I disagreed. As I have suggested through my various readings of Pratt's text, the interplay between "being at home" and "not being home" is much more complicated. These positions are intertwined not only in Pratt's narrative but in Miller's and my own. Both stances are always already present in each of our texts. For a somewhat different account of "being at home" and "not being at home" in Mohanty and Martin's text, see my "Reconfiguring Home: Jewish Feminist Identity/ies," in *Gender and Judaism: The Transformation of Tradition*, Tamar Rudavsky, ed. (New York: NYU Press, 1995), 39–51.

32. Despite the fact that there are other openly Jewish feminists on the faculty at Temple University teaching courses in women's studies and Jewish studies, we have few Jewish students. My Jewish feminist colleagues at Temple are Rebecca Alpert, cochair of Women's Studies, and Harriet Freidenreich, a full professor of history. It is unusual to be in an American university with more than one Jewish feminist scholar, and for this I am grateful to be at Temple. Despite having Jewish feminist colleagues, however, I am virtually the only Jew in the classrooms in which I teach.

33. The 1989 exchange is written in the form of letters. Peggy Kamuf and Nancy K. Miller, "Parisian Letters: Between Feminism and Deconstruction" in *Conflicts in Feminism*, Marianne Hirsch and Evelyn Fox Keller, ed. (New York: Routledge, 1990), 121–33.

34. The earlier exchange between Miller and Kamuf is also included in *Conflicts in Feminism*; Peggy Kamuf, "Replacing Feminist Criticism," 105–111, and Nancy K. Miller, "The Text's Heroine: A Feminist Critic and Her Fictions, " 112–20.

35. Hirsch and Keller, *Conflicts in Feminism*, 123–24.

36. Here I return to de Lauretis's notion of liberal opposition. In contrast to de Lauretis I do not believe that feminists must accept "the liberal allocation of a tiny amount of 'equal' time in which to present our 'opposing viewpoint'" (8). For a fuller account see de Lauretis, *Feminist Studies/Critical Studies*, 7–8 as well as my discussion of these issues in chapter 7.

37. Jane Gallop, Marianne Hirsch, and Nancy K. Miller, "Criticizing Feminist Criticism," in Hirsch and Keller, *Conflicts in Feminism*, 349–69.

Chapter Nine

1. Melanie Kaye/Kantrowitz, "Notes of an Immigrant Daughter: Atlanta," in *Nice Jewish Girls: A Lesbian Anthology*, 3d ed., Evelyn Torton Beck (Boston: Beacon Press, 1989), 124–28. All subsequent references to this poem will be included in the text.

2. Nancy K. Miller, "Dreaming, Dancing, and the Changing Locations of Feminist Criticism, 1988," *Getting Personal: Feminist Occasions and Other Autobiographical Acts* (New York: Routledge, 1991), 72–100.

3. Adrienne Rich, "Notes Towards a Politics of Location," *Blood, Bread,*

and Poetry: Selected Prose 1979–1985 (New York: Norton, 1986), 210–31. As Nancy K. Miller explains, Rich's essay was first given as a talk "at the First Summer School of Critical Semiotics, Conference on Women, Feminist Identity and Society in the 1980s at Utrecht. . ." (73–74) As she explains, she also presented a version of "Dreaming, Dancing" "[f]or a new graduate program in Women's Studies at the University of Utrecht (November 1988)." (72)

4. Miller, "Dreaming," 74.

5. It has been pointed out to me that there is a tension in this sentence that echoes many of the central concerns of this book, the shift from "shelter" to "move." As the reader explained, "this is a motif in your text—a little like the fear of finding that home isn't really home—and so the urgency to move on as soon as possible so the discovery can be postponed." I thank Ruth Tonner Ost for this insight. For a different account of this dilemma, see my preface.

6. At that time Rich's work was severely criticized for its essentialist tendencies. See for example, Linda Alcoff, "Cultural Feminism Versus Post Structuralism: The Identity Crisis in Feminist Theory," *Signs* (Spring 1988); 405–436.

7. In this sense, feminist or Jewish utopian dreams of another place are not possible. There is no conclusion. In a similar way, Adrienne Rich also questions her feminist desires for another place that does not yet exist. For a reading of Rich's dream about another place, a place that is always already inhabited by others, see Laura Levitt, "(The Problem) with Embraces," in *Judaism Since Gender*, Miriam Peskowitz and Laura Levitt, ed. (New York: Routledge, 1997).

8. Interestingly, this reading is somewhat anachronistic, a kind of backwards reading of the discursive move to "notes" since the Kaye/Kantrowitz poem was written in 1981. Rich wrote her "Notes" in 1984 and Miller reread them again in 1988, while I write about all of these texts together in 1995–1996 in ways that owe much to Miller's account of "notes" as a kind of reading strategy.

9. Again, the question of the differences between the African American experience of slavery in the United States and the legacy of the Shoah are complex and important. These issues demand a much fuller treatment than I can give them here. For a specific reading of next generations's writings, see Michelle Friedman's reading of Toni Morrison's *Beloved* and Cynthia Ozick's *The Shawl* in Michelle Friedman, "Transforming Acts of Witness," Ph.D. diss. Bryn Mawyr College, Bryn Mawyr, PA, 1997. As I have already noted, I hope to return to these questions about the relationship between African Americans and Jewish Americans in my next project.

10. I read these pieces in the order in which the poem was written.

11. Kaye/Kantrowitz, "Notes," 124.

12. In the original text there is an asterisk here with the following note added on the bottom of the page: "The grotesque look of Black people in this racist film is explained by the fact that they are really whites in blackface. Only in crowd scenes do a very few actual Blacks appear. Michelle Cliff's suspicions led me to this information" (124). For a different account of "blackface" and the history of American film see Michael Rogin, *Blackface, White Noise: Jewish Immigrants in the Hollywood Melting Pot* (Berkeley: University of California Press, 1996).

13. As Rogin explains, this narrative becomes a kind of encapsulated history of America, the birth of the nation as white. It does so in terms of the sanctity of America's whiteness. See Rogin, *Blackface*, especially 76–81. Reiteration is also crucial to this reference to the film, as the showing and reshowing of the film is itself a reiteration of the story. In this way film becomes a part of a kind of twentieth-century cinematic process of naturalization through repetition.

14. According to my father's first cousin Phil Pearl, whose father brought his brother Schmuel to the United States in 1948, my father's narrative was not correct. Not only was Schmuel not in a concentration camp, neither was his first wife. She too had escaped to the Soviet Union and survived the war in a far-off province. Schmuel and his first wife lost contact during the war and both believed that the other was dead. After the war, Schmuel remarried another Jewish women who had also survived the war in the Soviet Union. As Phil explained it to me, some years later, as if in an I. B. Singer short story, Schmuel and his first wife were reunited, both having already remarried other people. Apparently they were able to find a rabbi to intercede and write them a rabbinic bill of divorce, a *get*, to end their original marriage so that the second set of marriages would not be in jeopardy. Phone conversation, Phil Pearl, December 1995.

15. When I told my father's cousin Phil about my father's rendition of their uncle's story, he was surprised but then he also remembered that in 1947–1948 my father had suffered from a debilitating case of pleurisy and spent close to a year in bed. Phone conversation, Phil Pearl, December 1995.

16. On this point about the relative poverty of the entire extended family, I again thank Phil Pearl. Phone conversation, Phil Pearl, December 1995.

17. He was literally there as Bill Clinton came into the world. He is proud of this fact, repeating it more than once in this conversation: "Did you hear me, aren't you impressed?" This connects well with my father's desire to belong, to be a part of this country by connecting his own experience with later political events, politics, and power. My father has also been a loyal Democrat. He is a former chair of the Delaware Democratic Party for Kent County and a proud supporter of the president in the 1994 campaign. Both of my parents attended the inaugural gala for President Clinton in Washington, DC. Conversation, Irving and Phyllis Levitt, July 1995.

18. The full text of section five reads as follows:

5. a mother's voice booming across the TV miles
how many children going to lose their
lives mr mayor before you
do something

> the papers say the mothers just
> don't take care

mother of a murdered child, keening, they
didn't tell us about the danger, if
i'd known, i'd never have
let him out, my
baby be alive

> some people charge the mothers
> have done the killing

mother of children not yet dead shouts mr
mayor   we don't want to see you on TV
we don't want to see you next week
we want to see you
now about our
children

mother of a murdered child &
three still living, camille bell
says—if they were white children. . .

but, interrupts the white reporter, the
mayor the chief of police are
black (he means, aren't you
satisfied)

camille bell looks past him
says, these children were black
& poor

while newspapers i clip & save in a shoebox say
the klan practices guerrilla warfare
outside of atlanta
as outside nashville
as outside houston & dallas
as outside buffalo & kingston
as outside portland oregon
as outside youngstown ohio
the klan gathers

> *how will we die*
> *who will we kill*

klansmen on trial in greensboro
verdict: not guilty

if they were white children

if the mayor were on welfare
if the governor got pregnant
if the president had suckled babies instead of
sucking off the trilateral commission would
death's face be leering
all over the world

as in atlanta
where mothers
as always
teach children how to survive—
don't get in anyone's car   children   is that
correct— and to sing
with the preacher   in church
jesus loves the little children
all god's children in the world
red & yellow black & white
they are precious—

and in the sight of their mothers
they are precious—

mr mayor
mr president
mr chairman of the board

one of the klansmen acquitted in greensboro
has already been shot at

in atlanta
16   17   18   19   29   21   23   25   28 children
are dead   or missing

and we want to see you
now
about our children

April 1981 (126–28)

19. Douglas Lavin, "As 911 use rises, more callers to lifeline put on hold," *Atlanta Journal and Constitution*, May 27, 1990, A1, A14.
20. "If the mayor is serious about stopping crime, this is something concrete he can do. Change the 911 system, do whatever it takes." Lavin, "As 911 use rises," A14.
21. I was again reminded of these particular failings during the 1996 Summer Olympics in Atlanta when, despite a warning call to 911, a pipe bomb exploded in Centennial Olympic Park in downtown Atlanta.

22. As I completed this manuscript in the summer of 1996, President Bill Clinton signed legislation to "end welfare as we know it."

23. Even as I began writing these words in the summer of 1995, the tensions continued. On the radio one morning I heard that they don't want to put up a monument to Arthur Ashe, the African American tennis star who died of AIDS in his hometown in Virginia. The problem was that the place that was chosen in this particular Virginia town was reserved for historical monuments to Civil War heroes, the heroes of the Confederacy. National Public Radio, *Morning Edition*, July 17, 1995.

    Wasn't this a way to keep blacks out, to maintain continuity between this time and the past? This reminds me of the images the narrator invokes in the final section of the poem. In places like Atlanta, they don't just whistle dixie, there are restaurants called "plantation house" proclaiming their proud relationship to the lost South, to White hegemony. The narrator claims that those who go to these place mourn the demise of plantation culture.

Chapter Ten

1. Irena Klepfisz, *Keeper of Accounts* (Watertown, MA: Persephone Press, 1982), 74–87. I refer to this the original version of the poem since there are errors in the reprinted version in Irena Klepfisz, *A Few Words in the Mother Tongue: Poems Selected and New (1971–1990)* (Portland, OR: Eighth Mountain Press, 1990), 183–200. All subsequent references to the poem in the text will be from *Keeper of Accounts*.

2. This series includes three prose poems, "Glimpses of the Outside"; "*Bashert*," made up of two dedications, one to those who died and another to those who survived, as well as "1. Poland, 1944: My mother is walking down a road," "2. Chicago, 1964: I am walking home alone at midnight," "3. Brooklyn, 1971: I am almost equidistant from two continents," the section I have just described, and "4. Cherry Plain, 1981: I have become a keeper of accounts"; and finally the poem, "Solitary Acts." These poems appear in *Keeper of Accounts*, 59–96, as well as in Klepfisz, *A Few Words in the Mother Tongue*, 167–210.

3. The poem is attributed to "Melanie Kaye" in Klepfisz's original volume of poems. In *A Few Words* it is attributed to "Melanie Kaye/Kantrowitz. I will return to this issue in chapter 11.

4. At that time, I also found her poem "*Di rayze aheym*/The journey home" especially helpful. See Klepfisz, *A Few Words*, 216–24. See Laura Levitt and Sue Ann Wasserman, "*Mikvah* Ceremony for Laura (1989)," in *Four Centuries of Jewish Women's Spirituality: A Sourcebook*, ed. Ellen M. Umansky and Dianne Ashton (Boston: Beacon, 1992), 321–26.

5. This is a moment described in the first numbered section of the poem, "1. Poland, 1944: My mother is walking down a road."

6. There is an irony here since the title of the poem means "fate," that which is inevitable, as opposed to a choice.

7. For a longer and somewhat different reading of the poem see Laura Levitt, "Reconfiguring Home: Jewish Feminist Identity/ies," Ph.D. diss., Emory University, Atlanta, GA, 1993, with special attention to the conclusion.

8. This is not unlike the silent Holocaust described at a distance in the previous section of the poem, where the narrator writes:

> I see now the present dangers, the dangers of the void, of the American hollowness in which I walk calmly day and night as I continue my life. I begin to see the incessant grinding down of lines for stamps, for jobs, for a bed to sleep in, of a death stretched imperceptibly over a lifetime. I begin to understand the ingenuity of it. The invisibility. The Holocaust without smoke. (81)

9. See "1, Poland, 1944: My mother is walking down a road," 77–78.

10. Adrienne Rich, "Notes Towards a Politics of Location," *Blood, Bread, and Poetry: Selected Prose 1979–1985* (New York: Norton, 1986), 210–31.

Chapter Eleven

1. Irena Klepfisz, *Keeper of Accounts* (Watertown, MA: Persephone Press, 1982), 59.

2. Evelyn Torton Beck, ed., *Nice Jewish Girls: A Lesbian Anthology* (Watertown, MA: Persephone Press, 1982). The full poem was reprinted at that time with the permission of a small feminist journal called *Sisterlode*, where the poem first appeared in 1981.

3. In the 1984 edition of *Nice Jewish Girls* the poem is attributed to Melanie Kaye/Kantrowitz but the permission refers to her as Melanie Kaye. See Beck, *Nice Jewish Girls: A Lesbian Anthology*, 2d ed. (Trumansburg, NY: Crossing Press, 1984), 109–113. In 1986, Melanie Kaye/Kantrowitz and Irena Klepfisz published their own collection of Jewish women's writing, *Tribe of Dina: A Jewish Women's Anthology*, a special double issue of the journal *Sinister Wisdom* 29/30 (1986).

4. See Beck, *Nice Jewish Girls*, 3d ed., published by Beacon in 1989. Melanie's name is also changed in the reprinting of the passage from her poem in Irena Klepfisz's "Inhospitable Soil," republished in 1990. See Irena Klepfisz, *A Few Words*, in *The Mother Tongue: Poems Selected and New, 1971–1990* (Portland, OR: Eighth Mountain Press, 1990), 167. The opening quote is attributed to Melanie Kaye/Kantrowitz.

5. Part of what makes this so striking is that it is not about marriage, the "normal" case of a woman changing her name. This deliberative shift in names and the network of especially lesbian Jewish feminists who actively worked to enact it is significant, although when I spoke to both Evelyn Beck and Melanie Kaye/Kantrowitz to try to learn more about these efforts, I learned that they were a lot less conscious than I had believed them to be. Telephone conversations, May 1996.

6. As I was to learn from Melanie, this change is not "legal" in the sense that she never went to court to change her name. Thus, various official documents, passports, and the like continue to bear the name Melanie Kaye. What again moves me about this particular name change is its lack of formality. As Melanie explained to me, as long as she is not using this other name for fraudulent purposes it is legal. Thus, she has copyrights under both names. Telephone conversation, May 1996.

7. Here and elsewhere as I discuss this particular text, I will refer to the author as Melanie Kaye not only because the essay was written before the change but because the essay explicitly struggles with these issues. Here the author had not yet come to a solution. For some additional information about these issues see, Melanie Kaye/Kantrowitz, "Jews in the U.S.: The Costs of Whiteness," in *Names We Call Home: Autobiography on Racial Identity*, ed. Becky Thompson and Sangeeta Tyagi (New York: Routledge, 1996), 121–37.

8. Beck, *Nice Jewish Girls* (1989), 38. All subsequent references to this essay will be from this edition. Page numbers will be provided in the text.

9. I thank Melanie Kaye/Kantrowitz for speaking with me about these issues and the legal status of her current name. Telephone conversation, May 1996.

10. Please note that "Blanche" is also a made-up name: my grandmother's name was "Bluma." She changed it to Blanche but this took time. There are autograph books that belonged to my grandmother in high school with entries to a whole range of "B" names, Barbara, Betty, etc. I have no record of the official changing of this name. There is also some of this ambiguity in my father's family. My father's sister goes by the name "Muriel," but I am told that her real name is "Minnie." When my grandmother moved to Dover in the 1970s, she had a friend who decided that her name should also be Blanche, but she never acted on this. She remained, from the Polish, "Blanca" and not "Blanche."

11. I am so accustomed to writing it that it doesn't even strike me as odd, although I often confuse the slash with a dash. When I have taught texts written by Melanie Kaye/Kantrowitz at Temple, I have been reminded of the confusion. Students don't know how to verbalize the name, should they use one or both names. But, more interestingly, some of my students have been confused about whether or not the text was written by one or two different people, Kaye and Kantrowitz.

12. The "K" in Nancy K. Miller is also a trace of such a change. This "K" is for Kipnis, a name and identity that she says more about in her memoir, *Bequest and Betrayal: Memoirs of a Parent's Death* (New York: Oxford University Press, 1996). Personal correspondence, January 1996.

13. This connection is not without deep ambivalences. What is striking is the longing for and horror of such connections. I am grateful to Lorie Lefkowitz for helping me think some more about these tensions within

identification. We discussed these issues with particular reference to the Holocaust museum in Washington, DC, and complicated desires for identification in looking at the pictures in the tower of photographs. What is at stake in these acts of identification is both wanting and not wanting to make connections to those who died. Conversation at Haverford College, Haverford, PA, March 20, 1996.

14. Beck, *Nice Jewish Girls*, 39. She also describes experimenting with the name Melanie Kantrowitz during this time.

15. This move to the slash is reminiscent of my efforts to think about identities in both the singular and the plural in an earlier rendition of this project. See Laura Levitt, "Reconfiguring Home: Jewish Feminist Identity/ies," Ph.D. diss., Emory University, Atlanta, GA, 1993.

Conclusion

1. Irena Klepfisz, *Keeper of Accounts* (Watertown, MA: Persephone Press, 1982), 79–81; and Irena Klepfisz, *A Few Words in the Mother Tongue* (Portland, OR: Eighth Mountain Press, 1990), 190–93.

Selected Bibliography

Albert, Phyllis Cohen. "Israelite and Jew: How Did Nineteenth-Century French Jews Understand Assimilation?" In Frankel and Zipperstein, *Assimilation and Community*, 88–109.

Alcoff, Linda. "Cultural Feminism Versus Post Structuralism: The Identity Crisis in Feminist Theory." *Signs* (Spring 1988); 405–36.

Alexander, Jacqui M. "Redrafting Morality: The Postcolonial State and the Sexual Offenses Bill of Trinidad and Tobago." In *Third World Women and the Politics of Feminism*, ed. Chandra Talpade Mohanty, Ann Russo, and Lourdes Torres. Bloomington: Indiana University Press, 1991.

Bal, Mieke. *Lethal Love, Feminist Literary Readings of Biblical Love Stories*. Bloomington: Indiana University Press, 1987.

Baskin, Judith, ed. *Jewish Women in Historical Perspective*. Detroit: Wayne State University Press, 1991.

Beck, Evelyn Torton, ed. *Nice Jewish Girls: A Lesbian Anthology*. Boston: Beacon, 1989.

———. "The Politics of Jewish Invisibility." *NWSA Journal* 1.1 (1988); 93–102.

Begley, Adam. "Colossus Among Critics: Alan Bloom." *New York Times Magazine*, September 25, 1994.

Bell, Vikki. "Beyond the 'Thorny Question': Feminism, Foucault and the Desexualisation of Rape." *International Journal of the Sociology of Law* 19 (1991); 83–100.

Berkovitz, Jay R. "The French Revolution and the Jews: Assessing the Cultural Impact." *AJS Review* 20.1 (1995); 25–86.

Bhabha, Homi. "Of Mimicry and Man: The Ambivalence of Colonial Discourse." *October* 28 (1984), 125–33.

Biale, David, "Eros and the Jews," *Tikkun* 7.5 (September/October 1992), 49–52, 78–9.

Biale, Rachel. *Women and Jewish Law: An Exploration of Women's Issues in Halakhic Sources*. New York: Schocken, 1984.

Birnbaum, Pierre, and Ira Katznelson, ed. *Paths of Emancipation: Jews, States, and Citizenship*. Princeton: Princeton University Press, 1995.

Booth, Wayne. *Critical Understanding: The Powers and Limits of Pluralism*. Chicago: University of Chicago Press, 1979.

Borowitz, Eugene. *Choices in Modern Jewish Thought: A Partisan Guide*. 2d ed., West Orange NJ: Behrman House, 1995.

———. *Choosing a Sex Ethic: A Jewish Inquiry*. New York: Schocken, 1969.

———. *Exploring Jewish Ethics: Papers on Covenant Responsibility*. Detroit: Wayne State University Press, 1990.

———. *Liberal Judaism*. New York: Union of American Hebrew Congregations, 1984.

———. *Reform Judaism Today*. Vols. 1–3. New York: Behrman House, 1978.

———. *Renewing the Covenant: A Theology for the Postmodern Jew*. Philadelphia: Jewish Publication Society, 1991.

Bourne, Jenny. "Homelands of the Mind: Jewish Feminism and Identity Politics." *Race and Class* 29.1 (Summer 1987); 1–24.

Boyarin, Daniel. *Carnal Israel: Reading Sex in Talmudic Culture*. Berkeley: University of California Press, 1993.

———. *Unheroic Conduct*. Berkeley: University of California Press, forthcoming.

Boyarin, Jonathan. *Storm from Paradise: The Politics of Jewish Memory*. Minneapolis: University of Minnesota Press, 1992, 77–98.

Brownstein, Rachel M. *Tragic Muse: Rachel of the Comédie-Française*. Durham, NC: Duke University Press, 1995.

Buber, Martin. *I and Thou*. New York: Charles Scribner and Sons, 1958.

Bulka, Reuven. *Jewish Marriage: A Halakhic Ethic*. New York: Ktav, 1986.

Bulkin, Elly, Minnie Bruce Pratt, and Barbara Smith. *Yours in Struggle: Three Feminist Perspectives on Anti-Semitism and Racism*. Brooklyn: Long Haul Press, 1984.

Butler, Judith, "Against Proper Objects," introduction to "More Gender Trouble: Feminism Meets Queer Theory." Judith Butler, ed. *Differences: A Journal of Feminist Cultural Studies* 6.2–3 (Summer–Fall 1994); 1–26.

———, ed. "More Gender Trouble: Feminism Meets Queer Theory," 6:2–3 (Summer–Fall 1994).

Callaghan, Dympna. "The Vicar and Vigaro: Feminism and the Problem of Identity." In *Who Can Speak? Authority and Critical Identity*, ed. Judith Roof and Robyn Wiegman. Urbana and Chicago: University of Illinois Press, 1995.

Chazan, Robert, and Marc L. Raphael, ed. *Modern Jewish History: A Source Book*. New York: Schocken, 1969.

Clark, Ann. "Humanity or Justice? Wifebeating in the Eighteenth and Nineteenth Centuries." In *Regulating Womanhood: Historical Essays on Marriage, Motherhood and Sexuality*, ed. Carol Smart. New York: Routledge, 1991.

———. *Women's Silence, Men's Violence: Sexual Assault in England 1770–1845*. New York: Pandora, 1987.

Daiches, Samuel, Israel W. Slotki, and I. Epstein, ed. *Babylonian Talmud, Tractate Kethubot*. Hebrew-English edition. London: Soncino Press, 1971.

Davidovich, David. *The Ketuba: Jewish Marriage Contracts Through the Ages*. Jerusalem/New York: Adama Books, 1968, 1985.

Dayan, Joan. "Amorous Bondage: Poe, Ladies, and Slaves." *American Literature* 66.2 (June 1994); 239–271.

———. "Romance and Race." In *The Columbia History of the American Novel*, ed. Emory Elliot. New York: Columbia University Press, 1991.

de Lauretis, Teresa. *Feminist Studies/Critical Studies*. Bloomington: Indiana University Press, 1986.

———. "Feminist Studies/Critical Studies: Issues, Terms, and Contexts." In de Lauretis, *Feminist Studies/Critical Studies*.

———. *The Technologies of Gender: Essays on Theory, Film and Fiction*. Bloomington: Indiana University Press, 1987.

Diamant, Anita. *The New Jewish Wedding*. New York: Fireside, 1985.

Di Stefano, Christine. *Configurations of Masculinity: A Feminist Perspective on Modern Political Theory*. Ithaca: Cornell University Press, 1991.

Dohm, Christian Wilhelm. "Concerning the Amelioration of the Civil Status of the Jews." In *Modern Jewish History: A Source Book*, ed. Robert Chazan and Marc Lee Raphael. New York: Schocken, 1969, 1–13.

Downey, Sally A. "A decorative contract seals Jewish nuptials."*Philadelphia Inquirer*, June 7, 1996.

Eisenstein, Zillah. *The Radical Future of Liberal Feminism*. New York: Longman, 1981.

The Encyclopedia Judaica. Jerusalem: MacMillan, 1971.

Epstein, Gail and Bill Montgomery, "More Bombings threatened, Code appears to link writer to 2 Slayings," *Atlanta Journal/Constitution* December 29, 1989.

Estrich, Susan. *Real Rape: How the Legal System Victimizes Women Who Say No*. Cambridge: Harvard University Press, 1987.

Fauré, Christine. *Democracy Without Women: Feminism and the Rise of Liberal Individualism in France*. Bloomington: Indiana University Press, 1991.

Frankel, Jonathan, and Steven Zipperstein, ed. *Assimilation and Community: The Jews in Nineteenth-Century Europe*. Cambridge: Cambridge University Press, 1992.

Freud, Sigmund. "The 'Uncanny' (1919)." In *Studies in Parapsychology*. New York: Collier Books, 1963.

Friedman, Michelle. "Transforming Acts of Witness." Ph.D. diss., Bryn Mawyr College, Bryn Mawyr, PA, 1997.

Friedman, Mordechai Akiva. *The Jewish Marriage in Palestine, A Cairo Geniza Study. Vols. 1 and 2 , The Ketubba Traditions*. New York: Jewish Theological Seminary of America, 1980.

Funkenstein, Amos. *Perceptions of Jewish History*. Berkeley: University of California Press, 1993.

Fuss, Dianne. *Identification Papers*. New York: Routledge, 1995.

Gallop, Jane, Marianne Hirsch, and Nancy K. Miller. "Criticizing Feminist Criticism." In Hirsch and Keller, *Conflicts in Feminism*.

Gaster, Moses. *The Ketubah*. New York: Hermon, 1974.

Geiger, Abraham. "Prefaces to the Frankfort Prayerbook." In Chazan and Raphael, *Modern Jewish History*.

Ginsberg, Benjamin. *The Fatal Embrace: Jews and the State*. Chicago: University of Chicago Press, 1993.

Goiten, S.D. *A Mediterranean Society: The Jewish Communities of the Arab World as Portrayed in the Documents of the Cairo Geniza. Volume 3, The Family*. Berkeley: University of California Press, 1978.

Goldenberg, Robert. "Talmud." In *Back to the Sources. Reading the Classic Jewish Texts*. ed. Barry W. Holtz. New York: Summit, 1984.

Goldstein, Sidney E. *Meaning of Marriage and Foundations of the Family: A Jewish Interpretation*. New York: Blcoh, 1942.

Greenberg, Moshe. *Ezekiel 1–20. The Anchor Bible*. New York: Doubleday, 1983.

Gutwirth, Madelyn. *The Twilight of the Goddesses: Women and Representation in the French Revolutionary Era*. New Brunswick, NJ: Rutgers University Press, 1992.

Hadassah, August/September 1994.

Halbertal, Moshe, and Avishai Margalit. *Idolatry*, trans. Naomi Goldblum. Cambridge: Harvard Univeristy Press, 1992.

Hale, M. *The History of the Pleas of the Crown, volumes 1 and 2* (London: Professional Books, 1971).

Hertzberg, Arthur. *The French Enlightenment and the Jews*. New York: Columbia University Press, 1968.

Heschel, Susannah, ed. *On Being a Jewish Feminist: A Reader*. New York: Schocken, 1995, 1983.

Hirsch, Marianne, and Evelyn Fox Keller, eds. *Conflicts in Feminism*. New York: Routledge, 1990.

Hurston, Zora Neal. *Their Eyes Were Watching God*. Chicago: University of Illinois Press, 1978.

Hyman, Paula. *From Dreyfus to Vichy: The Remaking of French Jewry, 1906–1939*. New York: Columbia University Press, 1979.

———. *Gender and Assimilation in Modern Jewish History: The Roles and Representation of Women*. Seattle: University of Washington Press, 1995.

Jacobson, Israel. "The Association for the Reform of Judaism." In Chazan and Raphael, *Modern Jewish History*.

———. "A Dedication Address." In Chazan and Raphael, *Modern Jewish History*.

Jastrow, Marcus. *Dictionary of the Targumim, Talmud Babli, Yerushalmi and Midrashic Literature*. New York: Judaica Press, Inc., 1982.

Joselit, Jenna Weissman. *The Wonders of America: Reinventing Jewish Culture 1880–1950*. New York: Hill and Wang, 1994.

Jung, Leo. "The Jewish Way to Married Happiness." *The Jewish Forum* New York: 1930.

Kamuf, Peggy. "Replacing Feminist Criticism." In Hirsch and Keller, *Conflicts in Feminism*.

Kamuf, Peggy and Nancy K. Miller. "Parisian Letters: Between Feminism and Deconstruction." In Hirsch and Keller, *Conflicts in Feminism*.

Kaplan, Alice. *French Lessons: A Memoir*. Chicago: University of Chicago Press, 1993.

Kaplan, Aryeh. *Made in Heaven. A Jewish Wedding Guide*. New York: Moznaim, 1983.

Kaplan, Marion. *The Jewish Feminist Movement in Germany: The Campaigns of the Jüdischer Frauenbund, 1904–1938*. Westport, CT: Greenwood, 1979.

———. *The Making of the Jewish Middle Classes: Women, Family, and Identity in Imperial Germany*. New York: Oxford University Press, 1991.

Katz, Jacob. "The Term *Jewish Emancipation*: Its Origin and Historical Impact." In *Studies in Nineteenth-Century Jewish Intellectual History*, ed. Alexander Altman. Cambridge: Harvard University Press, 1964.

Kaufman, Michael. *Love, Marriage and Family in Jewish Law and Tradition*. Northvale, NJ: Jason Aronson, 1992.

Kaye/Kantrowitz, Melanie. "Jews in the U.S.: The Costs of Whiteness." In *Names We Call Home: Autobiography on Racial Identity*, ed. Becky Thompson and Sangeeta Tyagi. New York: Routledge, 1996.

———. "Notes of an Immigrant Daughter: Atlanta." In Beck, *Nice Jewish Girls*.

Kaye/Kantrowitz, Melanie, and Irena Klepfisz, eds. *The Tribe of Dina: A Jewish Women's Anthology*. Boston: Beacon, 1989.

Klepfisz, Irena. *A Few Words in the Mother Tongue: Poems Selected and New (1971–1990)*. Portland OR: Eighth Mountain Press, 1990.

———. *Keeper of Accounts*. Watertown MA: Persephone Press, 1982.

Klingenstein, Susanne. *Jews in the American Academy 1900–1940: The Dynamics of Intellectual Assimilation*. New Haven: Yale University Press, 1991.

Kritzman, Lawrence D., ed. *Auschwitz and After: Race, Culture, and "the Jewish Question" in France*, New York: Routledge, 1995.

Kuzmack, Linda Gordon. *Women's Cause, The Jewish Woman's Movement in England and the United States, 1881–1933*. Columbus: Ohio State University Press, 1990.

Lakritiz, Andrew. "Identification and Difference: Structures of Privilege in Cultural Criticism." In *Who Can Speak? Authority and Critical Identity*, ed. Judith Roof and Robyn Wiegman, Urbana and Chicago: University of Illinois Press, 1995.

Lamm, Maurice. *The Jewish Way in Love and Marriage*. San Francisco: Harper and Row, 1980.

Landes, Joan. *Women and the Public Sphere in the Age of the French Revolution.* Ithaca: Cornell University Press, 1988.

Lavin, Douglas. "As 911 Use Rises, More Callers to Lifeline Put on Hold." *The Atlanta Journal and Constitution*, Sunday May 27, 1990.

Lerner, Gerda. *The Creation of Patriarchy.* New York: Oxford University Press, 1987.

Levine, A.J. "A Jewess, More and/or Less." In Peskowitz and Levitt, *Judaism Since Gender.* New York: Routledge, 1996.

Levitt, Laura. "(The Problem with) Embraces." In Peskowitz and Levitt, *Judaism Since Gender.* New York: Routledge, 1996.

———. "Race, Gender and Jewish Excess: Rereading Jewish Cinematic Difference," Philadelphia, The American Academy of Religion, conference paper, November 1995.

———. "Reconfiguring Home: Jewish Feminist Identity/ies." In *Gender and Judaism: The Transformation of Tradition*, ed. Tamar Rudavsky, New York: NYU Press, 1995, 39–49.

———. "Reconfiguring Home: Jewish Feminist Identity/ies." Ph.D. diss., Emory University, Atlanta, GA, 1993.

———. "Rethinking Jewish Feminist Identity/ies: What Difference Can Feminist Theory Make?" In *Interpreting Judaism in a Postmodern Age*, ed. Steven Kepnes, New York: NYU Press, 1996.

———. "Review Essay: *Standing Again at Sinai: Judaism from a Feminist Perspective*," *Religious Studies Review* 20.1 (January 1994); 16–20.

———. "Speaking Out of the Silence Around Rape: A Personal Account." *Fireweed*, 41 (Fall 1993), 20–31.

———. "To Be Worthy of God's Love: Sin and Atonement in Franz Rosenzweig's *The Star of Redemption*," unpublished manuscript, February 1985.

Levitt, Laura and Miriam Peskowitz, ed. "Engendering Jewish Knowledges." Special issue, *Shofar: An Interdisciplinary Journal For Jewish Studies* 14.1 (Fall 1995).

Levitt, Laura and Sue Ann Wasserman. "*Mikvah* Ceremony for Laura (1989)." In *Four Centuries of Jewish Women's Spirituality: A Sourcebook*, ed. Ellen M. Umansky and Dianne Ashton. Boston: Beacon, 1992.

Lewittes, Mendell. *Jewish Marriage: Rabbinic Law, Legend, and Custom.* Northvale, NJ: Jason Aronson, 1994.

Lorde, Audre. "Age, Race, Class, and Sex: Women Redefining Difference." In *Out There: Marginalization and Contemporary Cultures*, ed. Russell Ferguson, Martha Gever, Trinh T. Minh-ha, and Cornel West. Cambridge: MIT Press, 1990.

———. "Uses of the Erotic: The Erotic as Power." In *Sister Outsider*. Trumansburg, NY: Crossing Press, 1984.

Martin, Biddy and Chandra Mohanty. "Feminist Politics: What's Home Got to Do with It?" In de Lauretis, *Feminist Studies/Critical Studies*.

McLaughlin, Andrée. "Black Women, Identity, and the Quest for Humanhood and Wholeness: Wild Women in the Whirlwind." In *Wild Women in the Whirlwind: Afra-American Culture and the Contemporary Literary Renaissance,* ed. Joanne M. Braxton and Andree Nicola McLaughlin. New Brunswick, NJ: Rutgers University Press, 1990.

Mendes-Flohr, Paul R., and Jehuda Reinharz, eds. *The Jew in the Modern World: A Documentary History.* New York: Oxford University Press, 1980.

Meyer, Michael. *The Origins of the Modern Jew: Jewish Identity and European Culture in Germany, 1749–1824.* Detroit: Wayne State University Press, 1979.

Michie, Helena. "The Greatest Story (N)Ever Told: The Spectacle of Recantation." In *Tatoo, Torture, Mutilation, and Abandonment: The Denaturalization of the Body in Culture and Text,* ed. Frances E. Mascia-Lees and Patricia Sharpe. Albany: State University of New York Press, 1992.

Miller, Nancy K. *Bequest and Betrayal: Memoirs of a Parent's Death.* New York: Oxford University Press, 1996.

———. "Dreaming, Dancing and the Changing Locations of Feminist Criticism, 1988." In *Getting Personal: Feminist Occasions and Other Autobiographical Acts.* New York: Routledge, 1991.

———. *French Dressing: Women, Men and Ancient Régime Fiction.* New York: Routledge, 1995.

———. "Hadassah Arms." In *People of the Book: Thirty Scholars Reflect on Their Jewish Identity,* ed. Jeffrey Rubin-Dorsky and Shelley Fisher Fishkin. Madison: University of Wisconsin Press, 1996.

———. "The Text's Heroine: A Feminist Critic and Her Fictions." In Hirsch and Keller, *Conflicts in Feminism.*

Miller, Nancy K., Jane Gallop, and Marianne Hirsch, "Criticizing Feminist Criticism." In Hirsch and Keller, *Conflicts in Feminism.*

Moore, Deborah Dash. *At Home In America: Second Generation New York Jews.* New York: Columbia University Press, 1981.

Mosse, George L., *Nationalism and Sexuality: Middle-Class Morality and Sexual Norms in Modern Europe.* Madison, WI: University of Wisconsin, 1985.

The New Oxford Annotated Bible, The Holy Bible. Revised Standard Version Containing the Old and New Testaments, ed. Herbert G. May and Bruce M. Metzger. New York: Oxford University Press, 1973.

Nicholson, Linda J. *Gender and History: The Limits of Social Theory in the Age of the Family.* New York: Columbia University Press, 1986.

Nochlin, Linda, and Tamar Garb, ed. *The Jew in the Text: Modernity and the Construction of Identity.* New York: Thames and Hudson, 1995.

Novak, David. *Jewish Social Ethics.* New York: Oxford University Press, 1992.

Orren, Dan. *Joining the Club: A History of Jews and Yale.* New Haven: Yale University Press, 1985.

Pateman, Carole. *The Disorder of Women: Democracy, Feminism and Political Theory.* Stanford, CA: Stanford University Press, 1989.

———. *The Problem of Political Obligation: A Critique of Liberal Theory.* Berkeley: University of California Press, 1979.

———. *The Sexual Contract*. Stanford, CA: Stanford University Press, 1988.

Peskowitz, Miriam. "Engendering Jewish Religious History." In Peskowitz and Levitt, *Judaism Since Gender.*

———. *Spinning Fantasies: Rabbis, Gender and History*. Berkeley: University of California Press, 1997.

Peskowitz, Miriam and Laura Levitt. ed. *Judaism Since Gender*. New York: Routledge, 1997.

Plaskow, Judith. *Standing Again At Sinai: Judaism from a Feminist Perspective*. San Francisco: Harper Collins, 1990.

———. "Special Section: Appropriation and Reciprocity,"*Journal of Feminist Studies in Religion* 8.2 (Fall 1992); 91–122.

———. "Towards a New Theology of Sexuality." In *Twice Blessed: On Being Lesbian, Gay, and Jewish*, ed. Christie Balka and Andy Rose. Boston: Beacon, 1989.

Pratt, Minnie Bruce. *Crimes Against Nature*. Ithaca: Firebrand, 1990.

———. "Identity: Skin Blood Heart." In Bulkin, Pratt, and Smith, *Yours in Struggle.*

———. *Rebellion: Essays 1980–1991*. Ithaca: Firebrand, 1991.

Rajan, Rajeswari Sunder. *Real and Imagined Women: Gender, Culture and Postcolonialism*. New York: Routledge, 1993.

Rich, Adrienne. *Blood, Bread, and Poetry: Selected Prose 1979–1985*. New York: W.W. Norton, 1986.

———. "Split at the Root." In Beck, *Nice Jewish Girls.*

Rifkin, Ellen. "*Fun di oysyes koyekh shepn*/Drawing Strength from Letters: Language and Land in the Diaspora." *Bridges* 5.2 (Winter 5756[1996]); 20–30.

Rogin, Michael. *Blackface, White Noise: Jewish Immigrants in the Hollywood Melting Pot*. Berkeley: University of California Press, 1996.

Russell, Diana E.H. *Rape in Marriage*. Bloomington: Indiana University Press, 1990.

Sabar, Shalom. *Ketubbah: Jewish Marriage Contracts of Hebrew Union College Skirball Museum and Klau Library*. Philadelphia: Jewish Publication Society, 1990.

Sanday, Peggy Reeves. *A Woman Scorned: Acquaintance Rape on Trial*. New York: Doubleday, 1996.

Scheid, Hayyim, ed. *Marriage*. Philadelphia: Jewish Publication Society, 1973.

Scheier, Barbara A. *Becoming American Women: Clothing and the Jewish Immigrant Experience*. Chicago: Chicago Historical Society, 1994.

Schwarzfuchs, Simon. *Napoleon, the Jews and the Sanhedrin*. London: Routledge & Kegan Paul, 1979.

Scott, Joan. "Universalism and the History of Feminism." *Differences: A Journal of Feminist Cultural Studies* 7.1 (1995); 1–14.

Shapiro, Susan E. "*Écriture judaique*: Where Are the Jews in Western Discourse?" In *Displacements: Cultural Identities in Question*, ed. Angelika Bammer, Bloomington: Indiana University Press, 1994.

———. "Troping Jews," Chicago; Modern Language Association, December 1995.

———. "The Uncanny Jew: A Brief History of an Image," *Judaism*, 46.1 (Winter 1997) forthcoming.

———. "Uncanny Jews: The History of an Image and Its Consequences," The Francis Thau Memorial Lecture, New York: The Jewish Theological Seminary, October 17, 1996.

Siegel, Richard, Sharon Strassfeld, and Michael Strassfeld. *The First Jewish Catalog*. Philadelphia: Jewish Publication Society, 1973.

Smart, Carol. *Feminism and the Power of Law*. New York: Routledge, 1989.

"Special Section: Appropriation and Reciprocity," *Journal of Feminist Studies in Religion* 8–2 (Fall, 1992).

Spencer, Sami I., ed. *French Women and the Age of Enlightenment*. Bloomington: Indiana University Press, 1984.

Spivak, Gayatri Chakravorty. *Outside in the Teaching Machine*. New York: Routledge, 1993.

Spurr, David. *The Rhetoric of Empire: Colonial Discourse in Journalism, Travel Writing and Imperial Administration*. Durham, NC: Duke University Press, 1993.

Suleiman, Susan Rubin. "The Jew in Sartre's *Reflexions sur la question juive*: Exercise in Historical Reading." In Nochlin and Garb, *The Jew in the Text*.

Synott, Marcia Graham. *The Half-Opened Door: Discrimination and Admissions at Harvard, Yale and Princeton, 1890–1970*. Westport, CT: Greenwood, 1979.

Steinsaltz, Adam. *The Talmud: The Steinsaltz Edition. Volume 9, Tractate Ketubot, Part 3*. New York: Random House, 1993.

Tama, Diogene, *Transactions of the Parisian Sanhedrin or Acts of the Assembly of Israelitish Deputies of France and Italy,* trans. I. D. Kitwan. London: C. Taylor, 1807.

Tanakh. Philadelphia: Jewish Publication Society, 1985. "To Have and To Hold: The Marital Rape Exemption and the Fourteenth Amendment." *Harvard Law Review* 99.6 (April 1986); 1255–73.

Torgovnick, Marianna, ed. *Eloquent Obsessions: Writing Cultural Criticism*. Durham, NC: Duke University Press, 1994.

———. "The Politics of the 'We'." In Torgovnick, *Eloquent Obsessions*.

Umansky, Ellen. "The Liberal Jew and Sex." *Response* 10:4 (Winter 1976–1977).

———. *Lily Montagu and the Advancement of Liberal Judaism: From Vision to Vocation*. New York: Edwin Mellen Press, 1983.

———. *Lily Montagu, Sermons, Addresses, Letters and Prayers*. New York: Edwin Mellen Press, 1985.

———. "Piety, Persuasion, and Friendship: Female Leadership in Modern Times." In *Embodied Love, Sensuality and Relationship as Feminist Values*, ed. P. Cooey, S. Farmer, and M. Ross. San Francisco: Harper and Row, 1987.

———. "Review of *Standing Again at Sinai: Judaism From a Feminist Perspec-*

tive," *Sh'ma, a journal of Jewish responsibility*, 20/390 (March 16, 1990); 78–79.

Weed, Elizabeth, ed. *Coming to Terms: Feminism, Theory, Politics*. New York: Routledge 1989.

Wenger, Beth. "Jewish Women and Voluntarism: Beyond the Myth of Enablers." *American Jewish History* 79.1 (Autumn 1989), 16–36.

West, Robin. "Equality Theory, Marital Rape, and the Promise of the Fourteenth Amendment." *Florida Law Review* 42.1 (January 1990), 45–79.

Young, James. *Writing and Rewriting the Holocaust: Narrative and the Consequences of Interpretation*. Bloomington: Indiana University Press, 1988.

Index